THE POETS OF GREECE.

THE

POETS OF GREECE.

BY

EDWIN ARNOLD

Essay Index Reprint Series

BOOKS FOR LIBRARIES PRESS
FREEPORT, NEW YORK

First Published 1869
Reprinted 1972

Library of Congress Cataloging in Publication Data

Arnold, Sir Edwin, 1832-1904.
The poets of Greece.

(Essay index reprint series)
Reprint of the 1869 ed.
1. Greek poetry--History and criticism. 2. Poets, Greek. I. Title.
PA3092.A7 1972 881'.01 70-39680
ISBN 0-8369-2738-9

PRINTED IN THE UNITED STATES OF AMERICA
BY
NEW WORLD BOOK MANUFACTURING CO., INC.
HALLANDALE, FLORIDA 33009

Dedication.

TO MY WIFE,

FANNIE M. A. ARNOLD,

I INSCRIBE ALL THAT IS WORTHY IN THESE PAGES

TO BE HONOURED WITH HER NAME.

Flowers from Greek gardens, Fannie!—old turned new,
    Doric, Æolic, Attic, planted here;
You made the happy sunshine, where they grew—
    Such as the growth is, have the blossoms, Dear!

INDEX OF POETS.

THE ALEXANDRIANS.

THE SICILIANS.

POETS OF THE DECLINE.

PREFACE.

INVITED by the eminent Firm which has published this volume to write "The Poets of Greece" for them, I might well have declined the task, both because of its magnitude and my unceasing literary duties. But the temptation of being thus gently obliged to wander once more in the myrtle-gardens of Greek Song was too strong to resist; and if my toil has been great, so has been my pleasure.

In the times which are coming the classical languages will be less studied, probably, than they have been. Modern life tends more and more towards practical or scientific education; and although nothing can ever depose Hellas from her throne of grace and power among nations of the past, there is fear that the "glory which was Greece" will have less and less influence upon young minds. Mr. Froude, Mr. Lowe, and many high authorities do not greatly deplore this change; yet that which the epic and lyric art of the Greeks gave to the student will never be given so perfectly by any other language; and if Plato were not still the greatest of philosophers, and Herodotus the best of antiquaries, the human intellect would nevertheless have to go back to Hellenic times for the most exquisite achievements in poetry as in sculpture and architecture.

These pages have been accordingly composed with the double hope of reminding the scholar of the variety and beauty of Greek verse, and of introducing these at the same time to the ordinary reader. A comparison of the poets cited with the complete list appended of Greek poetical authors, will at once show that no attempt has been made to go through that very long catalogue. The dramatic poets have been, moreover, omitted, for the reason that no proper justice could be done to their commanding merits in the space allotted; while they stand naturally apart from the epical, lyrical, didactic, and pastoral writers. I have attempted no more, in truth, than to pass down the ages of Hellenic song, mentioning with homage the names of the "chief musicians," and citing from their music enough to give a just idea of its character; while many of the minor minstrels are also noted, and some that were almost forgotten, even by students, are restored to their poetic rights. By quoting the Greek text of each passage, I have hoped to make the book a "florilegium" even for the learned—meantime, an English version under each citation renders it one from which the general reader may derive a fair view of the genius of Hellenic poesy. Wherever these translations are borrowed the author's name is given; where no name is annexed they are my own versions—and indeed the plan of the book has led me out of the pathway of most writers; by a road of considerable length and labour, although one made pleasant and rich by many rare and almost unknown flowers.

Aiming chiefly to facilitate a wider knowledge of Greek poetry, I have not gone very much into points of erudition; nor troubled my readers with "readings," "schools," and "eras." One would not thank the cicerone who lectured on the date and history of each painter in a gallery, instead of pointing out briefly the loveliest and most worthy pictures. Large, therefore, as the labour of this volume has been, it makes but slight pretensions. It merely seeks to popularise, if possible, the wealth of the scholar—to democratise classical learning a little; and if critics shall say, "He hath been at a great feast of languages and stolen the scraps," that is almost precisely what I wished to do on behalf of those for whom I have always written and thought most.

It remains to acknowledge my large obligations to

the "*Histoire de la Littérature Grecque,*" by Professor Alexis Pierron, of the Lycée Louis-le-Grand; one of those excellent and laborious aids to French education produced under the direction of M. Duruy. And craving pardon from the august company of scholars for the defects inseparable from the conditions of my task, I return, not without a sigh, from verse to prose—from Helicon to Fleet Street.

EDWIN ARNOLD.

THE POETS OF GREECE.

HOMER.

FROM the unparalleled inspiration which poured forth the "Iliad" and "Odyssey," down to Quintus of Smyrna—who very feebly tried to continue in Byzantine verse the "Song of Troy"—there are some fifteen hundred years. During this long life of Greece, her language was, well-nigh continuously, the language of the Muses; whether they spoke through the fresh morning airs of the Homeric hexameters, or the noon-tide iambics of Sophocles, or the soft afternoon pastorals of Bion and Theocritus, or the twilight murmurs of the hymns of Proclus. And into the beginning of this prolonged and beautiful day of Grecian Poetic Art the great light of Homer comes up as the sun comes. Rounded, finished, brilliant like the orb at its rising, Greek poetry seems born full-grown along with the first and greatest of the Grecian poets. Other literatures have faint day-breakings, rude ballad-beginnings, timid preludes upon the national lyre. Other nations practise with prose and break by-and-by into song. Greece was born musical, sweet in voice and quick in fancy; and she had her accomplished and perfect poets before any historian or philosopher appeared. From Homer to Tryphiodorus and Quintus the line of them, great and little, stretches down her history; but the first is greatest of all, and would be equally greatest had he written last. The verse of Homer is sufficient as the voices of nature are. It cannot be imagined as being better or completer, any more than the noise of the waving of the woods at dawn, or the rhythmical beating of the sea waves upon the shore. It appears as though his Achæan faith were true—as if the Goddess of Poesy, whom he invoked in his opening line, had indeed bowed her brows to him in visible favour; and given her own heaven-strung cithara into his hands, ready set and tuned.

Yet there were kings before Agamemnon, and there were poets before Homer. Perhaps there were singers of some kind or other upon this melodious soil of Hellas in the ages even of the Pelasgians, Dryopes, Abantes, and Leleges, when the language of Homer was still unformed. There must have been a time, probably a very long time, during which the migration which brought to Europe the colonising tribes from Asia was settling down, and preparing to make Greece famous. The speech of Homer and Thucydides, contrasted with the ancient inscriptions of Anadol, with the Zend scriptures, and with Sanskrit, is seen to be unmistakably Oriental along its course, and up to its source. The legend that Cadmus gave alphabetical letters to Hellas, only means that they came from "*Kadm*," *i.e.*, the East. By-and-by the pride of Greece made her people boast that they were Autochthones—"earth-born," "indigenous to the soil." The Athenian women wore grasshoppers of gold in their hair in sign of this pretension, because grasshoppers were thought to spring ready hatched and chirping out of the earth. They called every other people "barbarians;" but there could not have been much distinction, for all that, at first between the early Hellenes and the races of Anatolia and the Levantine coasts. Homer makes his Greeks talk very readily and glibly to the Trojans and all their allies from various parts of Asia—Lycians, Dardanians, with the rest. And if this be merely the licence of the bard—as Shakespeare shows us the Prince of Morocco conversing in English with the Venetian Portia, amid similar poetic liberties—yet there is a passage in Æschylus which proves that the early close relationship of Greece with Asia was deeply felt and known. The queen, Atossa, in the "Persæ," dreams a dream, and says—

> *ἐδοξάτην μοι δύο γυναῖκ' εὐείμονε,*
> *ἡ μὲν πέπλοισι Περσικοῖς ἠσκημένη,*
> *ἡ δ' αὖτε Δωρικοῖσιν, εἰς ὄψιν μολεῖν,*
> *μεγέθει τε τῶν νῦν ἐκπρεπεστάτα πολὺ,*
> *κάλλει τ' ἀμώμω, καὶ κασιγνήτα γένους*
> *ταὐτοῦ· πάτραν δ' ἔναιον ἡ μὲν Ἑλλάδα*
> *κλήρῳ λαχοῦσα γαῖαν, ἡ δὲ βάρβαρον.*
>
> *Æsch. Pers.* 181.

> It seemed two women of a stately mien—
> One in the garments of the Persians clad,
> One in the Dorian dress—came to my sight;
> Of stature greater than the women now;
> In beauty faultless; sisters of one house:
> And one had Hellas for her dwelling-place,
> And one the foreign lands.

There is no clear record of the gradual parting of these majestic sisters, nor any way of knowing how the seed of civilisation grew so quickly and richly on the west shores of the Ægean, while it produced comparatively little to the eastward. Homer speaks of the ages before the siege of Troy as if great cities and the ordered arts of government and society already existed then in Hellas. Yet the voyages of Jason must be half-mythical annals of early marauding and commercial ventures in the Greek seas. The tale of Helen's flight with Paris, and the consequent war of the Greek chiefs and people against the Trojans, is probably but the poetic recital of an especially eventful specimen of this piracy. What sort of age it was is shown by the words *φέρτατος* and *ἄριστος*, which prove that he alone was considered "excellent" and "best" who was the most daring robber and desperate fighter. The very earliest fragments of Greek poesy are, indeed, all about battles, and the "Iliad" duly keeps up the martial preferences of these primitive singers by its style and subject. Still the Trojan expedition must have been, after all, a great and serious event to its period, for half the Hellenic states seem to have been revolutionised either while the kings were fighting, or else during their long *νόστοι—i.e.*, the homeward voyages. Other absentees besides the sailors of Ulysses had reason to say, as our Laureate has made those say—

> "Is there confusion in the little isle?
> The gods are hard to reconcile;
> 'Tis hard to settle order once again."

And all can judge how the double story of the war and of these long homeward cruises must have filled the imagination of Greece, by the fact that Homer chose them before any others for the subjects of his two great poems. There were many mythical or legendary topics and established poetic models to attract him ; for long before there must have been poet-priests to invent and consolidate the mythology of the Greek Pantheon, perhaps to translate Aryan and Egyptian theologies into Hellenic creeds. Whether Zeus and Poseidon, Hephæstus and Artemis, came or did not come from Brahmanic or Thebaid temples—whether Narayan and Nereus, Osiris and Apollo, be identical or no, certainly many a genuine, albeit priestly, genius taught the early worship of her multiform and beautiful divinities to ancient Hellas. He was a sacerdotal poet who filled the green glens of Thessaly and the thickets of Arcadia with dryads and hamadryads, and made the still woods of Cyllene solemn with the unseen presence of Pan. He or they had surely the Muses for companions who first suited to every incident of the year its graceful religious fable—made out of the disappearance of the flowers, Proserpine's descent into Hades; from the rustling of the reeds, Syrinx's tale of peril and escape; from the waving laurels, Daphne's danger and safety; and out of the coincidence of two streams of the same name in different countries, a love-legend like that of Alpheus and Arethusa. The daily life and common country scenes of Greece were turned at once into poetry and religion by this exquisite polytheism, which Homer found ready to his hand. Besides all this, he certainly had teachers in the art, for the hexameter and trimeter were invented. The strings of the poetic shell must have been long stretched and practised upon, although we know so little about it. The ἀηδὴς, or religious poet—resembling the Brahman priest who to-day in every Indian village chants the Ramayana and Mahabharata—had been for centuries a great personage with Homer's countrymen. In the "Odyssey" Homer makes Ulysses spare such an one named Phemius, while he kills all the suitors in his hall. We read, too, of the *Linus*, an ancient chant of an elegiac kind, probably half erotic, half religious, like the song of the Syrian girls for Adonis; and in the same way, perhaps, figuring by a lament the departure of the bright half of the year. The *Pæan* was a song of war of still more antique origin, for hard knocks are older than sentiment or the sense of beauty and pathos in nature. There seem to have existed a *Hymenæum* also, or marriage song, and a *Threnos*, or funeral dirge; and Thrace especially appears to have been the land of these primæval essays. To Thrace belonged Orpheus, the first name upon the poetic roll not utterly mythical, although whether Orpheus ever lived is very doubtful. At least this name gave itself twice to a school of singers and of songs called "Orphic." Musæus is mentioned as the disciple of Orpheus, but this is possibly a generic title. Then there were, it is known, the Eumolpides, or "Sweet Singers" of Eleusis, priests of Demeter, while the oracle at Delphi had its choir and composers. Agamemnon, in leaving for Troy, confides Clytemnestra, his queen, to a poet-laureate of the palace. Achilles is found playing the lute in his tent when the Greek lords come to ask his aid in battle; Phemius and Demodocus sing in the "Odyssey," while weary captains and lovely princesses listen delighted and respectful. All this shows that poetry of some sort was established very early, and, indeed, these bards were the only historians as well as musicians of their times. Thus, Helen, not without justice, is made to say in the "Iliad" of herself and Paris—

> οἷσιν ἐπὶ Ζεὺς θῆκε κακὸν μόρον, ὡς καὶ ὀπίσσω
> ἀνθρώποισι πελώμεθα ἀοίδιμοι ἐσσομένοισι.
>
> *Il.* vi. 357.

> All for my guilt and his deed, Zeus gives us a doom that is dreadful,
> Ever to live in the songs, and to be a theme for the minstrels.

These same minstrels appear to have gone about as did the Jongleurs and Troubadours of Languedoc. They could have had no books or scrolls; the transmission of verse, however long or elaborate, was oral; and none will be wonder-struck at it who has heard a Hindoo repeat thousands of "shlokes" from the Sanskrit, not one of which he ever read in the original Devanagari character. The Rhapsodist, as this peripatetic singer was called by his contemporaries, came to be an improvisatore and rhymer on his own account, as may be seen by a passage in the "Ion" of Plato (ch. 5). Rhapsodist means "one who stitches together," and the word describes the way in which old poems were doubtless patched, pieced-up, and kept alive in the time of Homer—nay, indeed, thus Homer's own glorious chants were preserved, till the time when Peisistratus and Hipparchus, aided by Onomacritus the Athenian, "edited" all the floating passages; after which papyrus handed them to parchment, parchment to paper, and so down to print, a "κτῆμα ἐς ἀεὶ"; now a possession which the world will never "let die."

So, enough is said to show that Homer did not invent poesy for Greece. But was there ever any Homer at all? Is he a mere name, like Orpheus and Musæus, and are the "Iliad" and the "Odyssey" only compilations of ancient fragmentary song, stitched or strung together by Rhapsodists with such skill that the seams are not apparent? That audacious question has not only been put, but stoutly maintained. Fénélon chose this very duology, the "Iliad" and "Odyssey," as something human which helped, by analogy, to prove the existence of God from its indubitable internal signs of unity and individual design. Wolf, however, "denied the divinity" of Homer, and his pupil Lachmann declared there were in the twenty-four books but sixteen original passages of the primal poet, whoever this might have been. Nay! pushing this perturbing theory farther, the Wolfians refuse to believe that the "Iliad" and the "Odyssey" are by the same hand or hands. Their arguments are not very cogent: for example, the "separators" say that in the "Iliad" Cassandra is declared to be the fairest daughter of Priam, but Laodice in the "Odyssey." Crete has one hundred cities in the "Iliad," and only ninety in the "Odyssey." If upon such nibbling evidence the gentle reader will not abandon either poem as Homeric, he need not surrender the certainly reasonable belief that there *was* this great poet, and that he made both these noble things. It may very well be that the fine taste of the Greek Rhapsodists and Attic editors patched the royal purple here and there of Homer's mantle—filled up the broken mosaics of his pictures with new stones delicately and critically laid in. But unity is stamped upon the general conception of these poems. The style is singularly even and equal: take out a hundred lines of either work, from any book, and it is, unmistakably, wine of one vintage—gold of one assay. As a matter of probability it is harder to conceive many different lips singing in such harmony, than to accept the universal tradition that one pair poured forth this ancient music. As a matter of sentiment, it would be grievous to rob humanity of the sublime figure which it has ever set at the head of classical poets, the "Morning Star of Song," the "Chief Musician" of men. No! the world will believe in Homer—and it may! for albeit Niebuhr speaks of Plato's knowledge of Greek history with calm, contemptuous patronage, yet Plato, and Herodotus too, within four or five centuries of the poet's date, took him steadily for granted; Alexander carried about a copy of him wherever he marched, and would have impaled Frederick Augustus Wolf and his disciples for their uncomfortable suspicions. The two majestic productions came surely from one and the same rich source: the manners and dialect are the same; the morality, the sentiments, the touch, the *cachet* are identical. One presents the fighting times, the other the sea-journeyings of the pre-historic Greek age, and both are assuredly his for the honour of whose birth seven Hellenic cities contended. Did they contend about a myth? Do not credit it, good reader! This is one voice throughout which resounds in these magnificent chants—one hand which touches the many-stringed lyre into pathos or pæan

—one divinely-gifted heart which, in the dim first days, poured forth the diapason of this masculine Greek music.

What manner of man the great Ionian was cannot be certainly known. Of all the seven rival cities which disputed his birth, Smyrna and Chios showed the best claims. He belonged past doubt to that Asiatic Greece which lay along the east coast of the Ægean: he was an Ionic Greek. The well-known ancient bust represents him to us as a blind, venerable man, the forehead radiant with high thoughts, the face worn away with the fervour of their long strain and stress. Such might well have been the aspect of the author of the "Odyssey," the calmer and more peaceful of his two poems; but the "Iliad," with its martial fanfare of verse, and spirit that "saith ha! ha! amid the trumpets," flashing the fire of war like the helmet of Hector; that must have been struck at red-heat from the soul of Homer when he was more like the warrior-poet stamped on the Smyrniote coins, and painted on the bas-reliefs of Millin. The freshness, vigour, and variety, the melody and majesty, the lively narrative, and the tenderness alternated with manliness, of the "Iliad," have been noted very often, but sufficient attention has scarcely been given to the practical soldiership of the bard. His descriptions of engagements are not mere poetic pieces—except, perhaps, in the numerous single combats—and then even Homer writes like one who knew the "music of spears." But he tells of the movements and array of battle with a minuteness which is never wearisome; and at the same time with the air of one who knows the ground and the science of war. A recent writer, M. Nicolaides, native of Crete, has published an ingenious comment upon the strategics and military details of the "Iliad," which is almost the first critical recognition of a quality running distinctly throughout the twenty-four books. And it may be remarked as an additional reason to believe in the poet, as well as to study his work, that the cutting up of the "Iliad" into these twenty-four books is what has chiefly made it seem episodical and disconnected. This was done to suit the convenience of the Rhapsodists. Homer most probably divided his poem into the Epilogue, the Action, and the Prologue. The Prologue ends at the forty-sixth line of the second book; the Action of the poem continues to the death of Hector, after which what follows is but an Epilogue or tail-piece. Viewed thus, the work is a well-proportioned temple of art, with porch and peristyle complete; or, if there be stones inserted by other hands in after times, they do not affect the noble outlines of the edifice, nor lessen the eternal fame of the architect.

The story of the "Iliad" is briefly this. It commences at the moment when, the Greeks being encamped before Troy, Agamemnon, their leader, and Achilles, the chief of their warriors, have quarrelled about Briseis, a beautiful captive. Achilles retires to his tent in wrath, and the Greeks are worsted in battle by the Trojans while he is absent. A truce is made to bury the dead; but when the fighting begins again, the Trojans, under Hector, the son of King Priam, still obtain the general advantage, pushing the Greeks to their entrenchments with great slaughter. Discouraged and in peril, they send to ask Achilles to come forth, which he refuses. The combat recommences, and Patroclus, the friend of Achilles, reports to him that the very ships of the besiegers are endangered. At this moment the glare of the burning vessel of Protesilaus shines into the tent of the great chieftain, and Achilles permits Patroclus, his bosom companion, to go forth to their succour, wearing his own armour. The god Apollo strips Patroclus of these borrowed defences, Euphorbus wounds, and Hector kills him. The rage of Achilles at this news knows no bounds. He would rush into the battle unarmed, but Pallas, from heaven, arrests him, and the fight is suspended for the night. He now determines to take part in the endangered war, and Thetis, his mother, the ocean goddess, brings him divine armour forged by the god Vulcan. He dons it, and sweeps the Trojans from the field, dealing destruction on all sides. Only Hector dares to abide him in fight under the walls of Troy, whereupon Achilles slays him with the help of his tutelary deity, who deceives the gallant Trojan. Achilles drags the dead body of his victim at his chariot-tail thrice round the walls of Troy, and performs splendid but cruel death rites to Patroclus. Then, winding up the poem with a strain of solemn pathos, Priam comes to Achilles to beg the dead body of his heroic son. Achilles is finally persuaded to restore it, and it is carried back to the city, where the inhabitants celebrate the obsequies of their hero and protector with reverence and despair. Such is an epitome of the plot—simple and straightforward enough;—but the fighting books are diversified with all kinds of episodes and incidents, strung upon the thread of the main purpose.

And now, how shall the fine savour of this old wine of poetry be conveyed to those unlucky enough not to read Homer in his own tongue? He cannot be found, alas! in any translation. Pope's wonderful production is very properly called "Pope's Homer," for it is by no means Achilles' Homer, Helen's Homer, or Hector's Homer. It is a marvellous piece of work, and full of beauties of its own; but as unlike the sonorous, free, and massive Greek as Sarpedon in a full-bottomed wig would be unlike Sarpedon in his emblazoned armour. The marshalled lines of Homer cannot be broken up into such clinquant couplets without loss. The long hexameter is necessary for the expression, and, as it were, makes a natural music to much in the sense. Take any passage for example—take the oft-quoted prayer of Ajax for light:—

> *ποιήσον δ' ἄιθρην, δὸς δ' ὀφθαλμôισιν ἴδεσθαι*
> *ἐν δὲ φάει κὰι ὄλεσσον ἐπέι νύ τοι ἔυαδεν ὄυτως.*
>
> *Il.* xvii. 647.

Pope makes of this—very elegantly and neatly, no doubt—

> "If Greece must perish, we thy will obey;
> But let us perish in the face of day."

Yet, beside the lost glory of the music here, which cannot be wholly transferred, something of the bold and ardent supplication also evaporates. Not rivalling Pope, but vindicating Homer, let us try if a translation can preserve the gradual passion of the prayer. It should be seen how the fierce heart of Ajax climbs, as it were, to the foot-stool of Zeus, demanding a soldier's right with angry iteration:—

> "Bring us the daylight back, and give our eyes sunshine to see by;
> Then face to face make us die, sith it seems that thy will is to slay us!"

Pope's facility and terseness are admirable, and what the

rhymed couplet could do he has done—but Homer cannot thus be Englished. The manner of the "Iliad" is even more than its matter, and it has been well written that the result of such an attempt upon the oceanic greatness of the Greek is like a cross sea breaking up and confusing the majestic sweep of long rolling billows. Chapman's version is rugged, but powerful and rich, and, on the whole, the very best of the old essays at the vast task. In blank verse, which, next to the original metre, might most fairly represent the Greek, Cowper stands first; Lord Derby's over-praised edition wants everything which a translation should have, except good intentions. Homer—Mr. Conington's fine work and scholarship notwithstanding—should be done into the hexametric metre, which is his own, and which goes perfectly well with the genius of our language, as Longfellow has proved. The American poet, in truth, ought to have spent his latest labour of translation on the "Iliad," or, still better, on the "Odyssey," rather than upon that most difficult *terza rima* of Dante. "Evangeline's" skilful and eloquent singer lacks nothing but the antique strength which might partly arise from the task itself, to have given us a right noble version. An Oxford scholar and laureate, Mr. Dart, has recently published the "Iliad" in this metre. His book is a worthy attempt, although not so high in achievement as to be a "success." Yet, perhaps, the measure and style of the old singer will be sooner grasped by an extract from this translation than from any other. Below is given Mr. Dart's rendering of the deaths of Cebriones and Patroclus, which in the original are told in these stirring dactyls :—

βάλε δ' Ἕκτορος ἡνιοχῆα
Κεβριόνην, νόθον υἱὸν ἀγακλῆος Πριάμοιο,
ἵππων ἡνί' ἔχοντα, μετώπιον ὀξέϊ λᾶϊ·
ἀμφοτέρας δ' ὀφρῦς σύνελε λίθος, οὐδέ οἱ ἔσχεν
ὀστέον· ὀφθαλμοὶ δὲ χαμαὶ πέσον ἐν κονίῃσιν
αὐτοῦ πρόσθε ποδῶν· ὁ δ' ἄρ', ἀρνευτῆρι ἐοικὼς,
κάππεσ' ἀπ' εὐεργέος δίφρου· λίπε δ' ὀστέα θυμός.
τὸν δ' ἐπικερτομέων προσέφης, Πατρόκλεις ἱππεῦ·
Ὢ πόποι, ἦ μάλ' ἐλαφρὸς ἀνήρ· ὡς ῥεῖα κυβιστᾷ.
εἰ δή που καὶ πόντῳ ἐν ἰχθυόεντι γένοιτο,
πολλοὺς ἂν κορέσειεν ἀνὴρ ὅδε, τήθεα διφῶν,
νηὸς ἀποθρώσκων, εἰ καὶ δυσπέμφελος εἴη·
ὡς νῦν ἐν πεδίῳ ἐξ ἵππων ῥεῖα κυβιστᾷ·
ἦ ῥα καὶ ἐν Τρώεσσι κυβιστητῆρες ἔασιν.
Ὣς εἰπὼν, ἐπὶ Κεβριόνῃ ἥρωϊ βεβήκει,
οἶμα λέοντος ἔχων, ὅστε, σταθμοὺς κεραΐζων,
ἔβλητο πρὸς στῆθος, ἑή τέ μιν ὤλεσεν ἀλκή·

The sharp stone struck on the temples
Hector's charioteer : he was bastard offspring of Priam,
Son of the famous king. For, while he was holding the bright reins,
Full on the top of his face came the huge stone, smashing the eyebrows,
Crushing the solid skull ; and the eyeballs, forced from the sockets,
Fell in the dust at his feet ; while himself, as plunges a diver,
Plunged to the earth from the car, and the fierce soul fled from the carcass.
Loud, as he mark'd the act, thus scoffingly shouted Patroclus :—

"Gods ! what a nimble man ! How easy that shoot from the chariot !
Did he but happen to live by the ocean, where fish are abounding,
Many a mouth, through him, might be satisfied, diving for oysters ;
Even in times of storm, from his boat-side taking his headers :
Easy enough for one who on land dives thus from his war-steeds.
Who would have thought such tumblers had ever been found 'mid the Trojans ?"

Thus did Patroclus speak—then rush'd on the corpse to despoil it,
Like the tremendous rush of a lion first clearing the fold-yards ;

ὣς ἐπὶ Κεβριόνῃ, Πατρόκλεις, ἆλσο μεμαώς.
Ἕκτωρ δ' αὖθ' ἑτέρωθεν ἀφ' ἵππων ἆλτο χαμᾶζε.
τὼ περὶ Κεβριόναο, λέονθ' ὥς, δηρινθήτην,
ὥ τ' ὄρεος κορυφῇσι περὶ κταμένης ἐλάφοιο,
ἄμφω πεινάοντε, μέγα φρονέοντε μάχεσθον·
ὣς περὶ Κεβριόναο δύω μήστωρες ἀϋτῆς,
Πάτροκλός τε Μενοιτιάδης καὶ φαίδιμος Ἕκτωρ,
ἵεντ' ἀλλήλων ταμέειν χρόα νηλέϊ χαλκῷ.
Ἕκτωρ μὲν κεφαλῆφιν ἐπεὶ λάβεν, οὐχὶ μεθίει·
Πάτροκλος δ' ἑτέρωθεν ἔχε ποδός· οἱ δὲ δὴ ἄλλοι
Τρῶες καὶ Δαναοὶ σύναγον κρατερὴν ὑσμίνην.
Ὡς δ' Εὖρός τε Νότος τ' ἐριδαίνετον ἀλλήλοιϊν
οὔρεος ἐν βήσσῃς βαθέην πελεμιζέμεν ὕλην,
φηγόν τε, μελίην τε, τανύφλοιόν τε κράνειαν,
αἵ τε πρὸς ἀλλήλας ἔβαλον τανυήκεας ὄζους
ἠχῇ θεσπεσίῃ, πάταγος δέ τε ἀγνυμενάων·
ὣς Τρῶες καὶ Ἀχαιοὶ ἐπ' ἀλλήλοισι θορόντες

Then, with a wound on his breast, by his courage brought to destruction :
Thus on Cebriones dead did Patroclus rush to despoil him,
While on the opposite side leapt Hector to earth from his war-steeds.
As on a mountain peak two lions, roaring defiance
Over a slaughter'd stag, all raving and savage with hunger,
Wage unrelenting war for the coveted prize of the carcass,
So for Cebriones slain did these two lords of the battle,
Hector, mighty in war, and Patroclus, son of Menœtius,
Aim at each other's breasts with the points of their murderous weapons.
Hector held by the head to his brother's corpse, and retain'd it ;
While on the dead man's foot did Patroclus seize ; and around them
Deepen'd the roar of fight of the Trojan troops and the Argives.
As with opposing blasts, when the fury of Eurus and Notus
Falls upon some dense wood, in a glen deep down on a hill-side,
Beech or tough-grain'd ash, or the long-leaved boughs of the cornel,
And, as the blast drives over, the tall trees mingle their branches,
Rasping and grating together, or breaking, perchance, with a great crash,
So, and with equal din, did the armies of Troy and Achaia

δῄουν, οὐδ' ἕτεροι μνώοντ' ὀλοοῖο φόβοιο.
πολλὰ δὲ Κεβριόνην ἀμφ' ὀξέα δοῦρα πεπήγει,
ἰοί τε πτερόεντες ἀπὸ νευρῆφι θορόντες·
πολλὰ δὲ χερμάδια μεγάλ' ἀσπίδας ἐστυφέλιξε
μαρναμένων ἀμφ' αὐτόν· ὁ δ' ἐν στροφάλιγγι κονίης
κεῖτο μέγας μεγαλωστὶ, λελασμένος ἱπποσυνάων.
Ὄφρα μὲν Ἠέλιος μέσον οὐρανὸν ἀμφιβεβήκει,
τόφρα μάλ' ἀμφοτέρων βέλε' ἥπτετο, πίπτε δὲ λαός·
ἦμος δ' Ἠέλιος μετενίσσετο βουλυτόνδε,
καὶ τότε δή ῥ' ὑπὲρ αἶσαν Ἀχαιοὶ φέρτεροι ἦσαν·
ἐκ μὲν Κεβριόνην βελέων ἥρωα ἔρυσσαν
Τρώων ἐξ ἐνοπῆς, καὶ ἀπ' ὤμων τεύχε' ἕλοντο.
Πάτροκλος δὲ Τρωσὶ κακὰ φρονέων ἐνόρουσε·
τρὶς μὲν ἔπειτ' ἐπόρουσε, θοῷ ἀτάλαντος Ἄρηϊ,
σμερδαλέα ἰάχων· τρὶς δ' ἐννέα φῶτας ἔπεφνεν·
ἀλλ' ὅτε δὴ τὸ τέταρτον ἐπέσσυτο, δαίμονι ἶσος,
ἔνθ' ἄρα τοι, Πάτροκλε, φάνη βιότοιο τελευτή·

Seek each other's breasts, and fear was forgotten among them.
Over Cebriones' corpse was the clash and the crashing of lances,
Whizzing of arrow-shafts, that bounded in wrath from the bow-strings,
Clanging of pond'rous stones, that bruised and batter'd the bucklers
Of those fighting around him. He, mighty, and mightily stretch'd out,
Heedless of reins and steeds, slept sound 'mid the storm of the battle.

All such time as the sun stands high on his path 'mid the heavens,
Falls on each army the storm of the darts, and slain are the people.
But, when the sun stands low, and releases the labouring oxen,
Then, despite of fate, has Achaia the best in the struggle.
Dragging Cebriones off from the spears, in the face of the uproar
Made by Troy's foil'd host, they strip from his shoulders the armour.
Then on his foes once more, in his wild wrath, hurtles Patroclus :
Three times, dreadful as Ares, with terrible shouts, he assails them,
Charging them home. Three times, nine warriors perish before him ;
But when, great as a god, he a fourth time charges the phalanx,
This, of thy narrow life, is the finishing effort, Patroclus !

ἤντετο γάρ τοι Φοῖβος ἐνὶ κρατερῇ ὑσμίνῃ
δεινός. ὁ μὲν τὸν ἰόντα κατὰ κλόνον οὐκ ἐνόησεν·
ἠέρι γὰρ πολλῇ κεκαλυμμένος ἀντεβόλησε.
στῆ δ' ὄπιθε, πλῆξέν τε μετάφρενον, εὐρέε τ' ὤμω
χειρὶ καταπρηνεῖ· στρεφεδίνηθεν δέ οἱ ὄσσε.
τοῦ δ' ἀπὸ μὲν κρατὸς κυνέην βάλε Φοῖβος 'Απόλλων.
ἡ δὲ κυλινδομένη καναχὴν ἔχε ποσσὶν ὑφ' ἵππων
αὐλῶπις τρυφάλεια· μιάνθησαν δὲ ἔθειραι
αἵματι καὶ κονίῃσι· πάρος γε μὲν οὐ θέμις ἦεν,
ἱπποκόμον πήληκα μιαίνεσθαι κονίῃσιν·
ἀλλ' ἀνδρὸς θείοιο κάρη, χαρίεν τε μέτωπον
ῥύετ' 'Αχιλλῆος· τότε δὲ Ζεὺς Ἕκτορι δῶκεν
ᾗ κεφαλῇ φορέειν. σχεδόθεν δέ οἱ ἦεν ὄλεθρος.
πᾶν δέ οἱ ἐν χείρεσσιν ἄγη δολιχόσκιον ἔγχος,
βριθὺ, μέγα, στιβαρὸν, κεκορυθμένον· αὐτὰρ ἀπ' ὤμων
ἀσπὶς σὺν τελαμῶνι χαμαὶ πέσε τερμιόεσσα·
λῦσε δέ οἱ θώρηκα ἄναξ, Διὸς υἱὸς, 'Απόλλων.

For, through the midst of the fray, to assail thee, Phœbus Apollo
Moves—an unequal opponent. Patroclus never discerns him,
Since in a pile of cloud is the deity veil'd and enshrouded.
Standing in rear of the chief, on his back, 'mid his shoulders, the great god
Strikes with pond'rous hand. Swim dizzy the eyes of the hero,
Flies from his temples the helm, at the buffet of Phœbus Apollo;
Far, with a clash, to the earth, far away, 'mid the hoofs of the war-steeds
Rolls that crested helm; those bright plumes waving above it
Draggle in blood and dust. They have never been wont to be soil'd so,
Never before have dust and that proud helm been acquainted,
Used, as it is, to protect in the fight the high face of a hero,
Even Achilleus' self. Now Zeus upon Hector bestows it,
Gives it to him for awhile, as he stands on the brink of destruction:
All, in Patroclus' hand, does the huge spear shiver to splinters,
Stalwart, brass-headed beam as it is; and, afar from his shoulders,
Shield of ample orb to the earth comes down, with the shield-belt;
And from his gallant breast is the corslet loosed by Apollo.

τόν δ' ἄτη φρένας εἷλε, λύθεν δ' ὑπὸ φαίδιμα γυῖα·
στῆ δὲ ταφών· ὄπιθεν δὲ μετάφρενον ὀξέϊ δουρὶ
ὤμων μεσσηγὺ σχεδόθεν βάλε Δάρδανος ἀνὴρ,
Πανθοΐδης Εὔφορβος, ὃς ἡλικίην ἐκέκαστο
ἔγχεΐ θ', ἱπποσύνῃ τε, πόδεσσί τε καρπαλίμοισι·
καὶ γὰρ δὴ τότε φῶτας ἐείκοσι βῆσεν ἀφ' ἵππων,
πρῶτ' ἐλθὼν σὺν ὄχεσφι, διδασκόμενος πολέμοιο.
ὅς τοι πρῶτος ἐφῆκε βέλος, Πατρόκλεις ἱππεῦ,
οὐ δὲ δάμασσ', ὁ μὲν αὖτις ἀνέδραμε, μίκτο δ' ὁμίλῳ,
ἐκ χροὸς ἁρπάξας δόρυ μείλινον· οὐδ' ὑπέμεινε
Πάτροκλον, γυμνόν περ ἐόντ', ἐν δηϊοτῆτι.
Πάτροκλος δὲ θεοῦ πληγῇ καὶ δουρὶ δαμασθεὶς
ἂψ ἑτάρων εἰς ἔθνος ἐχάζετο, Κῆρ' ἀλεείνων.
Ἕκτωρ δ', ὡς εἶδε Πατροκλῆα μεγάθυμον
ἂψ ἀναχαζόμενον, βεβλημένον ὀξέϊ χαλκῷ,
ἀγχίμολον ῥά οἱ ἦλθε κατὰ στίχας, οὖτα δὲ δουρὶ
νείατον ἐς κενῶνα· διὰ πρὸ δὲ χαλκὸν ἔλασσε.

Mind and senses bewilder'd, his limbs unnerved by the buffet,
Stupid, aghast he remain'd. As he stood he was struck by a Dardan
Right 'mid his shoulder-blades, with a spear from behind by Euphorbus,
Panthous' gallant son, who headed the youths of his own age,
Both in the use of the spear, and in driving of steeds, and the foot-race;
Twenty the chiefs at least he had tumbled to earth from their war-steeds,
When with his car and horses he first took lessons in battle.
This man thus with his spear first wounded the back of Patroclus—
Nor with a fatal wound; and at once from the flesh of the hero
Tearing the spear, he retreated again to his friends, nor adventured
There to abide such a foe, though unarm'd, in the perilous death-gripe.
He, by the blow of the god and the spear-stroke stunn'd and enfeebled,
Shunn'd approaching fate, and retreated again to his comrades.
Hector remark'd from afar how Patroclus, sorely disabled,
Wounded by hostile steel, and his great soul cow'd, was retreating
Back to the Argive host; so, cleaving the ranks, overtook him,
Plunging the levell'd spear through his groin, right out on the far side.

δούπησεν δὲ πεσὼν, μέγα δ' ἤκαχε λαὸν 'Αχαιῶν.
ὡς δ' ὅτε σῦν ἀκάμαντα λέων ἐβιήσατο χάρμῃ,
ὥ τ' ὄρεος κορυφῇσι μέγα φρονέοντε μάχεσθον,
πίδακος ἀμφ' ὀλίγης· ἐθέλουσι δὲ πιέμεν ἄμφω·
πολλὰ δέ τ' ἀσθμαίνοντα λέων ἐδάμασσε βίηφιν·
ὣς πολέας πέφνοντα Μενοιτίου ἄλκιμον υἱὸν
Ἕκτωρ Πριαμίδης σχεδὸν ἔγχεϊ θυμὸν ἀπηύρα·
καί οἱ ἐπευχόμενος ἔπεα πτερόεντα προσηύδα·
Πάτροκλ', ἦ που ἔφησθα πόλιν κεραϊζέμεν ἁμὴν,
Τρωϊάδας δὲ γυναῖκας, ἐλεύθερον ἦμαρ ἀπούρας,
ἄξειν ἐν νήεσσι φίλην ἐς πατρίδα γαῖαν,
νήπιε· τάων δὲ πρόσθ' Ἕκτορος ὠκέες ἵπποι
ποσσὶν ὀρωρέχαται πολεμίζειν· ἔγχεϊ δ' αὐτὸς
Τρωσὶ φιλοπτολέμοισι μεταπρέπω, ὅς σφιν ἀμύνω
ἦμαρ ἀναγκαῖον· σὲ δέ τ' ἐνθάδε γῦπες ἔδονται.
ἆ δεῖλ', οὐδέ τοι, ἐσθλὸς ἐὼν, χραίσμησεν 'Αχιλλεὺς,
ὅς πού τοι μάλα πολλὰ μένων ἐπετέλλετ' ἰόντι·

Thundering he fell to the earth. Loud, deep, was the wail of Achaia.
Just as a stubborn boar is o'ermaster'd in fight by a lion,
When on a mountain-peak they have wrangled in terrible combat
Round some half-dried spring, which both have been eager to drink of,
Until the lion's might has master'd his snorting opponent :
Thus, having overthrown many foes, the brave son of Menœtius
Yielded at length his own strong soul to the weapon of Hector,
Who to his fallen foe thus vauntingly spake and address'd him :—

"Where is the boastful hope thou'st ventured to utter, Patroclûs,
Speaking of Troy's wall storm'd, and her proud dames carried as captives
Off in Achaia's barks, far away to the land of the fathers ?
Fool ! those dames and wall had protectors ready to guard them ;
Hector and his swift steeds—steeds eager for war—and their master,
First among Troy's fierce sons in the use of the spear ; a defender
Fitter to ward off fate. But thou shalt be prey to the vultures.
Wretch ! all brave as he is, not a jot has avail'd thee Achilleus,
He but urged thee to death, for he charged thee, methinks, when departing,

μή μοι πρὶν ἰέναι, Πατρόκλεις ἱπποκέλευθε,
νῆας ἐπὶ γλαφυράς, πρίν γ' Ἕκτορος ἀνδροφόνοιο
αἱματόεντα χιτῶνα περὶ στήθεσσι δαΐξαι·
ὥς πού σε προσέφη, σοὶ δὲ φρένας ἄφρονι πεῖθε.
Τὸν δ' ὀλιγοδρανέων προσέφης, Πατρόκλεις ἱππεῦ·
ἤδη νῦν, Ἕκτορ, μεγάλ' εὔχεο· σοὶ γὰρ ἔδωκε
νίκην Ζεὺς Κρονίδης καὶ Ἀπόλλων, οἵ με δάμασσαν
ῥηϊδίως· αὐτοὶ γὰρ ἀπ' ὤμων τεύχε' ἕλοντο.
τοιοῦτοι δ' εἴπερ μοι ἐείκοσιν ἀντεβόλησαν,
πάντες κ' αὐτόθ' ὄλοντο, ἐμῷ ὑπὸ δουρὶ δαμέντες.
ἀλλά με Μοῖρ' ὀλοή, καὶ Λητοῦς ἔκτανεν υἱός,
ἀνδρῶν δ' Εὔφορβος· σὺ δέ με τρίτος ἐξεναρίζεις.
ἄλλο δέ τοι ἐρέω, σὺ δ' ἐνὶ φρεσὶ βάλλεο σῇσιν,
οὔ θην οὐδ' αὐτὸς δηρὸν βέῃ, ἀλλά τοι ἤδη
ἄγχι παρέστηκε Θάνατος καὶ Μοῖρα κραταιή,
χερσὶ δαμέντ' Ἀχιλῆος ἀμύμονος Αἰακίδαο.
Ὣς ἄρα μιν εἰπόντα τέλος θανάτοιο κάλυψε.

Thus: 'To the hollow ships do not come again, knightly Patroclus!
Seek not again this face ere thou tear from the bosom of Hector
Corslet and blood-stain'd vest, and bear them as trophies before thee.'
Such were, perchance, his words; and thou, poor fool! wert the victim."

Then with his failing breath, thus answered knightly Patroclus:—
"It is thy season to boast, and thou boastest enough. But thy conquest
Comes from Zeus himself, and from Phœbus—they have subdued me
Easily, as gods could; themselves disarming my shoulders.
If twice ten such as thou had encounter'd me fairly in battle,
All had sunk in fight, and had bow'd to the brunt of my lance-point.
Fate overthrew me the first: it is Leto's son who has slain me;
Then came of men Euphorbus, and thou standest third in the death work.
But, take heed to my words, and ponder them well as I speak them:
Know that thyself, proud man, art doom'd not long to survive me.
Death and relentless fate are standing already beside thee,
Doom'd, ere long, to be slain by the hands of the noble Achilleus!"

Thus, as he spake, came death with its dark shade gloomily o'er him,

ψυχὴ δ' ἐκ ῥεθέων πταμένη 'Αϊδόσδε βεβήκει,
ὃν πότμον γοόωσα, λιποῦσ' ἁδροτῆτα καὶ ἥβην.

Il., Bk. 16.

Flitted the naked soul from the beautiful body to Hades,
Wailing its hapless fate, and the vigour and youth it abandon'd.

Dart's Iliad.

In that passage there are many of the chief characteristics of Homer; and such is the nature of all the fighting. The great chiefs stalk before the rank and file, and sustain almost alone the fortunes of the day. It is the oligarchy of battle—the monopoly of carnage! Ajax is a battalion on one side, Hector a *corps d'armée* on the other, while Achilles, when he does condescend to sally forth, slaughters Trojans by the score. The combatants proclaim their own merits like Red Indians, and insult the dead with bitter and barbarous taunts, as Patroclus in the above extract. There is a thoroughly savage element about the actual combats, which takes us back, indeed, to pre-civilised times; for scarcely a great soldier in the "Iliad," except Hector, comes up at all to the modern idea of "an officer and a gentleman." Achilles, in the opening quarrel of the poem, rails at Agamemnon (his king and general, be it remembered), in this classical Billingsgate :—

Οἰνοβαρὲς, κυνὸς ὄμματ' ἔχων, κραδίην δ' ἐλάφοιο,
οὔτε πότ' ἐς πόλεμον ἅμα λαῷ θωρηχθῆναι,
οὔτε λόχονδ' ἰέναι σὺν ἀριστήεσσιν 'Αχαιῶν
τέτληκας θυμῷ. *Il.* i. 225.

Wine-sodden sot, with the face of a dog, and the heart of a roe-buck!
Never once into the war, at the head of thy troops, in thine armour,—
Never once out on the ambush, along with the lords of Achaia—
Daredst thou to go!

But Achilles is simply a beautiful brutal creature—the apotheosis of animal force and passion—an incarnation of selfish anger, only redeemed by perfect grace and bodily excellence; though his very courage is marred by the knowledge that he has the protection of Athene, and of his goddess-mother, who have made him all but invulnerable. His friendship for Patroclus seems of a dubious elevation, and his rage at the death of his friend is rendered more furious, apparently, by personal pique than devotion. It may be said that the words which he exchanges with his horses (Iliad xix. 420) prove that he foresaw and recognised his fate by the arrow of Paris. If his prowess be rehabilitated by this passage, his ferocity remains at least undefended and indefensible. He is exactly as Horace paints him—

> "Impiger, iracundus, *inexorabilis*, acer."

No man gets mercy of him in war; valour does not make him respect it, nor youth win him to compassionate it. When he breaks forth at last "like a hungry lion" from his tent, he rages over the plain, inebriate with blood. A lion is not the right simile, for a lion has generosity: Achilles, in his grace and blood-thirstiness, resembles a panther rather, which slays for mere lust of slaughter when peril or appetite are over. Read the passage in which, after endless killing, he encounters and puts to the sword the son of Alastor:—

> *ὁ μὲν ἀντίος ἤλυθε, γούνων,*
> *εἴπως εὖ πεφίδοιτο, λαβὼν, καὶ ζωὸν ἀφείη,*
> *μηδὲ κατακτείνειεν, ὁμηλικίην ἐλεήσας·*
> *νήπιος, οὐδὲ τὸ ᾔδη, ὃ οὐ πείσεσθαι ἔμελλεν.*
> *οὐ γάρ τι γλυκύθυμος ἀνὴρ ἦν, οὐδ' ἀγανόφρων,*

ἀλλά μάλ' ἐμμεμαώς. ὁ μέν ἥπτετο χείρεσι γούνων,
ἱέμενος λίσσεσθ', ὁ δὲ φασγάνῳ οὖτα καθ' ἧπαρ·
ἐκ δέ οἱ ἧπαρ ὄλισθεν, ἀτὰρ μέλαν αἷμα κατ' αὐτοῦ
κόλπον ἐνέπλησε, τὸν δὲ σκότος ὄσσε κάλυψε,
θυμοῦ δευόμενον. *Il.* xix. 420.

Nor less unpitied young Alastor bleeds.
In vain his youth, in vain his beauty, pleads.
In vain he begs thee, with a suppliant moan,
To spare a form, an age so like thy own!
Unhappy boy! no prayer, no moving art,
E'er bent that fierce inexorable heart.
While yet he trembled at his knees, and cried,
The ruthless falchion oped his tender side.
The panting liver pours a flood of gore
That drowns his bosom, till he pants no more.

Pope's Iliad.

It is here Homer, his limner, who calls the Greek *ὀυ τὶ γλύκυθυμος*, "nothing sweet-natured," and Homer keeps all his painting consistent and equal, so that wherever we find Achilles we find this same insolent and heartless ideal of a "fighting man," the *ἄριστος* of the ancient pattern. When the unfair gods have given Hector into his hands, and the glorious Dardan lies, with the spear-wound in his neck, bleeding to death, he pleads with Achilles to let his body be buried. "By thy life, by thy knees, by thy father and mother," Hector entreats, "let not the dogs have my flesh. Take what ransom you will; Troy will pay any sum! But as you are brave and victorious, let my remains go to my own people." Whereupon the arrogant conqueror —the cannibal, rather—answers—

μή με, κύον, γούνων γουνάζεο, μηδὲ τοκήων.
αἳ γάρ πως αὐτόν με μένος καὶ θυμὸς ἀνήῃ

ὤμ' ἀποταμνόμενον κρέα ἔδμεναι, οἷά μ' ἔοργας·
ὣς οὐκ ἔσθ', ὃς σῆς γε κύνας κεφαλῆς ἀπαλάλκοι·
οὐδ' εἴ κεν δεκάκις τε καὶ εἰκοσινήριτ' ἄποινα
στήσωσ' ἐνθάδ' ἄγοντες, ὑπόσχωνται δὲ καὶ ἄλλα·
οὐδ' εἴ κεν σ' αὐτὸν χρυσῷ ἐρύσασθαι ἀνώγοι
Δαρδανίδης Πρίαμος· οὐδ' ὣς σέ γε πότνια μήτηρ
ἐνθεμένη λεχέεσσι γοήσεται, ὃν τέκεν αὐτή,
ἀλλὰ κύνες τε καὶ οἰωνοὶ κατὰ πάντα δάσονται.

Il. xix. 345.

No, wretch accurs'd ! (relentless he replies :
Flames, as he spoke, shot flashing from his eyes),
Not those who gave me breath should bid me spare,
Nor all the sacred prevalence of prayer,
Could I myself the bloody banquet join !
No—to the dogs that carcass I resign.
Should Troy to bribe me bring forth all her store,
And, giving thousands, offer thousands more ;
Should Dardan Priam and his weeping dame
Drain their whole realm to buy one funeral flame :
Their Hector on the pile they should not see,
Nor rob the vultures of one limb of thee.

Pope's Iliad.

"Right well," the dying hero sighs, "I knew you were iron-hearted!" Once, truly, the strong and savage nature melts, when the reaction of rage sets in, and he sees Priam kneeling before him, kissing the hands which have killed the hope of Troy, and imploring that the precious body may be surrendered. Achilles softens then, and it is well-nigh the only time in the "Iliad" when he is not as hateful as he is fair, and as fierce as he is swift and splendid.

Hector is the "Christian soldier," as far as such a type could exist before the strange doctrine astonished the world that we should "love our enemies." He is even braver than Achilles, for he has no charm against spears and arrows except the favour of those few Gods who happen to take sides with Troy; yet he sustains the fortunes of his native city from the first to the last with generous and manly valour. The noblest sentiments of the poem come all from his mouth. It is he who laughs at the auguries when they forbid the battle, saying—

εἷς οἰωνὸς ἄριστος ἀμύνεσθαι περὶ πατρῆς.

Without a bird his sword the brave man draws,
And asks no omen but his country's cause.

It is he who is ever ready to expose himself for the common cause against the most doughty champion offering, and his anger is seldom roused except towards cowardice. For that his patriotic soul has no manner of patience. When Paris, the cause of all the war, turns back from the face of Menelaus in the fight, the great warrior rebukes him very sternly:—

Δύσπαρι, εἶδος ἄριστε, γυναιμανὲς, ἠπεροπευτὰ
αἴθ' ὄφελες ἄγονός τ' ἔμεναι, ἄγαμός τ' ἀπολέσθαι.
καί κε τὸ βουλοίμην, καί κεν πολὺ κέρδιον ἦεν,
ἢ οὕτω λώβην τ' ἔμεναι καὶ ὑπόψιον ἄλλων.
ἦ που καγχαλόωσι καρηκομόωντες 'Αχαιοὶ,

Unhappy Paris! but to women brave!
So fairly form'd, and only to deceive!
Oh! hadst thou died when first thou saw'st the light,
Or died at least before thy nuptial rite!
A better fate than vainly thus to boast,
And fly, the scandal of thy Trojan host.
Gods! how the scornful Greeks exult to see
Their fears of danger undeceiv'd in thee!
Thy figure promis'd with a martial air,

φάντες ἀριστῆα πρόμον ἔμμεναι, οὕνεκα καλὸν
εἶδος ἔπ᾿· ἀλλ᾿ οὐκ ἔστι βίη φρεσὶν, οὐδέ τις ἀλκή.
ἦ τοιόσδε ἐὼν ἐν ποντοπόροισι νέεσσι
πόντον ἐπιπλώσας, ἑτάρους ἐρίηρας ἀγείρας,
μιχθεὶς ἀλλοδαποῖσι, γυναῖκ᾿ εὐειδέ᾿ ἀνῆγες
ἐξ ᾿Απίης γαίης, νυὸν ἀνδρῶν αἰχμητάων ;
πατρί τε σῷ μέγα πῆμα, πόληΐ τε, παντί τε δήμῳ,
δυσμενέσι μὲν χάρμα, κατηφείην δέ σοι αὐτῷ ;
οὐκ ἂν δὴ μείνειας ᾿Αρηΐφιλον Μενέλαον ;
γνοίης χ᾿, οἵου φωτὸς ἔχεις θαλερὴν παράκοιτιν.
οὐκ ἄν τοι χραίσμῃ κίθαρις, τά τε δῶρ᾿ ᾿Αφροδίτης,
ἥ τε κόμη, τό τε εἶδος, ὅτ᾿ ἐν κονίῃσι μιγείης.
ἀλλὰ μάλα Τρῶες δειδήμονες· ἦ τέ κεν ἤδη
λάϊνον ἕσσο χιτῶνα, κακῶν ἕνεχ᾿, ὅσσα ἔοργας.

Il. iii. 39—57

But ill thy soul supplies a form so fair.
In former days, in all thy gallant pride,
When thy tall ships triumphant stemm'd the tide,
When Greece beheld thy painted canvas flow,
And crowds stood wondering at the passing show ;
Say, was it thus, with such a baffled mien,
You met th' approaches of the Spartan queen ;
Thus from her realm convey'd the beauteous prize,
And both her warlike lords outshin'd in Helen's eyes?
This deed, thy foes' delight, thy own disgrace,
Thy father's grief, the ruin of thy race ;
This deed recalls thee to the proffer'd fight;
Or hast thou injur'd whom thou dar'st not right?
Soon to thy cost the field would make thee know
Thou keep'st the consort of a braver foe.
Thy graceful form instilling soft desire,
Thy curling tresses, and thy silver lyre,
Beauty and youth, in vain to these you trust,
When youth and beauty shall be laid in dust.
Troy yet may wake, and one avenging blow
Crush the dire author of his country's woe.

Pope's Homer's Iliad.

But when Paris, ashamed and reminded of himself, offers to engage Menelaus in single combat, Hector's heart leaps up for joy to find his brother no poltroon: *ἐχάρη μέγα.* He is mightily glad, for he harbours no petty feeling, and will fight twice ten years, if necessary, after that, for Paris and Helen. Towards the beautiful Greek who is the cause of such woe to his country, Hector is ever exquisite in manner. The few passages wherein they encounter represent him as gravely courteous, and her as in turn sincerely respectful; and though we must not mistake their age for one of much "morality" in the modern sense, it is plain, from Hector's well-marked deference, and the mild language of King Priam, that Helen was meant by Homer to seem no wanton "light o' love." Obviously

> "The face that launched a thousand ships,
> And sacked the topless towers of Ilium"

appeared to the Trojan generalissimo—one of a breed of sea-pirates himself—excuse for a good deal. Yet in his grave and dutiful speeches, and far different estimate of love, as evinced towards Andromache; as well as in Homer's obvious preference for the gallant chieftain, we see the light of a purer principle very clear. Perhaps the most lovely passage of the "Iliad" is that oft-cited one in which Hector bids adieu to his wife and child before joining battle. It is this:—

> *Δαιμόνιε, φθίσει σε τὸ σὸν μένος, οὐδ' ἐλεαίρεις*
> *παῖδά τε νηπίαχον, καὶ ἔμ' ἄμμορον, ἣ τάχα χήρη*
> *σεῦ ἔσομαι. τάχα γάρ σε κατακτανέουσιν 'Αχαιοὶ,*

> Too daring prince! ah! whither dost thou run?
> Oh! so forgetful of thy wife and son!
> And think'st thou not how wretched we shall be,

πάντες ἐφορμηθέντες. ἐμοὶ δέ κε κέρδιον εἴη,
σεῦ ἀφαμαρτούσῃ, χθόνα δύμεναι. οὐ γὰρ ἔτ' ἄλλη
ἔσται θαλπωρή, ἐπεὶ ἂν σύγε πότμον ἐπίσπῃς,
ἀλλ' ἄχε'. οὐδέ μοι ἐστὶ πατὴρ καὶ πότνια μήτηρ·
ἤτοι γὰρ πατέρ' ἁμὸν ἀπέκτανε δῖος Ἀχιλλεύς,
ἐκ δὲ πόλιν πέρσε Κιλίκων εὖ ναιετάωσαν,
Θήβην ὑψίπυλον· κατὰ δ' ἔκτανεν Ἠετίωνα,
οὐδέ μιν ἐξενάριξε· σεβάσσατο γὰρ τόγε θυμῷ·
ἀλλ' ἄρα μιν κατέκηε σὺν ἔντεσι δαιδαλέοισιν,
ἠδ' ἐπὶ σῆμ' ἔχεεν· περὶ δὲ πτελέας ἐφύτευσαν
Νύμφαι Ὀρεστιάδες, κοῦραι Διὸς αἰγιόχοιο.
οἳ δέ μοι ἑπτὰ κασίγνητοι ἔσαν ἐν μεγάροισιν,
οἱ μὲν πάντες ἰῷ κίον ἤματι Ἄϊδος εἴσω·
πάντας γὰρ κατέπεφνε ποδάρκης δῖος Ἀχιλλεύς,
βουσὶν ἐπ' εἰλιπόδεσσι καὶ ἀργεννῇς ὀΐεσσι.

A widow I, a helpless orphan he?
For sure such courage length of life denies;
And thou must fall, thy virtue's sacrifice.
Greece in her single heroes strove in vain;
Now hosts oppose thee, and thou must be slain.
Oh! grant me, gods! ere Hector meets his doom,
All I can ask of Heaven, an early tomb!
So shall my days in one sad tenor run;
And end with sorrows as they first begun.
No parent now remains my griefs to share,
No father's aid, no mother's tender care.
The fierce Achilles wrapp'd our walls in fire;
Laid Thebè waste, and slew my warlike sire!
His fate compassion in the victor bred.
Stern as he was, he yet rever'd the dead;
His radiant arms preserv'd from hostile spoil,
And laid him decent on the funeral pile:
Then rais'd a mountain where his bones were burn'd.
The mountain nymphs the rural tomb adorn'd.
Jove's sylvan daughters bade their elms bestow
A barren shade, and in his honour grow.

μητέρα δ', ἣ βασίλευεν ὑπὸ Πλάκῳ ὑλήεσσῃ,
τὴν ἐπεὶ ἂρ δεῦρ' ἤγαγ' ἅμ' ἄλλοισι κτεάτεσσιν,
ἂψ ὅγε τὴν ἀπέλυσε, λαβὼν ἀπερείσι' ἄποινα·
πατρὸς δ' ἐν μεγάροισι βάλ' Ἄρτεμις ἰοχέαιρα.
Ἕκτορ, ἀτὰρ σύ μοι ἐσσὶ πατὴρ καὶ πότνια μήτηρ,
ἠδὲ κασίγνητος, σὺ δέ μοι θαλερὸς παρακοίτης.
ἀλλ' ἄγε νῦν ἐλέαιρε, καὶ αὐτοῦ μίμν' ἐπὶ πύργῳ,
μὴ παῖδ' ὀρφανικὸν θείης, χήρην τε γυναῖκα·
λαὸν δὲ στῆσον παρ' ἐρινεὸν, ἔνθα μάλιστα
ἄμβατός ἐστι πόλις, καὶ ἐπίδρομον ἔπλετο τεῖχος.
τρὶς γὰρ τῇ γ' ἐλθόντες ἐπειρήσανθ' οἱ ἄριστοι
ἀμφ' Αἴαντε δύω, καὶ ἀγακλυτὸν Ἰδομενῆα,
ἠδ' ἀμφ' Ἀτρείδας, καὶ Τυδέος ἄλκιμον υἱόν·
ἤπου τίς σφιν ἔνισπε θεοπροπίων εὖ εἰδὼς,
ἤ νυ καὶ αὐτῶν θυμὸς ἐποτρύνει καὶ ἀνώγει.

By the same arm my seven brave brothers fell,
In one sad day beheld the gates of hell.
While the fat herds and snowy flocks they fed,
Amid their fields, the hapless heroes bled!
My mother liv'd to bear the victor's bands.
The queen of Hippoplacia's sylvan lands,
Redeem'd too late, she scarce beheld again,
Her pleasing empire and her native plain,
When, ah! oppress'd by life-consuming woe,
She fell a victim to Diana's bow.
Yet, while my Hector still survives, I see
My father, mother, brethren, all in thee.
Alas! my parents, brothers, kindred, all
Once more will perish, if my Hector fall.
Thy wife, thy infant, in thy danger share:
Oh! prove a husband's and a father's care!
That quarter most the skilful Greeks annoy,
Where yon wild fig-trees join the wall of Troy.
Thou from this tower defend th' important post.
There Agamemnon points his dreadful host.
That pass Tydides, Ajax, strive to gain;
And there the vengeful Spartan fires his train.
Thrice our bold foes the fierce attack have given,

Τὴν δ' αὖτε προσέειπε μέγας κορυθαίολος Ἕκτωρ·
ἦ καὶ ἐμοὶ τάδε πάντα μέλει, γύναι· ἀλλὰ μάλ' αἰνῶς
αἰδέομαι Τρῶας καὶ Τρωάδας ἑλκεσιπέπλους,
αἴ κε, κακὸς ὥς, νόσφιν ἀλυσκάζω πολέμοιο.
οὐδ' ἐμὲ θυμὸς ἄνωγεν· ἐπεὶ μάθον ἔμμεναι ἐσθλὸς
αἰεὶ, καὶ πρώτοισι μετὰ Τρώεσσι μάχεσθαι,
ἀρνύμενος πατρός τε μέγα κλέος, ἠδ' ἐμὸν αὐτοῦ.
εὖ μὲν γὰρ τόδε οἶδα κατὰ φρένα καὶ κατὰ θυμὸν,
ἔσσεται ἦμαρ, ὅτ' ἄν ποτ' ὀλώλῃ Ἴλιος ἱρὴ,
καὶ Πρίαμος, καὶ λαὸς ἐϋμμελίω Πριάμοιο.
ἀλλ' οὔ μοι Τρώων τόσσον μέλει ἄλγος ὀπίσσω,
οὔτ' αὐτῆς Ἑκάβης, οὔτε Πριάμοιο ἄνακτος,
οὔτε κασιγνήτων, οἵ κεν πολέες τε καὶ ἐσθλοὶ
ἐν κονίῃσι πέσοιεν ὑπ' ἀνδράσι δυσμενέεσσιν,
ὅσσον σεῖ', ὅτε κέν τις Ἀχαιῶν χαλκοχιτώνων

Or led by hopes, or dictated from heaven.
Let others in the field their arms employ;
But stay my Hector here, and guard his Troy.
The chief replied: That post shall be my care,
Nor that alone, but all the works of war.
How would the sons of Troy, in arms renown'd,
And Troy's proud dames, whose garments sweep the ground,
Attaint the lustre of my former name,
Should Hector basely quit the field of fame!
My early youth was bred to martial pains.
My soul impels me to th' embattled plains.
Let me be foremost to defend the throne,
And guard my father's glories and my own.
Yet come it will, the day decreed by fates,
(How my heart trembles, while my tongue relates!)
The day when thou, imperial Troy! must bend,
And see thy warriors fall, thy glories end.
And yet no dire presage so wounds my mind,
My mother's death, the ruin of my kind,
Not Priam's hoary hairs defil'd with gore,
Not all my brothers gasping on the shore,

δακρυόεσσαν ἄγηται, ἐλεύθερον ἦμαρ ἀπούρας·
καί κεν, ἐν Ἄργει ἐοῦσα, πρὸς ἄλλης ἱστὸν ὑφαίνοις,
καί κεν ὕδωρ φορέοις Μεσσηΐδος ἢ Ὑπερείης,
πόλλ' ἀεκαζομένη· κρατερὴ δ' ἐπικείσετ' ἀνάγκη·
καί ποτέ τις εἴπησιν, ἰδὼν κατὰ δάκρυ χέουσαν·
Ἕκτορος ἥδε γυνή, ὃς ἀριστεύεσκε μάχεσθαι
Τρώων ἱπποδάμων, ὅτε Ἴλιον ἀμφεμάχοντο.
ὥς ποτέ τις ἐρέει· σοὶ δ' αὖ νέον ἔσσεται ἄλγος
χήτεϊ τοιοῦδ' ἀνδρὸς, ἀμύνειν δούλιον ἦμαρ.
ἀλλά με τεθνειῶτα χυτὴ κατὰ γαῖα καλύπτοι,
πρίν γε τι σῆς τε βοῆς, σοῦ θ' ἑλκηθμοῖο πυθέσθαι.
Ὣς εἰπὼν, οὗ παιδὸς ὀρέξατο φαίδιμος Ἕκτωρ.
ἂψ δ' ὁ πάϊς πρὸς κόλπον ἐϋζώνοιο τιθήνης
ἐκλίνθη ἰάχων, πατρὸς φίλου ὄψιν ἀτυχθεὶς,
ταρβήσας χαλκόν τ', ἠδὲ λόφον ἱππιοχαίτην,

As thine, Andromache! thy griefs I dread.
I see thee trembling, weeping, captive led,
In Argive looms our battles to design,
And woes of which so large a part was thine:
To bear the victor's hard commands, or bring
The weight of waters from Hyperia's spring.
There, while you groan beneath the load of life,
They cry, behold the mighty Hector's wife!
Some haughty Greek, who lives thy tears to see,
Embitters all thy woes, by naming me.
The thoughts of glory past and present shame,
A thousand griefs shall waken at the name!
May I lie cold, before that dreadful day,
Press'd with a load of monumental clay!
Thy Hector, wrapt in everlasting sleep,
Shall neither hear thee sigh, nor see thee weep.
Thus having spoke, th' illustrious chief of Troy,
Stretch'd his fond arms to clasp the lovely boy.
The babe clung crying to his nurse's breast,
Scar'd at the dazzling helm and nodding crest.
With secret pleasure each fond parent smil'd;

δεινὸν ἀπ' ἀκροτάτης κόρυθος νεύοντα νοήσας·
ἐκ δὲ γέλασσε πατήρ τε φίλος, καὶ πότνια μήτηρ.
αὐτίκ' ἀπὸ κρατὸς κόρυθ' εἵλετο φαίδιμος Ἕκτωρ,
καὶ τὴν μὲν κατέθηκεν ἐπὶ χθονὶ παμφανόωσαν.
αὐτὰρ, ὅγ' ὃν φίλον υἱὸν ἐπεὶ κύσε, πῆλέ τε χερσὶν,
εἶπεν ἐπευξάμενος Διΐ τ', ἄλλοισί τε θεοῖσι·
    Ζεῦ, ἄλλοι τε θεοὶ, δότε δὴ καὶ τόνδε γενέσθαι
παῖδ' ἐμὸν, ὡς καὶ ἐγώ περ, ἀριπρεπέα Τρώεσσιν,
ὧδε βίην τ' ἀγαθὸν, καὶ Ἰλίου ἶφι ἀνάσσειν.
καί ποτέ τις εἴπῃσι· πατρὸς δ' ὅγε πολλὸν ἀμείνων·
ἐκ πολέμου ἀνιόντα· φέροι δ' ἔναρα βροτόεντα,
κτείνας δήϊον ἄνδρα, χαρείη δὲ φρένα μήτηρ.
    Ὣς εἰπὼν, ἀλόχοιο φίλης ἐν χερσὶν ἔθηκε
παῖδ' ἑόν· ἡ δ' ἄρα μιν κηώδεϊ δέξατο κόλπῳ,

And Hector hasted to relieve his child ;
The glittering terrors from his brows unbound,
And placed the beaming helmet on the ground :
Then kiss'd the child, and, lifting high in air,
Thus to the gods preferr'd a father's prayer :
    O thou ! whose glory fills th' ethereal throne,
And all ye deathless powers ! protect my son !
Grant him, like me, to purchase just renown,
To guard the Trojans, to defend the crown ;
Against his country's foes the war to wage,
And rise, the Hector of the future age !
So when, triumphant from successful toils,
Of heroes slain he bears the reeking spoils,
Whole hosts may hail him with deserv'd acclaim,
And say, This chief transcends his father's fame :
While, pleas'd amidst the general shouts of Troy,
His mother's conscious heart o'erflows with joy.
    He spoke, and, fondly gazing on her charms,
Restor'd the pleasing burden to her arms.
Soft on her fragrant breast the babe she laid,
Hush'd to repose, and with a smile survey'd.
The troubled pleasure soon chastis'd by fear,
She mingled with the smile a tender tear.

D

δακρυόεν γελάσασα. πόσις δ' ἐλέησε νοήσας,
χειρί τέ μιν κατέρεξεν, ἔπος τ' ἔφατ', ἐκ τ' ὀνόμαζε·
Δαιμονίη, μή μοί τι λίην ἀκαχίζεο θυμῷ.
οὐ γάρ τίς μ' ὑπὲρ αἶσαν ἀνὴρ Ἄϊδι προϊάψει.
μοῖραν δ' οὔτινά φημι πεφυγμένον ἔμμεναι ἀνδρῶν,
οὐ κακὸν, οὐδὲ μὲν ἐσθλὸν, ἐπὴν ταπρῶτα γένηται.
ἀλλ' εἰς οἶκον ἰοῦσα τὰ σαυτῆς ἔργα κόμιζε,
ἱστόν τ', ἠλακάτην τε, καὶ ἀμφιπόλοισι κέλευε
ἔργον ἐποιχεσθαι· πόλεμος δ' ἄνδρεσσι μελήσει
πᾶσιν, ἐμοὶ δὲ μάλιστα, τοὶ Ἰλίῳ ἐγγεγάασιν.

Il. vi. 394—494.

The soften'd chief with kind compassion view'd,
And dried the falling drops, and thus pursued :
Andromache ! my soul's far better part !
Why with untimely sorrows heaves thy heart ?
No hostile hand can antedate my doom,
Till fate condemns me to the silent tomb.
Fix'd is the term to all the race of earth ;
And such the hard condition of our birth.
No force can then resist, no flight can save ;
All sink alike, the fearful and the brave.
No more—but hasten to the tasks at home ;
There guide the spindle, and direct the loom.
Me glory summons to the martial scene ;
The field of combat is the sphere for men.
Where heroes war, the foremost place I claim,
The first in danger, as the first in fame.

Pope's Homer's Iliad.

The quotation is long, but Hector well deserves it ; for what can be finer than the strong soldier's tenderness, the gentle manliness which he displays towards his wife, and that sweet touch of nature, linking the far-off day with all which is soft and loving in human spirits for ever, when he takes off his nodding helmet-plume that the little Astyanax may not be frightened ? What can be more eloquent, either, than the δακρυόεν γελάσασα, the "tearful smile" of Andromache? Usage has wrought this noble Trojan much wrong in making the verb "to hector" imply, as it does, "to swagger," "to bluster." The chief talks fiercely and big at times, like the others; but from first to last he is the Bayard of the "Iliad," "sans peur et sans reproche."

This identity in the personal qualities of the Homeric heroes is to a just mind one of the greatest proofs of the unity of the work. It is preserved through all the leading characters. Ajax is ever blunderingly brave—a "heavy" of the Greek foot-guards; a "beef-witted lord," "good at need," in truth, but with muscle somewhat cumbrously overlying mind. Paris is light, womanish, sensitive, graceful, and unstable; Diomed, quick in council and agile in the fight—a Greek Paris without the feminine element. We are nowhere jarred by such inconsistencies as patchwork composition would have brought in. Ulysses, doubly important because he is the hero of the second poem of this duology, never once loses his character as πολυμητὶς. He fights like a cunning man, and plots like a brave one; he has neither any cowardice in him, nor any imprudence—nor, to speak the truth, very much true elevation of soul. He is Common Sense in splendid armour—a mailed *père de famille;* wise, substantial, unvulgar, but as practical as a British tax-payer. The clear, broad lines in which Homer paints this favourite of Pallas—as also the companion-portrait of Æneas, the Trojan prince—are almost as strong as proof can be to the careful student that one and the same genius created or recalled to life the grand company of captains amid which these live and move. It may be seen by the "Æneid" and in "Troilus and Cressida" how perfectly easy it was to identify and transfer such vitalised and consistent individualities.

But the women of Homer must have due mention. First in beauty and world-wide fame—not in virtue, alas! comes that fair plague of men—

Ἑλένας, ἕλανδρος, ἑλέπτολις,

the "*causa teterrima belli*"—HELEN. Homer takes care that we shall know how glorious her charms were, and why so many Greeks and Trojans died gladly for their sake. When she passes out upon the wall among the old men of the city, even they chirrup praises at her like grasshoppers, τεττίγεσσιν ἐοικοτες. They say, with effusion of admiration—

Οὐ νέμεσις, Τρῶας καὶ ἐϋκνήμιδας Ἀχαιοὺς
τοιῇδ' ἀμφὶ γυναικὶ πολὺν χρόνον ἄλγεα πάσχειν·
αἰνῶς ἀθανάτῃσι θεῇς εἰς ὦπα ἔοικεν.
ἀλλὰ καὶ ὧς, τοίη περ ἐοῦσ', ἐν νηυσὶ νεέσθω,
μηδ' ἡμῖν τεκέεσσί τ' ὀπίσσω πῆμα λίποιτο.

Il. iii. 155.

Sure 'tis no marvel that Troy and the well-greaved men of Achaia
All this while should struggle and bleed for a woman like that one!
Awfully lovely she is, and like the immortals to look on;
Still, it were well she went back in the ships with her terrible beauty,
Rather than tarry, a curse upon us, and our children hereafter.

And Helen—her history notwithstanding, and notwithstanding that she has to look out from the Trojan wall and point below it to Menelaus, her deserted husband—is in Homer no wanton, but a gentle, though sinful, and sorrowful dame. Priam comforts her with pious words about the "power of the gods;" Hector is, as has been said, invariably respectful and polite; Antenor, and all the chiefs—full allowance being made for the laxer morality of the old days—are still particularly tender and pitiful towards her, as if Priam's view of the matter were upon all their minds—

> *οὔτι μοι αἰτίη ἐσσὶ, θεοι νυ μοι αἴτιοι ἐισιν.*
>
> *Il.* iii. 160.
>
> 'Tis not you are the cause—the gods are the cause—the gods only.

Her best plea for consideration throughout the carnage which takes place around and on account of her, is, that she never forgives herself. Others may see in her but the victim of the will of Zeus—she for herself is deeply ashamed and penitent; even in her tenderest passages with Paris, she retains enough of the Greek princess in her to upbraid him for his cowardice and to regret her guilt; while before Hector's face she abases herself into the dust with the agony of self-reproach, and pours out all a woman's burning pity for her thousands of bleeding victims. In the "Odyssey" these qualities in her, so carefully emphasised by the great artist, have brought her as much peace of mind as the dreadful war can have left. She is discovered to us restored, and not without honour and happiness, to the court of her husband Menelaus—modest, hospitable, but high-serious with her past shame and present forgiveness. Very tender and full of a later wisdom are those last words of Helen in the "Odyssey"—

> *ἔνθ' ἄλλαι Τρωαὶ λίγ' ἐκώκυον· αὐτὰρ ἐμὸν κῆρ*
> *χαῖρ', ἐπεὶ ἤδη μοι κραδίη τέτραπτο νέεσθαι*

ἂψ οἶκόνδ', ἄτην δὲ μετέστενον, ἣν Ἀφροδίτη
δῶχ', ὅτε μ' ἤγαγε κεῖσε φίλης ἀπὸ πατρίδος αἴης,
παῖδά τ' ἐμὴν νοσφισσαμένην θάλαμόν τε πόσιν τε
οὔ τευ δευόμενον, οὔτ' ἂρ φρένας οὔτε τι εἶδος.

Od. iv. 261.

Troy and the Trojan dames were sad. But I then the rather
Gladdened, because my heart was turned to sail the sea over
Back to my home—for I mourned the sweet mischief the goddess had done me,
Aphrodite the strong, in tempting me far from my country,
Far from my child, my home—far, worst of all, from my lord here,
Second to no one—ah me ! in heart, nor in beauty of body.

But, indeed, if virtue had its rights of precedence, Hector's wife should come first. Andromache, shrined in the very loveliest verses wherever her name occurs, and heroine of that already-quoted passage which breaks the clouds of war like the evening star, is therein sufficiently pourtrayed. Andromache is one of those perfect wives whose instinctive honour and purity taught the world the happy lesson of such words as honour and purity in times when constancy and wedded troth were only being learned. None of the goddesses in the Iliadic heaven are so divine as this Trojan mother and wife, whose grace and goodness, pourtrayed so early, and belonging to an age so far removed, help us to believe that "sweetness and light" were among the most ancient of the possessions of the world, and, above all, of that sex which the other treats as "inferior."

The morality of Homer has been a subject of much discussion in all ages, from Plato down to Mr. Gladstone. The Athenian philosopher, who drove the poets from his republic, makes no exception in favour of the Father of them. He condemns him for a theology where the Gods are of like passions with men; sharing their angers; hot with their foolish factions; fighting in unfair disguise amid their ranks; and even wounded by their spears. This, however, is no fault of the poet. He found the religion of his time anthropomorphic, and he merely turned it into charming verse. Nor is there always wanting an esoteric meaning in his melange of gods and chieftains. If Apollo favours Hector, and Pallas aids Ulysses, this was the old-world way of teaching that "Heaven helps those who help themselves." Judged by the religious thought of later days, or even by the high and clear light of Plato's intellect and conscience, Homer no doubt was but a "heathen-man." The machinery of the blind singer's creed is clumsy—his Jove is overmastered by Fate, and weighs the lives of contending lords against each other with no more power of control than a grocer possesses to make two pounds of one commodity lighter than a pound and a half of another. His heroes fight like Chinese braves for swagger, like cannibals for ferocity; and Diomed and Ulysses, upon a midnight reconnoitring expedition, kill sleeping men without the smallest compunction. But making reservation for the age and the training of Homer, his work is to be unhesitatingly declared as one of a clear and pronounced morality. Horace has not praised him too much in saying that he "teaches the noble and ignoble, the becoming and unbecoming, better than Chrysippus and Crantor." He pourtrays his warriors very much, in truth, *au naturel*—they eat and drink, fight and repose, jest roughly or weep with effusion, like the sons of nature that they were. He is not answerable, however, for them, nor for his uxorious Jove, nor yet for the tiger-like fighting-men who tear the spear from the entrails of their enemy, and deride him as he sobs and dies. But the chivalry of Sarpedon, the patriotic devotion of Hector, the perfect wifehood of Andromache, and the heart-felt repentance of Helen, with many a passage of lofty honour, and much sentiment, rich with the spirit of knighthood before its time, show Homer to have been true to his "divine mission" as a poet. For a real poet is divine, and priest of God by better consecration than any which the churches can confer. St. Basil did very well, therefore, to cite "the blind old man" as one who always upheld virtue and high ends and thoughts in life. To this chief merit must be added his radiant cheerfulness of mind, and simple delight in the world of objects and of actions—the true and glad Greek nature—in itself a virtue. He tells us of the Fates, the Gods, the scenes of camp and city, the joys and troubles, the tears and smiles of his heroes and heroines, with that serene calm which only the best singers have. He will no more be affected by the carnage of his theme than a river will be always stained with the blood from a battle. There is the melancholy, indeed, of early religious thought about him when he speaks of "the races of men falling like the leaves;" and the awe of mankind's eternal wonder at the "for ever" when he describes soul after soul of his fighting men "unwillingly seeking the gloomy shades below." Yet, like the Greek he was, he turns for ever to the light—for ever to the lovely things which are in the world—to this gay, picturesque, sufficing, delightful, many-coloured existence of mankind; and though Jove sports with mortals, and

Fate controls Jove, the sense of some sweeter and holier *ἄναξ*, of some more just and potent God above both, is rather felt than read in these his two grand pagan epics.

Their style, as has been said, cannot be conveyed, for the old wine, in this case, truly bursts the new bottles. The study of Greek might well be undertaken were it only for the possession of Homer's music and manner. His Achæan hexameters have the utmost vigour, puissance, and billow-like might and flow of which this powerful metre is capable. It carries itself with such swing and skill, that one forgets the art, which is all the while exquisite, though never finical. Solemn or sweet, majestic or simple, slow as the march of legions, or fiery as the charge of fight, the dactyls and spondees roll along, their very syllables making the music to the sense, as if the verses broke—which doubtless most of them did—straight from the lips of the bard, while his blind eyes worked with the splendour of the vivid vision of each scene. The way in which the spirit of Homer thus drives along the rolling vocables of his Greek in rhythmic flood, is like the action of the wind upon the wide sea. The nature-like power of the poet is, indeed, his central quality; he has so much to tell, and goes the nearest way to tell it, with no apparent art, and no pomp of diction but the glorious language of his race, and the poetry inherent in his theme. He possesses the qualities of a narrator sufficiently to excite and assure attention—but you must sit down and listen; he will not bribe you with artifices and surprises; when the action demands it, he will tell a message twice over, or repeat a long speech; if one word serves his purpose, he will use it as often as he wants it, not hunting for synonyms. He is the freshest, easiest, serenest, and simplest bard, as he was the first; the colours of his page are clear and strong as those of the dawn; the air of him is like the breath of morning moving over a waking earth; the light upon him lies like the light of heaven upon the highest alpine peaks—white, broad, beautiful, unbroken.

The "Odyssey" deals with a theme as interesting and momentous for Greece as the siege of Troy, namely, the *νόστοι*, or home voyages of the Achæan leaders. It is easy to see in the early history of Hellas that the prolonged return of Agamemnon, Teucer, Ulysses, and many other chieftains, led to all sorts of revolutions in their states. For his second epic Homer takes the adventurous cruise of Ulysses, or "Odysseus," as he is always called in the Greek. It is many years since Troy was taken when we find Ulysses still afar from Ithaca, which he for ever desires to reach. Penelope, his wife, left on the island with her son Telemachus, is besieged by the suits of the princes ruling the Ionian Archipelago, who live in her palace upon the belongings of the absent hero, behaving in an abominable manner, and are, in truth, on the point of forcing her to choose one of them as husband. Telemachus denounces the conduct of these rioters before the Ithacans, and then goes away to seek for his father in the courts of Nestor and Menelaüs. Ulysses has, meanwhile, been in many places, and last of all languishing in the isle of Ortygia, the residence of Calypso; but a reviving impulse constrains him to break away from the enchanting goddess, and he escapes upon a raft. The wrath of Neptune follows him over the sea in the shape of a terrible tempest, which casts him away upon the islets inhabited by the Phæacians. Alcinous, the king, receives him with great hospitality, and here Ulysses relates a series of his past maritime adventures, which makes the "Odyssey" a mine of delightful fables, as fascinating—but as little veracious—as those of the "Arabian Nights." The Greek warrior and mariner recounts how the winds have tossed him from peril to peril, from sea to sea; how he has been with the Circonians, reclined with his sailors along the sleepy rills of Lotus-land, escaped the awful clutches of the Cyclops Polypheme, lodged with King Æolus, and the Lestrygonians (classic cannibals), and feasted safely in that magic isle of Æea where Circe, the fair and wicked witch, turns men into beasts. Spell-bound, the Phæacians listen to him—as does his reader now—while he descends into the very shades, and speaks with souls of the dead, athirst for the scent of the sacrifices. He tells how he came past the bewitching but deadly seductions of the Sirens; avoided the double danger of Scylla and Charybdis; and fled from the wrath of the Deity of the Sun, whose bullocks his companions had rashly eaten. All these tales of the sea, full of the flavour of strange voyaging—when the world was young, and anything might very well be true—follow one another in a charming recitation. We listen yet to our Greek Sindbad with an attention which becomes intense and youthful; and we forget to disbelieve him—we forget even Penelope and the wicked suitors—tracking these weird and wondrous travels by the lips of the cunning and brave island-prince. It is Lotus-land of the mind to sit and hear the long hexameters rolling, like the measured sea curling on the placid beach of the real golden-lighted Lotus-land—

τῶν δ' ὅς τις λωτοῖο φάγοι μελιηδέα καρπόν,
οὐκέτ' ἀπαγγεῖλαι πάλιν ἤθελεν οὐδὲ νέεσθαι,
ἀλλ' αὐτοῦ βούλοντο μετ' ανδράσι Λωτοφάγοισιν
λωτὸν ἐρεπτόμενοι μενέμεν νόστου τε λαθέσθαι.

Od. ix. 94.

Whoso has tasted the honey-sweet fruit from the stems of the lotus,
Nevermore wishes to leave it, and never once longs to go homeward;
There would he stay if he could, content, with the eaters of lotus,
Plucking and eating the lotus, forgetting that he was returning.

We forget that Ulysses must return, and we awake half-sadly to a life where the charm of the fables fades away into their abiding lessons—where the Sirens are, as we perceive, the perilous pleasures of sense; and Circe is the ensnaring witchery of animal appetites; and Calypso is no fiction at all, nor Ortygia a mythical prison-house of temptations. However, the Phæacians presently send their guest away in a new ship, and lay him asleep on his own island, with his presents and property beside him. He wakes and thinks he is again deserted, and far from Ithaca; but soon meets and recognises his old servant Eumæus the swineherd, who reports all the enormities of the suitors to him, and brings Telemachus, by this time returned home, to his father's side. The three concert together a plan for the punishment of the suitors, and Ulysses is introduced as a beggar to the palace among these personages; who are eating and drinking his substance and persecuting his queen. No one guesses that the ragged stranger is the island King, except an old nurse about the palace and the dog Argos, which wags its tail at sight of its master, and dies outright for joy. The situation is here extremely dramatic, and the interest of the poem most absorbing.

Penelope, ignorant of her husband's return—doubtful, indeed, of his existence—has engaged, after all kinds of evasions, to give her assent to that one of the Ithacan suitors who can win the prize in a match at the targets. But the bow used must be the one which Ulysses left when he sailed away for Troy, and not a man of them can so much as string it. Telemachus obtains permission for the ragged beggar to try his hand; whereupon, to the astonishment of all, this vagabond stranger strings and manages the weapon with ease, and sends an arrow from it clean and straight into the distant mark. Now commences as moving a piece of description in the Greek as ever has been put in words, and it is a marvel that no great painter has yet essayed to fix upon his canvas this splendid and terrible scene of the vengeance of Ulysses. The hero strides from the shooting-ground, bow in hand, to the threshold of the hall where the suitors are revelling; and there he flings the mendicant's dress from off his armour, and flashes out upon the princely robbers like an armed vision of Nemesis. There can be no better passage quoted to show the power and music of the "Odysseiad." Thus begins the twenty-second book, and afterwards are given such words as come to the author's pen, anxious but not able to convey a full taste of the rich pleasure of this Greek :—

Αὐτὰρ ὁ γυμνώθη ῥακέων πολύμητις Ὀδυσσεύς,
ἆλτο δ' ἐπὶ μέγαν οὐδὸν ἔχων βιὸν ἠδὲ φαρέτρην
ἰῶν ἐμπλείην, ταχέας δ' ἐκχεύατ' ὀϊστοὺς
αὐτοῦ πρόσθε ποδῶν, μετὰ δὲ μνηστῆρσιν ἔειπεν·
“οὗτος μὲν δὴ ἄεθλος ἀάατος ἐκτετέλεσται·
νῦν αὖτε σκοπὸν ἄλλον, ὃν οὔ πώ τις βάλεν ἀνὴρ,
εἴσομαι, αἴ κε τύχωμι, πόρῃ δέ μοι εὖχος Ἀπόλλων.”
Ἦ, καὶ ἐπ' Ἀντινόῳ ἰθύνετο πικρὸν ὀϊστόν.
ἤτοι ὁ καλὸν ἄλεισον ἀναιρήσεσθαι ἔμελλεν,
χρύσεον ἄμφωτον, καὶ δὴ μετὰ χερσὶν ἐνώμα,
ὄφρα πίοι οἴνοιο· φόνος δέ οἱ οὐκ ἐνὶ θυμῷ
μέμβλετο· τίς κ' οἴοιτο μετ' ἀνδράσι δαιτυμόνεσσιν
μοῦνον ἐνὶ πλεόνεσσι, καὶ εἰ μάλα καρτερὸς εἴη,
οἷ τεύξειν θάνατόν τε κακὸν καὶ κῆρα μέλαιναν;
τὸν δ' Ὀδυσεὺς κατὰ λαιμὸν ἐπισχόμενος βάλεν ἰῷ,
ἀντικρὺ δ' ἁπαλοῖο δι' αὐχένος ἤλυθ' ἀκωκή.
ἐκλίνθη δ' ἑτέρωσε, δέπας δέ οἱ ἔκπεσε χειρὸς
βλημένου, αὐτίκα δ' αὐλὸς ἀνὰ ῥῖνας παχὺς ἦλθεν

Thereupon, stripping his tatters away, many-counselled Ulysses
Strode to the threshold, and stood there, upholding his bow, and his quiver
Brim-full of shafts; on the ground he poured forth the light-wingèd arrows
All in a pile at his feet, then turned to the suitors and spake this:
“Yonder match has been played; ye have seen my skill at the target:
Now I will shoot a shot that no man, I fancy, will better,
Into a different mark—if I may—and Apollo shall aid me.”

Straight at Antinous then a keen-bladed arrow he levelled.
Grasping a golden cup stood the chief—a cup with two handles;
Deep in the draught he was, no thought in his mind of destruction!
How should a lord at the feast, in the midst of the banquetters, drinking,
Dream that, one against many—nay, though the strongest of mortals,
Thus could do him to death, and send him to sudden perdition?
Even as he quaffed, in the jowl the shaft of Odusseus transfixed him:
Right thro' the soft o' the neck the steel point travelled; his body
Tottered, bent, and fell; from his fingers the two-handled goblet

αἵματος ἀνδρομέοιο· θοῶς δ' ἀπὸ εἶο τράπεζαν
ὦσε ποδὶ πλήξας, ἀπὸ δ' εἴδατα χεῦεν ἔραζε·
σῖτός τε κρέα τ' ὀπτὰ φορύνετο· τοὶ δ' ὁμάδησαν
μνηστῆρες κατὰ δώμαθ', ὅπως ἴδον ἄνδρα πεσόντα,
ἐκ δὲ θρόνων ἀνόρουσαν ὀρινθέντες κατὰ δῶμα,
πάντοσε παπταίνοντες ἐϋδμήτους ποτὶ τοίχους·
οὐδέ πῃ ἀσπὶς ἔην, οὐδ' ἄλκιμον ἔγχος ἑλέσθαι.
νείκειον δ' Ὀδυσῆα χολωτοῖσιν ἐπέεσσιν·
"ξεῖνε, κακῶς ἀνδρῶν τοξάζεαι· οὐκέτ' ἀέθλων
ἄλλων ἀντιάσεις· νῦν τοι σῶς αἰπὺς ὄλεθρος.
καὶ γὰρ δὴ νῦν φῶτα κατέκτανες ὃς μέγ' ἄριστος
κούρων εἰν Ἰθάκῃ· τῷ σ' ἐνθάδε γῦπες ἔδονται."
Ἴσκεν ἕκαστος ἀνήρ, ἐπεὶ ἦ φάσαν οὐκ ἐθέλοντα
ἄνδρα κατακτεῖναι· τὸ δὲ νήπιοι οὐκ ἐνόησαν,
ὡς δή σφιν καὶ πᾶσιν ὀλέθρου πείρατ' ἐφῆπτο.
τοὺς δ' ἄρ' ὑπόδρα ἰδὼν προσέφη πολύμητις Ὀδυσσεύς·
"ὦ κύνες, οὔ μ' ἔτ' ἐφάσκεθ' ὑπότροπον οἴκαδ' ἱκέσθαι

Clattered ; a gush of blood burst thick and hot from his nostrils !
Sprawling and writhing, the feet of him kicked the board and o'erset it,
Spilling the viands and wine, overturning the roast meat and boiled meat,
Mixing the cates and fruit with his blood. The suitors, affrighted,
Sprang from the benches on this side and that side, and ran to the dead man,
Glaring for shield or for spear along the walls of the palace :
Not one spear there was, nor sword, nor target to help them ;
Then they turned with furious words on Odusseus, and cursed him.
"Stranger, thou shootest too well ; but this is the last of thy shooting !
Death shall have thee for this ! Thou hast killed with thy villanous arrow
One of the Ithaca princes, as noble and lordly as any,
Great in birth and deed : for this thing the vultures shall pick thee."

Each of them waited, expecting the man would surely crave pardon,
Saying, "the arrow slipped," that "the deed was wrought maladventure."
Fools, who did not feel Death's portals yawning to take them !
Then with terrible eyes broke forth the wrathful Odusseus :
"Dogs ! ye did not think I should ever live to come hither,

δήμου ἄπο Τρώων, ὅτι μοι κατεκείρετε οἶκον,
δμωῇσιν δὲ γυναιξὶ παρευνάζεσθε βιαίως,
αὐτοῦ τε ζώοντος ὑπεμνάασθε γυναῖκα,
οὔτε θεοὺς δείσαντες, οἳ οὐρανὸν εὐρὺν ἔχουσιν,
οὔτε τιν' ἀνθρώπων νέμεσιν κατόπισθεν ἔσεσθαι.
νῦν ὕμιν καὶ πᾶσιν ὀλέθρου πείρατ' ἐφῆπται."
Ὣς φάτο, τοὺς δ' ἄρα πάντας ὑπὸ χλωρὸν δέος εἷλεν.
[πάπτηνεν δὲ ἕκαστος ὅπῃ φύγοι αἰπὺν ὄλεθρον.]
Εὐρύμαχος δέ μιν οἶος ἀμειβόμενος προσέειπεν·
" εἰ μὲν δὴ 'Οδυσεὺς 'Ιθακήσιος εἰλήλουθας,
ταῦτα μὲν αἴσιμα εἶπας, ὅσα ῥέζεσκον 'Αχαιοί,
πολλὰ μὲν ἐν μεγάροισιν ἀτάσθαλα, πολλὰ δ' ἐπ' ἀγροῦ.
ἀλλ' ὁ μὲν ἤδη κεῖται ὃς αἴτιος ἔπλετο πάντων,
'Αντίνοος· οὗτος γὰρ ἐπίηλεν τάδε ἔργα,
οὔ τι γάμου τόσσον κεχρημένος οὐδὲ χατίζων,
ἀλλ' ἄλλα φρονέων, τά οἱ οὐκ ἐτέλεσσε Κρονίων,
ὄφρ' 'Ιθάκης κατὰ δῆμον ἐϋκτιμένης βασιλεύοι

Back from the city of Troy ; and so ye harried my palace,
Ravished my handmaids, and, I being breathing, ye dared to beset her—
Her ! my wife, Penelope—her ! with your impudent suings,
Nothing regarding the gods, who reign in infinite heaven,
Neither believing that any man lived who would shrewdly requite you.
Now for all of you—all !—the hour is arrived of your judgment."

Sickly their visages waxed with fear as his accents resounded ;
Hither and thither they rolled their eyes to find any refuge ;
Only Eurymachus gathered his breath, and answered in this way :
"If, of a truth, thou art he, the Odusseus of Ithaca, living,
Just are thy words, and rightful thy wrath at the deeds of the princes,
Done without shame in thy halls, and done in thy fields, without number.
Yet this dead man here was the head and front of the sinning :
He, Antinous, set us on to the worst of our doings ;
Caring not half so much for thy beauteous queen, nor to win her,
As that this thing might be, the which dread Zeus has forbidden,
Namely, to reign alone over all thine Ithacan kingdom,
King and Lord—having slain thy son and gotten his birthright.

αὐτος, ἀτὰρ σὸν παῖδα κατακτείνειε λοχήσας.
νῦν δ' ὁ μὲν ἐν μοίρῃ πέφαται, σὺ δὲ φείδεο λαῶν
σῶν· ἀτὰρ ἄμμες ὄπισθεν ἀρεσσάμενοι κατὰ δῆμον,
ὅσσα τοι ἐκπέποται καὶ ἐδήδοται ἐν μεγάροισιν,
τιμὴν ἀμφὶς ἄγοντες ἐεικοσάβοιον ἕκαστος,
χαλκόν τε χρυσόν τ' ἀποδώσομεν, εἰς ὅ κε σὸν κῆρ
ἰανθῇ· πρὶν δ' οὔ τι νεμεσσητὸν κεχολῶσθαι."
Τὸν δ' ἄρ' ὑπόδρα ἰδὼν προσέφη πολύμητις 'Οδυσσεύς·
" Εὐρύμαχ', οὐδ' εἴ μοι πατρώϊα πάντ' ἀποδοῖτε,
ὅσσα τε νῦν ὔμμ' ἔστι, καὶ εἴ ποθεν ἄλλ' ἐπιθεῖτε,
οὐδέ κεν ὧς ἔτι χεῖρας ἐμὰς λήξαιμι φόνοιο
πρὶν πᾶσαν μνηστῆρας ὑπερβασίην ἀποτῖσαι.
νῦν ὑμῖν παράκειται ἐναντίον ἠὲ μάχεσθαι
ἢ φεύγειν, ὅς κεν θάνατον καὶ κῆρας ἀλύξῃ.
ἀλλά τιν' οὐ φεύξεσθαι ὀΐομαι αἰπὺν ὄλεθρον."
"Ως φάτο, τῶν δ' αὐτοῦ λύτο γούνατα καὶ φίλον ἦτορ.
τοῖσιν δ' Εὐρύμαχος προσεφώνεε δεύτερον αὖτις·

Now he is dead for his scheme ; but do thou have mercy and spare us—
Liegemen of thine and submissive—then we, going home to our houses,
Thence will bring for whatever was eaten or drunk in thy palace
Each of us twenty-fold back to thee here, a great restitution.
Brass and gold we will fetch, and whatsoever may please thee,
Only be merciful now, and let not thine anger o'erwhelm us."

Him, with a look of fire, the mighty Odusseus thus answered :—
" Not if ye brought me, Eurymachus, all that ye have on the islands,
All that is yours to-day, and all ye may ever own after,
Would I for this hold back my hand from its office of death here.
Deed for deed I will have my price in the blood of your bodies.
Now, then, choose ye your way to die, and face me and fight me ,
Else turn about and fly from the fates that I send from my bowstring—
If, indeed, ye can fly—for I think my shafts will go faster."

Hearing his words, their knees grew loose and their hearts were like water.
Yet once more Eurymachus spake—this time to the suitors :

"ὦ φίλοι, οὐ γὰρ σχήσει ἀνὴρ ὅδε χεῖρας ἀάπτους,
ἀλλ' ἐπεὶ ἔλλαβε τόξον ἐΰξοον ἠδὲ φαρέτρην,
οὐδοῦ ἄπο ξεστοῦ τοξάσσεται, εἰς ὅ κε πάντας
ἄμμε κατακτείνῃ· ἀλλὰ μνησώμεθα χάρμης.
φάσγανά τε σπάσσασθε, καὶ ἀντίσχεσθε τραπέζας
ἰῶν ὠκυμόρων· ἐπὶ δ' αὐτῷ πάντες ἔχωμεν
ἀθρόοι, εἴ κέ μιν οὐδοῦ ἀπώσομεν ἠδὲ θυράων,
ἔλθωμεν δ' ἀνὰ ἄστυ· βοὴ δ' ὤκιστα γένοιτο.
τῷ κε τάχ' οὗτος ἀνὴρ νῦν ὕστατα τοξάσσαιτο."
Ὣς ἄρα φωνήσας εἰρύσσατο φάσγανον ὀξὺ
χάλκεον, ἀμφοτέρωθεν ἀκαχμένον, ἆλτο δ' ἐπ' αὐτῷ
σμερδαλέα ἰάχων· ὁ δ' ἁμαρτῇ δῖος Ὀδυσσεὺς
ἰὸν ἀποπροϊεὶς βάλλε στῆθος παρὰ μαζὸν,
ἐν δέ οἱ ἥπατι πῆξε θοὸν βέλος· ἐκ δ' ἄρα χειρὸς
φάσγανον ἧκε χαμᾶζε, περιρρηδὴς δὲ τραπέζῃ
κάππεσε δινηθεὶς, ἀπὸ δ' εἴδατα χεῦεν ἔραζε
καὶ δέπας ἀμφικύπελλον· ὁ δὲ χθόνα τύπτε μετώπῳ

"Friends, the man is in earnest ; he will not be stayed from his purpose,
But while an arrow is left he will shoot from his terrible bow there
Shot upon shot from the threshold, till each of us fall by his fellow,
Slain in a pile. Recall, then, our manhood ! Stand not to be butchered !
Draw what swords we have, and hold the board up before us,
So, with its fence, let us rush in close order upon him ! If one man
Thrust his way past the door, he may come to the town and call succour,
Then peradventure this shooter will pull his bow for the last time."

So, as he spoke, from its scabbard Eurymachus drew forth his falchion,
Bronze in the blade, two-edged, and rushed with a yell to the portal,
Waving it high ; but right as he came the watchful Odusseus
Let go a whistling shaft which took him under the breast-bone,
Plunging barb-deep in the liver. Down out of his grasp fell the falchion,
Clattering he rolled in the wreck of the festival, screaming and twisting :
Platters and food flew about, and cups whirled hither and thither,
While the wretch hit this way and that his head on the pavement,
Mad with the anguish, and struck with his feet the boards and the benches,
Beating a horrid tune, till death's fog clouded his eyeballs.

θυμῷ ἀνιάζων, ποσὶ δὲ θρόνον ἀμφοτέροισιν
λακτίζων ἐτίνασσε· κατ' ὀφθαλμῶν δ' ἔχυτ' ἀχλύς.
'Αμφίνομος δ' 'Οδυσῆος ἐείσατο κυδαλίμοιο
ἀντίος ἀΐξας, εἴρυτο δὲ φάσγανον ὀξὺ,
εἴ πώς οἱ εἴξειε θυράων· ἀλλ' ἄρα μιν φθῆ
Τηλέμαχος κατόπισθε βαλὼν χαλκήρεϊ δουρὶ
ὤμων μεσσηγὺς, διὰ δὲ στήθεσφιν ἔλασσεν·
δούπησεν δὲ πεσὼν, χθόνα δ' ἤλασε παντὶ μετώπῳ.
Τηλέμαχος δ' ἀπόρουσε, λιπὼν δολιχόσκιον ἔγχος
αὐτοῦ ἐν 'Αμφινόμῳ· περὶ γὰρ δίε μή τις 'Αχαιῶν
ἔγχος ἀνελκόμενον δολιχόσκιον ἢ ἐλάσειεν
φασγάνῳ ἀΐξας ἠὲ προπρηνέϊ τύψας.
βῆ δὲ θέειν, μάλα δ' ὦκα φίλον πατέρ' εἰσαφίκανεν,
'Αγχοῦ δ' ἱστάμενος ἔπεα πτερόεντα προσηύδα·
"ὦ πάτερ, ἤδη τοι σάκος οἴσω καὶ δύο δοῦρε
καὶ κυνέην πάγχαλκον, ἐπὶ κροτάφοις ἀραρυιαν,
Αὐτός τ' ἀμφιβαλεῦμαι ἰὼν, δώσω δὲ συβώτῃ
καὶ τῷ βουκόλῳ ἄλλα· τετευχῆσθαι γὰρ ἄμεινον."
Τὸν δ' ἀπαμειβόμενος προσέφη πολύμητις 'Οδυσσεύς·

Next Amphinomus faced his fate, and ran at Odusseus
Headlong, drawing his keen-edged blade, and desperately hoping
If he might break his way ; but him Telemachus dealt with,
Striking him quick as he passed with the bronze-barbed spear in the shoulders—
Right through the back it drove, and out at the ribs made its passage.
Down with a crash he fell, full-front on the stones of the pavement :
Nay, and Telemachus left him so, with the spear in his shoulders,
Dreading lest one of the suitors, the while he tugged at the weapon,
Either with sword or club should find him helpless, and slay him ;
Therefore back to his father he came, and spoke in his ear this :

"Father, 'twere good I fetched thee shield and spears and a helmet ;
Armed thou shouldst be for the rest of this matter, and I, having donned it,
Armour will bring for the swineherd and cowherd, if thou canst abide here."

Answered him, under his breath, the watchful and mighty Odusseus :

"οἶσε θέων, εἵως μοι ἀμύνεσθαι πάρ' ὀϊστοὶ,
μή μ' ἀποκινήσωσι θυράων μοῦνον ἐόντα."

Od. xxii. 1—107.

"Go for them quickly, Telemachus ! while I have arrows to stop them,
Lest the dogs should see me in straits, and push their way past me."

Telemachus hastens to the upper apartments, and brings the weapons and armour, while Ulysses shoots still into the affrighted flock of princes.

αὐτὰρ ἐπεὶ λίπον ἰοὶ ὀϊστεύοντα ἄνακτα,
τόξον μὲν πρὸς σταθμὸν ἐϋσταθέος μεγάροιο
ἔκλιν' ἑστάμεναι, πρὸς ἐνώπια παμφανόωντα,
αὐτὸς δ' ἀμφ' ὤμοισι σάκος θέτο τετραθέλυμνον
κρατὶ δ' ἐπ' ἰφθίμῳ κυνέην εὔτυκτον ἔθηκεν,
ἵππουριν· δεινὸν δὲ λόφος καθύπερθεν ἔνευεν·
εἵλετο δ' ἄλκιμα δοῦρε δύω κεκορυθμένα χαλκῷ.

Od. xxii. 119—125.

So, when the arrows were shot—each arrow a death for the suitors –
Calmly he set down his bow at the porch, in the nook of the door-post ;
Then about his arm a shield of four thicknesses bracing,
Over his brows a helmet he fastened, dreadfully nodding
'Thwart his countenance fierce with its black plumes of horse-hair, and each hand
Grasped a spear of bronze, keen-sharpened, awful to smite with.

But Telemachus has left the door of the armoury open, and there is a back way by which the princes send Melanthius to fetch them lances and mail. Ulysses perceives the danger when some of them are already equipped ; so by his orders the swineherd and cowherd go up to surprise and bind Melanthius. Upon this Minerva appears in the form of Mentor to encourage Ulysses, and afterwards perches upon the roof in the likeness of a swallow. The suitors agree to hurl six javelins at a time against Ulysses, but Minerva renders the first shower vain, and the return spears of the four at the door kill four more princes. In the next exchange Amphimedon indeed strikes Telemachus upon the left wrist, and Ctesippus grazes the left shoulder of Eumæus; but Telemachus kills Amphimedon in return, and each of the others slays his man. Hereupon abject terror falls upon the guilty lords. They herd together and rush about, "like cattle when the days are long and hot, and the gad-fly stings," and Ulysses, with his three companions, chases and dispatches them "like a hawk striking fluttering birds." Two only are spared, Phemius the poet, and Medon. By this time the end of the bloody work is come and revenge is complete. Odusseus looks round, but none are left alive to dispatch.

τοὺς δὲ ἴδεν μάλα πάντας ἐν αἵματι καὶ κονίῃσιν
πεπτεῶτας πολλούς, ὥς τ' ἰχθύας, οὕς θ' ἁλιῆες
κοῖλον ἐς αἰγιαλὸν πολιῆς ἔκτοσθε θαλάσσης
δικτύῳ ἐξέρυσαν πολυωπῷ· οἱ δέ τε πάντες
κύμαθ' ἁλὸς ποθέοντες ἐπὶ ψαμάθοισι κέχυνται·
τῶν μέν τ' ἠέλιος φαέθων ἐξείλετο θυμόν.
ὣς τότ' ἄρα μνηστῆρες ἐπ' ἀλλήλοισι κέχυντο.

Od. xxii. 383—389.

All, wherever he gazed, lay motionless, bloody, and dusty,
Tumbled together and foul; like fish that the fisherman gathers
Out of the foamy sea, and hales on the brink of the shingle.
There they sprawl, gills wide, heaped head and tail, and the sunshine
Dries them where they lie on the yellow bend of the sea-shore:
Just so the suitors lay, like a haul of fish, on the pavement.

The debt so long due to gods and men is paid. The insulters of Penelope are no more: nothing remains but to drag the carcases away, clean the stained floor, and punish the servants who had helped the princes in their outrages. This splendid and varied poem ends hereupon in the recognition of Ulysses by his wife. The last book seems to be an unnecessary and unsuitable sequel: the dramatic construction and moral interest of the "Odyssey" alike close with the faithful Penelope's words of calm and proud love at line 285 of Book xxiii. What follows appears to be the work of another and a weaker hand—or must be taken patiently, as the last faint notes of a noble measure, dying slowly away, the better to break the passage for the ear from perfect music to silence.

HESIOD.

HESIOD the Eolian is a classic and an antiquary, but not a poet. A magnificent accident has linked his name through all the ages with the Ionian Homer, and he enjoys a kind of reflected light from the circumstance; but Homer and Hesiod are not so much to be compared as the sun and the moon. Standing prominent in the early times of Grecian poesy, he is, of course, *clarum et venerabile nomen*, and he has certain merits which are by no means to be denied; but the veritable *afflatus* is not upon his spirit; and he would not occupy a higher pedestal among his compatriots, except for his ancient date, than Dr. Darwin or Bloomfield among English poets. The resemblance which exists between the style of Homer and Hesiod is superficial chiefly, and limited to expressions, epithets, and methods which both in common borrowed from the earlier minstrels. The probability is strong that "the Ascræan" lived before the singer of the Iliad and Odyssey, although there was a tradition that he had contended with Homer at Chalcis for a prize; but nothing can be affirmed from the doubtful *data* existing with regard to his exact period.

He does not interest us personally like his grand countryman. Bœotia, wherein he was born, was the Essex of Greece, *vervecum patria*, a land of dull folks and heavy atmospheres; and Hesiod's verse has something about it of the fogs of Ascra. He was poet enough, nevertheless, to have detested the bucolic locality, situated though it was at the foot of Mount Helicon. It was miserably damp in winter, and burning hot in summer; therefore nothing but the business of the paternal estate kept him, he tells us, at such a place. By the style in which he addresses his fellow-townsmen in the "Theogony," they must have been true Bœotians, naturally suitable to the spot. He makes his muses say—

> Ποιμένες ἄγραυλοι, κάκ' ἐλέγχεα, γαστέρες οἶον,
> ἴδμεν ψεύδεα πολλὰ λέγειν ἐτύμοισιν ὁμοῖα,
> ἴδμεν δ', εὖτ' ἐθέλωμεν, ἀληθέα μυθήσασθαι.
>
> *Theog.* 26—28.

> Hinds of the field, and mock'ries of men, living still for the belly,
> We can tell you lies that you would take to be true things ;
> Yea ! and things which are truly true, if we list to recount them.

But it may be that the Bœotians were better than the poet makes out, and that their fault was mainly inappreciation of their townsman, for there are passages which prove him to have been vain to a degree—and at any rate, he himself has no doubt about his own inspiration. "Three celestial Muses," he says—

> σκῆπτρον ἔδον, δάφνης ἐριθηλέος ὄζον,
> δρέψασαι θηητόν· ἐνέπνευσαν δέ μοι αὐδὴν
> θείην, ὡς κλείοιμι τά τ' ἐσσόμενα πρό τ' ἐόντα·
> καί με κέλονθ' ὑμνεῖν μακάρων γένος αἰὲν ἐόντων,
> σφᾶς τ' αὐτὰς πρῶτόν τε καὶ ὕστερον αἰὲν ἀείδειν.
>
> *Theog.* 16.

> A branch of laurel gave, which they had plucked,
> To be my sceptre ; and they breathed a song
> In music on my soul, and bade me set

Things past and things to be to that high strain;
Also they bade me sing the race of gods,
Themselves, at first and last, ever remembering.

However, if the Ascræans neglected their laureate in his life, they paid public honours to him afterwards. They raised him a statue at Thespiæ, and another upon Mount Helicon. They gave out that his ashes had put a stop to a pestilence in Orchomenus, when they were transported there, and pilgrims used to go to visit his tomb in this place. Thus Hesiod was well reputed with posterity, if not amid his especial public. What else we know of him is little, and it is not even certain whether he died by violence, as was always believed. He had a younger brother named Perses, to whom he addresses his "Works and Days," and who seems to have been a somewhat troublesome relation. Add to this dearth of personal interest, that the religious part of Hesiod's writings is either dry catalogue or unrelieved superstition, while the didactic section of them seems practical and shrewd rather than elevated; and it becomes natural that Hesiod bears no commanding presence in Grecian literature like the great Ionian generally coupled with him. He presents himself to the fancy of a modern student as a grave and quiet composer of very respectable versicles—with a sacerdotal mind, marked by agricultural tastes and tendencies; never exactly "inspired," but not wanting a certain skilfulness of speech occasionally, and power of expression, combined with a strong rural substantiality of thought, which unite to make the little that remains of him a portion of the roll of song that the student, and especially the historic student, cannot neglect. He has no flights of imagination; his language, *crasso sub aere nata*, displays the Ascræan air of heaviness about it; and he shows very little poetic art in the composition of his paragraphs—unless, indeed, time has done him much more wrong than we know, and broken up his labour into fragments. He never carries the mind along like the wave of Homer's line, crested with its sparkling epithets; we follow him, rather, slowly and tediously, as if his verse were a ploughshare, turning up the fat clay of Bœotia.

Once or twice only—if, indeed, these passages be his—we come upon spirited descriptions, as, for example, the war of the Titans in the "Theogony," and it must be allowed that such exhibit a vigour of outline and strong trick of colour, recalling, in another field of art, the broad manner of the Dutch painters, who also gave themselves, like Hesiod, impartially to boors and theology. But he is essentially a moralist and adviser-general, and may perhaps be regarded as the inventor of the didactic fable—at any rate, as regards Greece. He introduces his poetic apologues in an abrupt manner, wherever and whenever they strike him. The subjoined is suddenly interpolated into the "Works and Days" after such a fashion, and gives a fair idea of the rather melancholy and unexalted morality of the poet:—

ὧδ' ἴρηξ προςέειπεν ἀηδόνα ποικιλόδειρον,
ὕψι μάλ' ἐν νεφέεσσι φέρων ὀνύχεσσι μεμαρπώς·
ἡ δ' ἐλεόν, γναμπτοῖσι πεπαρμένη ἀμφ' ὀνύχεσσι,
μύρετο· τὴν δ' ὅγ' ἐπικρατέως πρὸς μῦθον ἔειπε·

Δαιμονίη, τί λέληκας; ἔχει νύ σε πολλὸν ἀρείων·
τῇ δ' εἶς ᾗ σ' ἂν ἐγώ περ ἄγω, καὶ ἀοιδὸν ἐοῦσαν·
δεῖπνον δ', αἴ κ' ἐθέλω, ποιήσομαι, ἠὲ μεθήσω.
ἄφρων δ' ὅς κ' ἐθέλῃ πρὸς κρείσσονας ἀντιφερίζειν.
νίκης τε στέρεται πρός τ' αἴσχεσιν ἄλγεα πάσχει.

Works and Days, 201—209.

Once a hawk said this to a nightingale ;—
The robber had the singer in his claws,
High up among the clouds, and Philomel,
Trembling, and nipped in those sharp crooked talons,
Bewailed ; whereat the hawk savagely screamed :
"Why pipe, my friend? I am too strong to heed ;
I take you where I will, for all your singing ;
To eat you if I like, or let you go ;
And he's a fool that fights against his fate.
He loses, and gets shame, beside his tears."

The poem of the "Works and Days" begins with a brief litany to Zeus, strongly reminding the oriental scholar of the religious preface to all Sanskrit hymns and writings. Then Hesiod favours his brother with a dissertation on good and evil rivalries, and seeks to impress upon him the duties of industry and probity. He describes the successive ages of the human race—the gold, the silver, the brazen, and the iron age—that ever comfortless "now," in which such weather as the abominable fogs of Ascra, and such folks as the Bœotians, were so much as possible. Amid these ill times and hard societies he counsels prudence to the feeble, but warns the strong that "there are gods." He teaches, not without emphasis and faith, that "it is measured to each as each metes," and his idea of an avenging Providence is even stricter than the Mosaic doctrine. "A whole town," he declares, "is often punished because there is one wicked man in it." "Thirty thousand watchful angels," Hesiod declares, are detailed to observe the deeds of men in authority: and Justice, he boldly and nobly proclaims, has her place in heaven "beside the right hand of Zeus himself." A very striking passage, and one which will recall the parallel teaching in the New Testament, is subjoined:—

τήν μὲν τοι κακότητα καὶ ἰλαδὸν ἔστιν ἑλέσθαι
ῥηϊδίως· λείη μὲν ὁδός, μάλα δ' ἐγγύθι ναίει.
τῆς δ' ἀρετῆς ἱδρῶτα θεοὶ προπάροιθεν ἔθηκαν
ἀθάνατοι· μακρὸς δὲ καὶ ὄρθιος οἶμος ἐπ' αὐτὴν
καὶ τρηχὺς τὸ πρῶτον· ἐπὴν δ' εἰς ἄκρον ἵκηαι,
ῥηϊδίη δὴ ἔπειτα πέλει, χαλεπή περ ἐοῦσα.

Works and Days, 286.

Evil is manifold and quickly reached;
Smooth is the road thereto, and nigh the way;
But the high gods do make us sweat for Good;
Strait is the gate to that, and long the road,
And steep at first—but when the top is won,
All then is easy that was hard before.

After much of this not unworthy moral teaching—prolonged till about the middle of the poem—Hesiod proceeds to descant upon agricultural *works*, and the *days* of good and ill luck in the rural calendar. Here his love of nature comes forth, and whatever the Royal Society might think of his farming, he paints with the eye of a landscape artist the rude winters of the Bœotian mountains, the green Greek spring, and again the joyous time of harvest—

Ἦμος δὲ σκόλυμός τ' ἀνθεῖ, καὶ ἠχέτα τέττιξ
δενδρέῳ ἐφεζόμενος λιγυρὴν ἐπιχεύετ' ἀοιδὴν

πυκνὸν ὑπὸ πτερύγων, θέρεος καματώδεος ὥρῃ,
τῆμος πιόταταί τ' αἶγες καὶ οἶνος ἄριστος.

Works and Days, 580—583.

When worts are yellow, and the grasshopper
Sings his shrill song upon the tree—his wings
Quick beating—in the toilsome summer-time,
When goats are fullest, and the wine is best.

Then, although he confesses himself no sailor, Hesiod proceeds to dilate on maritime commerce, the choice of a good craft, and the seasons favourable to navigation. Afterwards he falls into a very remarkable vein of didactic maxims, some of which are more practical than elegant in their character, but all very well intended, and furnishing a perfect code of etiquette for a Bœotian gentleman, such as was Perses. The poem—if certain graceful snatches of music in it can earn for it this title—ends with a very bare and dry enumeration of lucky and unlucky days for rural and domestic pursuits, a kind of "Ascræan Tenant-Farmer's Almanack," probably the oldest specimen of the sort extant. It will be seen that there is not much connection between the various divisions of the composition, and those who have never made a study of the "Works and Days" in the original may be disappointed to find a mighty classic described as so jejune. But such is Hesiod, although he must not be refused a sincere tribute for his moral teaching, which is well-meaning and pure, albeit melancholy in tone and sombre with superstition; and he has, indeed, left in this rather disjointed little literary monument, "tricks of a master's touch," vigorous bits of Bœotian simplicity and quiet pastoral feeling, which have sufficed to keep it existing and even celebrated.

His "Theogony"—a higher work in scheme—is not so free from interpolations; and the side notes of grammarians and commentators have been obviously worked into the text. One even finds stray lines and passages of Homer inlaid with the Hesiodic material; and it is probable that neither the introduction nor the disconnected finish of this poem are by the same hand which wrought the central and genuine portion. Only the antiquarian, or the resolute student of Greek for its mythological and ethnological treasures, could pretend to speak of the "Theogony" as a whole with any enthusiasm. The prefatory lines to the Muses are perhaps in the best manner of the old poet. After that exordium the main part of the hexameters creak and groan along, like over-laden wagons on the dusty roads of Ascra, burdened with the names and attributes of gods and goddesses, nymphs, nereids, dryads, and hamadryads, till the poet disappears entirely, and nothing is left of him except a catalogue-maker. He repeats—and perhaps did very much to crystallise into a faith such mythological tales of the deities—the quarrel of Uranus and his children; how Saturn mutilated his father and devoured his own offspring; how Rhea saved Jupiter, and how Jupiter, with the aid of the Titans, deposed Saturn—in fact, all that strange labyrinth of celestial fable, which must have made Greek orthodoxy far more forbidding as a subject for examination at Delphi or Elis than even our own Athanasian theology in the Divinity Schools at Oxford or Cambridge. The poet dwells most of all upon this mythic battle between the elder and younger gods and Titans. Here he truly rises to something like Miltonic fervour of description; and his gods—who, to tell the truth, are generally very earthly deities in attribute and tone—become grand and solemn by the vastness of the field of battle, the terror of its weapons, the awfulness of the shock of Earth with Heaven, and the picturesque nature of the combatants. The language is remarkably sonorous, and the images imposing, when Jupiter makes his great onset.

οὐδ' ἄρ' ἔτι Ζεὺς ἴσχεν ἑὸν μένος· ἀλλά νυ τοῦγε
εἶθαρ μὲν μένεος πλῆντο φρένες, ἐκ δέ τε πᾶσαν
φαῖνε βίην· ἄμυδις δ' ἄρ' ἀπ' οὐρανοῦ ἠδ' ἀπ' Ὀλύμπου
ἀστράπτων ἔστειχε συνωχαδόν· οἱ δὲ κεραυνοὶ
ἴκταρ ἅμα βροντῇ τε καὶ ἀστεροπῇ ποτέοντο
χειρὸς ἄπο στιβαρῆς, ἱερὴν φλόγα εἰλυφόωντες
ταρφέες, ἀμφὶ δὲ γαία φερέσβιος ἐσμαράγιζεν
καιομένη, λάκε δ' ἀμφὶ πυρὶ μεγάλ' ἄσπετος ὕλη.
ἔζεε δὲ χθὼν πᾶσα καὶ Ὠκεανοῖο ῥέεθρα,
πόντος δ' ἀτρύγετος· τοὺς δ' ἄμφεπε θερμὸς ἀϋτμὴ

Then Zeus let loose his wrath ! his awful heart,
Brimfull of anger, gave his will its way !
From Heaven's vault and high Olympus' crags
Impetuous he bade start the leashed-up fires :
Lightning and thunder and the thunderbolts
Flew from his mighty hand—flame with the crash,
And bolts with both—fire, noise, and bolts all mixed !
Groaned fruitful Mother Earth, wrapped in the war ;
All her vast forests crackled, lightning-scorched ;
The parched fields heaved and split ; the ocean-floods
Bubbled, with all the streams, and lurid smoke
Curled round the Titans fighting—whence the glare
Blazed up across and through the infinite air ;

Τιτῆνας χθονίους, φλὸξ δ' ἠέρα δῖαν ἵκανεν
ἄσπετος, ὄσσε δ' ἄμερδε καὶ ἰφθίμων περ ἐόντων
αὐγὴ μαρμαίρουσα κεραυνοῦ τε στεροπῆς τε.

Theog. 687—699.

So that those warrior-ranks, albeit like gods,
Were blinded with the dazzle of the flash,
And deaf with leaping peals.

Hesiod is here almost Homeric, and the description continues in the same sustained splendour of terror and trouble, concluding thus with the imprisonment of the giants :—

Κόττος τε Βριάρεώς τε Γύης τ' ἄατος πολέμοιο.
οἵ ῥα τριηκοσίας πέτρας στιβαρῶν ἀπὸ χειρῶν
πέμπον ἐπασσυτέρας, κατὰ δ' ἐσκίασαν βελέεσσι
Τιτῆνας· καὶ τοὺς μὲν ὑπὸ χθονὸς εὐρυοδείης
πέμψαν καὶ δεσμοῖσιν ἐν ἀργαλέοισιν ἔδησαν,
νικήσαντες χερσὶν ὑπερθύμους περ ἐόντας,
τόσσον ἔνερθ' ὑπὸ γῆς, ὅσον οὐρανός ἐστ' ἀπὸ γαίης
ἐννέα γὰρ νύκτας τε καὶ ἤματα χάλκεος ἄκμων
οὐρανόθεν κατιὼν δεκάτῃ ἐς γαῖαν ἵκοιτο·
ἐννέα δ' αὖ νύκτας τε καὶ ἤματα χάλκεος ἄκμων
ἐκ γαίης κατιὼν δεκάτῃ ἐς Τάρταρον ἵκοι.

Theog. 714—724.

Cottus, Briareus, and Gyes strong
Gluttons of war, let fly a hail of rocks,
Three hundred thick, from their enormous hands,
And 'whelmed the Titans with a cloud of spears.
Then underneath the earth they drove the crew,
And caged them there, and loaded them with chains
Ponderous and pitiless, for all their might.
As deep their dungeon was below the earth
As heaven is above ; nine days and nights
A brazen anvil falling from the sky
Would need to reach the ground, and then nine more
Would bring it the tenth morn to Tartarus.

A noticeable point about the Æolian bard is his misogynism. He was no "Frauenlob," as the best poets have been; no eulogist and defender of noble and good ladies. It is true that he tells Perses, in the "Works and Days," how nothing is better than a good woman; but then his very praise, like Iago's, has this reservation, "if ever such wight were;" and in the subjoined account of the creation of the Greek Eve, Pandora, his last line is very ungallant:—

Ὣς ἔφαθ'· οἱ δ' ἐπίθοντο Διὶ Κρονίωνι ἄνακτι.
αὐτίκα δ' ἐκ γαίης πλάσσε κλυτὸς Ἀμφιγυήεις
[παρθένῳ αἰδοίῃ ἴκελον, Κρονίδεω διὰ βουλάς·
ἀμφὶ δέ οἱ Χάριτές τε θεαὶ καὶ πότνια Πειθὼ
ὅρμους χρυσείους ἔθεσαν χροΐ· ἀμφὶ δὲ τήνγε
Ὧραι καλλίκομοι στέφον ἄνθεσιν εἰαρινοῖσι·
πάντα δέ οἱ χροῒ κόσμον ἐφήρμοσε Παλλὰς Ἀθήνη.
ἐν δ' ἄρα οἱ στήθεσσι διάκτορος Ἀργειφόντης
ψεύδεά θ' αἱμυλίους τε λόγους καὶ ἐπίκλοπον ἦθος
τεῦξε Διὸς βουλῆσι βαρυκτύπου· ἐν δ' ἄρα φωνὴν
θῆκε θεῶν κῆρυξ· ὀνόμηνε δὲ τήνδε γυναῖκα

He spake, and all obeyed the king of gods:
And straight from clay the lame Hephaistus thumbed
A figure beautiful and virginal.
The Graces three and soft Persuasion hung
Chains of wrought gold upon her lovely skin;
The fair-haired Hours adorned her brow with flowers
Plucked from the spring; Pallas Athenë brought
A pleasing majesty to all her form,
And wily Hermes, Heaven's quick messenger,
Filled her heart full with all his deep deceits,
With subtlest ways and cunning stratagems.
So Hermes did, obedient; and he gave
A voice sweet-toned; and thus the first of Shes

F

Πανδώρην, ὅτι πάντες 'Ολύμπια δώματ' ἔχοντες
δῶρον ἐδώρησαν, πῆμ' ἀνδράσιν ἀλφηστῇσιν.
Works and Days, 69—81.

Was called "the gift of all," for all had given,
And her they sent to be a plague to man.

But to return to the "Theogony" and the poet's more elevated themes. After the celestial battle the piece subsides again, through a series of mythical genealogies and anecdotes of Olympian annals, to the instances of goddesses who have given birth to mortals, and of mortal women who have been loved by immortals. There is not much of the lively and bright Greek belief in the contact of Heaven and Earth about all these enumerations of the heavenly personages. Hesiod writes like a priest rather than a poet; and polytheism was still a creed, in his days, upon which the glorious genius of Athenian art had not yet stamped deep the beauty of the Anadyomene, the majesty of the Pallas of Phidias, the sylvan mystery of Pan's cloven feet and wreathed horns. There is an emptiness about it all, and a sense of insufficiency;—a melancholy and un-Greek-like tone—notably those lines upon Sleep and Death.

τῶν ἕτερος μὲν γῆν τε καὶ εὐρέα νῶτα θαλάσσης
ἥσυχος ἀνστρέφεται καὶ μείλιχος ἀνθρώποισι,
τοῦ δὲ σιδηρέη μὲν κραδίη, χάλκεον δέ οἱ ἦτορ
νηλεὲς ἐν στήθεσσιν· ἔχει δ' ὃν πρῶτα λάβῃσιν
ἀνθρώπων εχθρος δε καὶ αθανατοὶσι θεοισιν.
Theog. 762—766.

Of whom the one soothes all the earth, and calms
The broad back of the sea; gentle to men:

> The other has a heart of steel—a breast
> Brazen and pitiless, and clutches all,
> Hateful to men and to th' immortal gods.

A later age of Hellenic thought mocked these poor "immortal" Gods who died; laughed at the mystery of death with Socrates; and twisted garlands of smiling flowers about the funeral urn: but the blossoms of that bright unbelief were not blown in Hesiod's time and town.

There remains to be noticed a probably spurious poem, called the "Shield of Hercules." It is a torso, not without dignity and good work, but hardly from the Hesiodic chisel. In the middle of the combat of Hercules with Cycnus, son of Mars—abruptly commenced—begins, yet more abruptly, the description of the shield which the son of Alcmena carried. Hesiod would not have spent so much time upon the piece in continuation of his narrative of *'Hoῖαι*, or Heroines; and unless he plagiarised from himself, the poem can hardly be his, for there are verses of the "Works and Days" inserted bodily, and many expressions intercalated from the same source. The description of the shield is, at the same time, too ample and careful for an episode; it must have made part of a special poem, of which we have only the moiety. Some Rhapsodist, perhaps, composed it, with Homer's picture of the shield of Achilles in his mind; for the language is Homeric, and some of the turns of verse identical with the great Ionian's. Assuredly the "Shield of Hercules" was chased by no mean hand; no slight artist beat up the repoussé-work of this poetic buckler. The two hundred hexameters which paint it for us have energy, movement, and music; but the nameless poet who wrote it, or pieced it together, has lost his spray of laurel; while Hesiod has gained that honour, as well as the credit for many other ancient poems quite lost now, or else fragmentary, like the "Lessons of Chiron," "The Melampodia," "The Marriage of Ceyx," and "The Descent of Theseus and Pirithous into Hades." In fact, the name of Hesiod was long a centre of gravity for the stray asteroids of poesy in his age, especially throughout Bœotia; and he is thus a literary accretion, in regard of which we cannot always tell what is fly and what is amber. His own countrymen in Pausanias' time doubted whether even the "Theogony" belonged to him. In so cold and foggy an atmosphere of scepticism, uncomfortable as Hesiod has told us that of Ascra was; it is reassuring to be tolerably certain that the "Works and Days," with their homely wisdom and pastoral sincerity, are the Æolian poet's; and to agree that, for the sake of that alone, he will ever deserve to wear the myrtles gathered from the majestic Helicon which overshadowed his home.

THE HOMERIC HYMNS.

In these ancient and often beautiful fragments of Greek poetry we have doubtless many that are as old as the "Iliad" and "Odyssey," and others which were probably inspired long afterwards by the spirit of Homer, and composed by the most skilful of the Rhapsodists. Some of the shorter poems of the group known by this name may have been portions of lost epic pieces—the prefatory dedication common to all antique verse-making. Others are *per se* important and self-sufficient works, of considerable length and constructive art; complete in themselves, as mythological litanies in honour of some one or other deity. The fact that Thucydides ascribes to Homer himself the "Hymn to the Delian Apollo" shows, indeed, that the golden age of Greece was nowise so critical as ours, and also that the style of these poems is by no means low. These hymns are of a comparatively modern date in Grecian literature whenever we find them perfect; and in some cases appear to be new crystallisations of verse around old poetic remains. In the Hymn to the Delian Apollo, Homer, truly, is made to call himself its author—but this is probably the artifice of an unknown writer. The opening of the hymn is wanting; but it proceeds, after an invocation of Latona and her son, to describe how Delos gave shelter to the goddess, and how Apollo was born at the foot of a palm-tree; and then it paints a fine Poussin-like picture of the feasts of the worshippers of the Sun God. The "Hymn to the Pythian Apollo" is probably older than this, and celebrates the Deity of the valley of Crissa. It relates how the God of Day descended from Olympus to find a spot in Greece for his temple; and how Telphusa, the Bœotian Naiad, recommended him to repair to Crissa. This she did, knowing that a great serpent ravaged the lands there, and wishing ill to the god. Apollo killed the monster, and built a temple among the rocks; but to punish the perfidious maiden he made the waters of her fountain disappear. Such is the matter of this hymn—the manner has nothing to deserve particular attention; it is smooth and skilful, a neatly written liturgy of a very old church.

The "Hymn to Venus" may have been composed, as is thought, as late as the Messenian war, to flatter some of the princes of Mount Ida, who called themselves descendants of Æneas; but the supposition is far-fetched. What remains of it seems to have belonged to a series of sacred poems, the work of the Homeric imitators and reciters. It relates the loves of Aphrodite and the Trojan Anchises. The Goddess of Love appears to the happy hero upon Mount Ida under the form of a Phrygian princess. At her leave-taking she reveals herself, and tells Anchises that she shall bear a son to him, but he must never divulge its mysterious origin, under pain of the wrath of Jupiter. This piece of heathendom is extremely lively and easy in its versification, but not otherwise remarkable.

A far more valuable relic is the "Hymn to Ceres"—if,

indeed, the work be veritably antique—which Ruhnkenius, the philologist, dug up from the rubbish of oblivion. The *lacunæ* in it, as well as its style and nature, compel the conclusion that it is genuine. It is a religious poem devoted to that profoundest of all the Grecian cults, the worship of Ceres or Demeter, "Mother Earth." The writer was probably initiated into the Eleusinian mysteries, although he dared not write of them exoterically. His nearly perfect litany celebrates the glories of the fane at Eleusis—it praises the wisdom of the initiated, and urges the acquisition of philosophic and spiritual knowledge, while it narrates the mystical tale of Ceres. It is here sung how she lost her daughter Proserpine, and refused the gifts of corn and grass to men, till Zeus gave her back her child; with licence to stay half of each year beside her mother, and then to return for the other half to her dreary spouse, the Lord of Hell. This legend, deeply engrafted in the East, and shadowing forth the changes of the year from summer with its flowers to bare winter, and from winter again to summer, is told with poetic grace and enthusiasm. To any ear it must have sounded sweetly—to those of the initiated at Eleusis every line probably bore a delicate and transcendental meaning.

Whoever will see one of these curious liturgical pieces translated to the very best advantage should read the exquisite "Hymn to Mercury," by Shelley. The Greek is very bright and graceful, and loses nothing whatever in the delicious Spenserian stanza, except its form. Indeed, the only fault of such verses as the following is that they are a little too rich:—

To whom thus Hermes slily answered : "Son
Of great Latona, what a speech is this!
Why come you here to ask me what is done
With the wild oxen which it seems you miss?
I have not seen them ; nor from any one
Have heard a word of the whole business.
If you should promise an immense reward,
I could not tell more than you now have heard.

"An ox-stealer should be both tall and strong;
And I am but a little new-born thing,
Who, yet at least, can think of nothing wrong.
My business is to suck, and sleep, and fling
The cradle-clothes about me all day long;
Or, half asleep, hear my sweet mother sing,
And to be washed in water clean and warm,
And hushed and kissed, and kept secure from harm.

"Oh, let not e'er this quarrel be averred!
The astounded gods would laugh at you if e'er
You should allege a story so absurd,
As that a new-born infant forth could fare
Out of his home after a savage herd.
I was born yesterday; my small feet are
Too tender for the roads so hard and rough;
And will you think that this is not enough?

THE CYCLIC POETS.

THIS name was given to a group of mediocre imitators of Homer, who wrote upon the episodes of the Trojan war: some of them in admiration, some in jealousy of the great Ionian—one or two, it may be, with grace and skill sufficient to get a place for a bar or so of their work amid the immortal music of the "blind old man." There were also other "Cyclic poems," reflecting the style of Hesiod, and all beginning, like one of the old Spanish tragedies, with the creation of the world. Such as they were, these productions are lost, but the world is probably not very much the poorer. They were never called classical by the critics of the golden age of Greece; and Horace, who lived near enough to the writers to have seen them on parchment or papyri, selects from one of them his example of utterly bad taste and literary bombast. Perhaps he was alluding to STASINUS when he remarks that, "to relate the wrath of Achilles, Homer does not remount to the eggs of Leda." Stasinus, one of these Cyclic minstrels, was said, however, to have received the copy of his "Cyprian Songs" from Homer himself. He narrated the incidents preceding the Trojan war from the birth of Helen downwards. According to this writer, Zeus caused the Trojan war to arise out of pity for the earth, which was overloaded with inhabitants. Judging from the conduct of kings and aristocracies in all history, this view is far from unparalleled or devilish. But

Stasinus never learned such a theory from the noble intellect and heart of Homer. ARCTINUS was another improver or legatee of Homer. He carried on the "Iliad" *haud passibus æquis,* in a poem entitled the "Ethiopiad," a work old enough to be also ascribed, by uncritical tradition, to Homer. It commences with the arrival of the Amazons before Troy, after the obsequies of Hector. The writer describes the deaths of Memnon and of Achilles, the stratagem of the wooden horse, and the capture of Ilion—and doubtless from such sources the "Æneid" of Virgil and the many sequels of the "Tale of Troy" were largely drawn. There were nine thousand lines in the "Ethiopiad," but almost all are gone, *nocte premuntur;* and the scholiast who preserves us a fragment of the perished mass calls it "The Sack of Ilium," by a wrong title. Another Cyclic, called LESCHES, wrote or patched together a "Little Iliad." Aristotle quotes it as a rude and undigested mass of matter, and what remains of this Lesbian shows that he was but a mere chronicler in rhyme of old Grecian traditions. "The Homeward Voyages" of AGIAS, with the "Telegonid" of EUGAMON, are two other Cyclic poems, of no greater artistic value; although they would have immense archæological interest, could we recover them, as relics in verse of very ancient fables. The first relates the return of Atrides and other chiefs; the second is the complement of the "Odyssey." It recounts the adventures of Telegonus, the son of Ulysses and Circe; how he wandered over the earth seeking out his father, to wreak upon him the spite of the Enchantress; how he landed at last upon Ithaca, and took to highway robbery for his living; till in one of his encounters he waylays Ulysses and kills him unknowingly. The "Thebaid" and the "Heracleïd" are names of antique works, pertaining to this same period of the Rhapsodists and Cyclics, who sprang as thickly from the great stem of Homer, as saplings do from an oak. The first was occupied with the wars of Thebes; of the second, called also "The Taking of Œchalia," but one line remains. The "Phoronid," the "Europæa," and the "Corinthiaci," are titles of works wholly lost; and to complete this list of faded human labour and forgotten singing, CHERSIAS of Orchomenus, and ARIAS of Tamos, were also Cyclic poets, of whom positively not so much as the author's signature survives. *Stant nominum umbræ:* their very names are blotted.

THE ELEGIAC POETS.

THE hexameter was the metre of the epical poems of Greece—but Poesy now stretched her wings wider, and invented the Elegiac measure. The etymology of the word, and a certain plaintive fall which the pentameter has in succeeding the hexameter, have attached a definite tradition of sadness to the couplet thus composed. *Ἔλεγος* is derived from the verb of woe, *'ελέγειν*, or the word ἔλεος, "pity." And perhaps the first use of this mixed metre was to enshrine a funeral song—the checked and broken utterance of mourning. The beautiful wailing chants of Corsica have the same musical sob in them, the same slow burial-pace. But if the original Elegiac of Greece bore this character, it soon became enlarged. The hexameter and pentameter together was virtually made to serve for the step from epical to lyrical singing; and the most ancient relics of this second measure of Greek poesy are devoted as much to light or stirring themes as to sad and solemn ones. Some of the elegiac poets of the mid-age of Hellas are satirical, some martial and patriotic. Let two of these last appear!

CALLINUS.

CALLINUS of Ephesus lived about seven hundred years before the Christian era. The particular city of Ionia in which he resided was much threatened by the martial people of the north, who had destroyed Magnesia and other places, and hung like a storm-cloud over the effeminate Greeks of the coast. The neighbouring lands had already been overrun when Callinus took up his lyre; the Ionians were in danger, and the Ephesian poet appears to have devoted his undoubted genius to the task of animating and reproving his degenerate countrymen. His verses are full of an energetic and manly spirit, and descant upon the miseries of cowardice, the value and joy of courage, and the bounden duty of fighting for country, kindred, and honour. Here is a specimen of the strong and gallant strain of the Ionian :—

τιμῆέν τε γάρ ἐστι καὶ ἀγλαὸν ἀνδρὶ μάχεσθαι
γῆς πέρι καὶ παίδων κουριδίης τ' ἀλόχου
δυςμενέσιν. θάνατος δὲ τοτ' ἔσσεται, ὁππότε κεν δὴ
Μοῖραι ἐπικλώσωσ'. ἀλλά τις ἰθὺς ἴτω

Fair and becoming it is for a man
To fight for home and children and wife ;
And death, that comes when the Fates please, can
Come never but once. To the glorious strife

ἔγχος ἀνασχόμενος καὶ ὑπ' ἀσπίδος ἄλκιμον ἦτορ
ἔλσας τὸ πρῶτον μιγνυμένου πολέμου.
οὐ γάρ πως θάνατόν γε φυγεῖν εἱμαρμένον ἐστὶν
ἀνδρ' οὐδ' εἰ προγόνων ᾖ γένος ἀθανάτων.

Let each, then, go with a heart of brass,
As hard as the blade that his fingers draw !
Die well ! for die we must, alas,
Though the gods were our fathers. 'Tis Heaven's law !

We do not know what effect the verses of Callinus had upon the soft Ephesians. They were good enough to have put spirit into sensualists or slaves.

TYRTÆUS.

THIS was another and a still more famous singer of warlike lays, the contemporary of Callinus, and an Ionian. His martial muse found her theme in the events of the Messenian war, which was waged from 685 B.C. to 668. The outbreak of this conflict found him at Athens, and it is said that he came to take part in it, from a very singular incident. The Spartans, who were fighting with the Messenians, were advised by the oracle to seek a leader from Athens. The "city of the violet-crown" sent them in derision the obscure Tyrtæus, who was a schoolmaster, and lame of one leg. But if it were so, the oracle and the Spartans had the best of the jest, for Tyrtæus turned out a hero of the first water, and his spirited verses were worth whole battalions of peltasts to Lacedæmon. All this may signify something very different from the tradition. Tyrtæus was more likely a "master" of a school of philosophy, politics, and poetry, than a mere pedagogue; and the story of his lameness may possibly—though, perhaps, not very probably—have arisen from the fact that he wrote the elegiac, or "halting" verse, which limps from hexameter to pentameter, and was new at this date to continental Greece. Tyrtæus, at any rate, came to Sparta, and rendered noble services to his adopted country. If it be true, as is reported, that he calmed popular riots with his poetic writings, Plato ought to blush in that he has excluded poets from the model republic. Unluckily, nothing remains of a labour so remarkable, and so desirable for certain modern governments. What remains to us of Tyrtæus is but little, yet that little is full of martial incentives and the praise of patriotism and courage. Even from these fragments we must conclude that the bard well deserved the laurels which surround his brow in all classical pages. Ionian by birth, the character of his genius was rather Dorian—Dorian in its stern eulogy of fortitude, its austere contempt of pleasure and selfishness, its fear of shame, its defiance of death. Here are four clarion-like lines in praise of the brave soldier :—

ἀνδράσι μεν θηητὸς ἰδεῖν, ερατὸς δε γυναιξὶ
ζωὸς ἐών, καλὸς δ' ἐν προμάχοισι πεσών.
ἀλλά τις ἒυ διαβὰς μενέτω ποσὶν ἀμφοτέροισιν
στηριχθεὶς ἐπὶ γῆς, χεῖλος οδοῦσι δακών.

Envied by men, by women praised and loved ;
Alive, a king ; a hero, dead on shield ;
Stand like him to the front, with hearts unmoved !
Bite the lip grimly—root the foot to the field !

Three of the stirring war-songs of Tyrtæus survive, from the first of which the above is an extract. In the second the poet reminds the Spartans that they are descendants of Zeus himself, and ought to fight like demi-gods. A certain sad and desperate courage, a stoic and melancholy calm of soul, is in these elegiacs. They have the Pagan's contempt for "the life that now is," rather than the Christian soldier's faith in "the life which is to come." One understands how the souls of

Leonidas and the three hundred of Thermopylæ might be suckled upon this strong and cold milk of the Muses. The men who combed their hair smooth, to die by the Persian lances; and thanked Heaven that the arrows flew so thickly, "because they could fight in the shade," were well weaned from the weakness of life upon such lines as these:—

καὶ πόδα παρ' ποδὶ θεὶς καὶ ἐπ' ἀσπίδος ἀσπίδ' ἐρείσας
ἐν δὲ λόφον τε λόφῳ καὶ κυνέην κυνέῃ
καὶ στέρνον στέρνῳ πεπλημένος ἀνδρὶ μαχέσθω,
ἢ ξίφεος κώπην ἢ δόρυ μακρὸν ἑλών.

Foot against foot, buckler to buckler pressed;
Plumes tossed on plumes, helmet with helmet clashing;
Breast in the reeling fight knit close to breast,
So wield the blade and send the long lance flashing!

On such stern stuff were nourished the minds of those Spartan dames, who bade their sons go forth to battle; and for a maternal blessing and farewell said, "Come back with your shield, or come back upon it." The mother of Brasidas taught these elegiacs to her boy; she who observed, when the news of his glorious death was brought, "Sparta hath many better soldiers than he." For the songs of Tyrtæus became "household words" in Lacedæmon. Living, he was honoured with every distinction and respect; and dead, he was made a dear and famous name for ever in Sparta. He was their war-poet long after his death, and in many other battles beside those at Ithome; and when the Lacedæmonians went out into the field, they were always wont to sing the stirring couplets of their old leader and laureate to the Spartan flute. Tyrtæus gained many a bloody day for the Dorians with verses like these and their like, "singing of death and of honour that cannot die."

οὐδέ ποτε κλέος ἐσθλὸν ἀπόλλυται οὐδ' ὄνομ' αὐτοῦ,
 ἀλλ' ὑπὸ γῆς περ ἐὼν γίγνεται ἀθάνατος
ὅντιν' ἀριστεύοντα μένοντά τε μαρνάμενόν τε
 γῆς περὶ καὶ παίδων θοῦρος Ἄρης ὀλέσῃ.
εἰ δὲ φύγῃ μὲν κῆρα τανηλεγέος θανάτοιο
 νικήσας δ' αἰχμῆς ἀγλαὸν εὖχος ἕλῃ,
πάντες μιν τιμῶσιν ὁμῶς νέοι ἠδὲ παλαιοί,
 πολλὰ δὲ τερπνὰ παθὼν ἔρχεται εἰς Ἀΐδην.

Never the glorious tale of him dies, nor the deeds of him ever!
 Under the earth he may lie, yet he is greater than Fate,
Whomso, firm in the battle, unyielding, awaiting his death-blow,
 Fighting for children and home, Mars the omnipotent slew.
But if he 'scape the message of death—the far-reaching slayer—
 'Scape it and come safe home, bringing the garland of war;
Then in his town he is honoured, by old men and young men together,
 Many a glory and joy hath he, or ever he dies.

ARCHILOCHUS.

An unkind mistress and an unbending father made Archilochus, the Parian, a satirist and writer of what Horace calls *furentes iambos.* He was contemporary of Tyrtæus, and composed the war-songs peculiar to his age for the battles between the Naxians and Parians. The islander fought himself, but his fame does not live only in consequence of his valour or valorous verses. He loved a maiden of Paros, called Neobule, the daughter of Lycambes. Records of his early passion for this damsel are to be found among the ruins of his writings. She must have been beautiful. Here are something like stray threads from the tresses of this antique beauty:—

ἡ δε οἱ κόμη
ὤμους κατεσκίαζε καὶ μετάφρενα.

Her flowing hair
Shaded her shoulders and her neck and waist.

And again—

εσμυρισμένας κόμας
καὶ στῆθος ὡς ἂν καὶ γέρων ἠράσσατο.

Her scented hair
And bosom, sweet enough to stir old blood.

But great love and great hatred tremble into each other from either side of an invisible line, and Archilochus came to write things as bitter of fair Neobule as these are sweet. Lycambes had promised Neobule to the poet, but subsequently changed his mind; or else the young lady was fickle, and had a heart after all of Parian marble. Archilochus took a poetic and merciless vengeance. He had strung his cithara with new chords to make the iambic line, and he used them like whip-lashes upon the unlucky family. He was less than gentlemanly in his epigrams upon Neobule; and satirised the unfortunate father till tradition says that that aggrieved Parian hanged himself in sheer despair. It will be seen that these Greeks of the middle ages of Hellas, whether they wrote battle chants or hymns; love songs or songs of hatred, put fervour into them and living stuff. The lampoons of Archilochus had such a disastrous success that iambics and satire came to mean the same thing. Neobule should have kept her word, but then poetic art would have waited longer for the development of the flowing line, which the tragedians afterwards borrowed from the angry muse of Archilochus to employ in the noblest uses. The disappointed lover pressed into the service of his rage a fine sense of epithet, a simple, clear, lively style, and a deep knowledge of the weak places in human nature; as well as an originally noble and poetic spirit, which this hapless passion warped. In Archilochus is first found that generous sentiment—

οὐ γὰρ ἐσθλὸν κατθανοῦσι κερτομέειν ἐπ' ανδρασι.

It is not good to speak ill of the dead.

And the following verse breathes a better religion than hatred:—

Ὦ Ζεῦ, πάτερ Ζεῦ, σὸν μὲν οὐρανοῦ κράτος.
σὺ δ' ἔργ' ἐπ' ἀνθρώπων ὁρᾶς

λεωργὰ καὶ θεμιστά, σοὶ δὲ θηρίων
ὕβρις τε καὶ δίκη μέλει.

Oh, Father Zeus, the Heavens are thine,
And thou dost know all works of men,
Evil and good. Thine edicts shine
All-potent, in the wild-beasts' den.

But little except broken samples of the man's goodness or badness remains—enough, no doubt, to show that Archilochus had mastered the iambic and the tetrametric line, and that "epode" which Horace imitated, as he himself allows in the "Epistles." Here is one fragment of the "raging iambics:"—

Αἶνός τις ἀνθρώπων ὅδε,
ὡς ἆρ' ἀλώπηξ καἰετὸς ξυνωνίην
ἔμιξαν.

Of monstrous birth and terrible this man,
As if an eagle and a fox had mixed
To get him.

No wonder Lycambes hanged himself; Paros is a little place, and he was "between the devil and the deep sea."

SIMONIDES OF AMORGOS.

THERE is no new idea! We are plagiarists from our ancestors in the most modern novelties of thought, and Dr. Darwin's theory of "Natural Selection" was anticipated in the time of Archilochus by his imitator, Simonides of Amorgos! The iambic line which the poet of Paros employed for private resentments, Simonides used for public satire. He is especially notable for a poem upon women, *περὶ γυναικῶν*. In this production a very curious view is broached, to the effect that all womankind is derived from the lower animals, and that the various characters and caprices of the sex are due to the differences between the nature of the creatures from which they are developed. This is very rude, however philosophical; but Simonides never pretended to be gallant. He twice repeats in this little satire of only ninety couplets the line—

Ζεὺς γὰρ μέγιστον τουτ' ἐπόιησεν κακὸν γυναῖκας.

For Zeus hath sent the worst of all his plagues in womankind.

Certainly everybody must have noticed among the countenances of the passengers in any thronged street, how strangely and frequently the features recall the characteristics of some animal. The horse-face, the squirrel-face, the cat-face, the bird-face are quite common. And when a dog-picture of Sir Edwin Landseer is studied—as, for instance, the "Laying down the Law," or "Alexander and

Diogenes"—we are curiously sensible of a hidden and subtle likeness between the canine race and mankind, which the skilful artist has rather noted than invented. That poodle, how grave, judicial, and ponderously wise he looks! That she "King Charles," what a *dame du cour* the little coquette is! and the blood-hound, what a heavy-jowled "plunger" of the canine Horse Guards! Simonides worked the idea out upon a broader poetical canvas than the painter. His view is that every woman has been in a previous life some bird, beast, or insect; for of the men he said nothing. The ill-favoured and sluttish one was a sow, the cunning one a vixen-fox, the busybody a bitch, the greedy and dull an ass, the gay and vain a mare, the pinched and malicious one an ape. Let us hasten, however, from these unkind genealogies to the single poor little piece of praise which the Iago of Amorgos awards to that sex which has ever been the victim, first of male tyranny, and afterwards of male sarcasm and abuse. One sort of woman *is* good and sweet, the woman born from a bee:—

> φίλη δὲ σὺν φιλεῦντι γηράσκει πόσει,
> τεκοῦσα καλὸν κοὐνομάκλυτον γένος·
> κάριπρεπὴς μὲν ἐν γυναιξὶ γίγνεται
> πάσῃσι, θείη δ' ἀμφιδέδρομεν χάρις·
> οὐδ' ἐν γυναιξὶν ἥδεται καθημένη,

> Dear to her spouse from youth to age she grows;
> Fills with fair girls and sturdy boys his house;
> Among all women womanliest seems,
> And heavenly grace about her mild brow gleams.
> A gentle wife, a noble spouse she walks,

ὅκου λέγουσιν ἀφροδισίους λόγους.
τοίας γυναῖκας ἀνδράσιν χαρίζεται
Ζεὺς τὰς ἀρίστας καὶ πολυφραδεστάτας.

Nor ever with the gossipmongers talks ;
Such women sometimes Zeus to mortals gives,
The glory and the solace of their lives.

But it is too plain that Simonides believed very little in the existence of these "bee-women." His style, however, was better than his life, there is reason to believe, and such kinds only swarm into clean and honest hives.

MIMNERMUS.

DANGER is good for nations as for men. When Ionia was delivered from the constant menace of invasion, by being made a subject province of Lydia, the fire and the bright honour flashing in the elegiacs of Callinus died out. Then came a race of soft, effeminate singers like Mimnermus, who "flourished" B.C. 600. Sweet and eloquent was this Colophonian, and his countrymen called him λιγυσταδὴς, "the melodious." But the strings of his cithara thrill only with the passions which enervate. Ionia had no glories left, and her poets no pride. The verses of Mimnermus are tender and skilful, but they exhibit a voluptuous soul abandoned to pleasure, a light and fine Greek nature, finding youth, love, beauty, wine and feasting, joys bountiful enough for contented existence, if only the black shadow of death did not overhang them. Here is a strain from the sorely-changed minstrelsy of Ionia :—

Τίς δὲ βίος, τί δὲ τερπνὸν ἄτερ χρυσέης 'Αφροδίτης ;
τεθναίην ὅτε μοι μηκέτι ταῦτα μόλοι,
κρυπταδίη φιλότης καὶ μείλιχα δῶρα καὶ εὐνή.
ἄνθεα τῆς ἥβης γίγνεται ἁρπαλέα
ἀνδράσιν ἠδὲ γυναιξίν· ἐπεὶ δ' ὀδυνηρὸν ἐπέλθῃ

Life without golden love—what bliss in this?
Oh, let me die when I can love no more!
The stolen words, the honeyed gifts, the kiss,
These are the blossoms that youth's branches pour

γῆρας ὅ τ' αἰσχρὸν ὁμῶς καὶ κακὸν ἄνδρα τιθεῖ,
αἰεὶ μὲν φρένας ἀμφὶ κακαὶ τείρουσι μέριμναι.

On lovers and their loved ones ; but vile time
Spoils the glad heart, and makes the bright eyes dim.

This antique epicurean fixed sixty years of age as the time at which he would wish to die. Did he keep to his wish when threescore years had drifted their snows upon his head? We know little more of him than that he was still poet and lover enough to win the heart of beautiful Nanno, a flute-player, when he was near that age; and that Solon, the law-giver, thought him worthy of a poetic remonstrance, while Horace has embalmed his roseate philosophy in the lines—

"Si, Mimnermus uti censet, sine amore jocisque
Nil est jucundum—vivas in amore jocisque."

Hor. Ep. i. vi. 65.

SOLON.

BUT place for a greater name! Solon, the legislator of the Athenians, was among these elegiac poets, and no mean competitor either of the very best. If Plutarch's story be true about his poem upon Salamis—as may well be believed from the noble verses which survive—Solon might have won a name as great in poetry as he has left in the architectonic art of government. The Athenians, weary with their long struggle against the people of Megara for the possession of the island of Salamis, had passed an impatient law, decreeing death against any one who should mention the name of the place. Solon's patriotic heart chafed at this unworthy prohibition, and, according to the story, he let it go about that he was out of his senses. One day he broke forth from his house into the market-place, and mounting the stone, he commenced reciting a poem that he had composed, in which the shame of losing so beautiful an islet was pictured with such force, that almost before the verses could be finished the young men of the city exploded in cries of indignation, and the law was repealed by acclamation, an expedition determined upon almost on the spot, and Salamis was finally regained and added to Attica. We retain still the fiery words which kindled this spirit in the young Athenians ;—*ἴομεν*, the Law-giver poet, cried :—

ἴομεν εἰς Σαλαμῖνα μαχησόμενοι περὶ νήσου
ἱμερτῆς· χαλεπόν τ' ἆισχος ἀπωσόμενοι.

To Salamis! sail we to Salamis!
To win the lovely isle, and end our shame!

Solon, it is declared, conceived the idea at first of writing his laws in metre; and if ever jurisprudence could be versified, his was certainly the two-fold genius to have accomplished that curious feat. We have some relics—too few, alas!—of his didactic and moral poems. All breathe a lofty and faithful spirit—not austere, never narrow, but "of large discourse"—full of a strong belief in the eternal principles of the good and the true, the singing of one who

"Heard in his soul the music
Of wonderful melodies."

Indeed, none can rightly honour Solon the law-maker in history, who have not met him upon the slopes of Parnassus. The fervour and humanity of the poet are explanations thrown upon the justice and wisdom of his statutes; round about his Greek brow there shone the glory of a heavenly inspiration, as, like a Greek Moses, he stood before his people with the tablets of the law in hand.

PHOCYLIDES.

MILETUS gave birth to this Ionian, who may be called the Tusser of the elegiac style—at any rate, as far as he can be judged of by his remnants. He wrote something very much like the "Five Hundred Points," except that his theme was moral and social instead of agricultural. He dealt in "wise saws" and ancient "instances," and has an egotistic way of announcing every fresh dictum or gnome with *καὶ τοδε Φωκυλιδέω*, "Phocylides also saith this." A certain finish and neatness characterise these proverbs, among which the subjoined is perhaps a fair specimen of his manner and generally unexceptionable philosophy :—

Γνήσιός εἰμι φίλος, καὶ τὸν φίλον ὡς φίλον οἶδα,
τοὺς δὲ κακοὺς διόλου πάντας ἀποστρέφομαι.
οὐδένα θωπεύω πρὸς ὑπόκρισιν· οὓς δ' ἄρα τιμῶ,
τούτους ἐξ ἀρχῆς μέχρι τέλους ἀγαπῶ.

A friendly friend I am, who love my lover ;
The bad I hate, and wholly keep at bay.
No man I court for show—but those I honour
I honour from the first to the last day.

THEOGNIS.

WHAT has come down to us as the bequest of Theognis in literature is apparently a mosaic from all sorts of elegiac writers; and, on the other hand, Theognis has probably parted to Phocylides and others with something which belonged to himself. True, he was a Dorian, but the Ionic dialect was so thoroughly the language of verse at this date, that nobody yet thought of composing except in this, which was the classical vernacular for all the Hellenic peoples. Theognis belonged to the aristocratic class of Megara, which Theagenes thrust from power in the sixth century before Christ, amid which revolution the poet lost everything, and was obliged to go into exile. His soul is, therefore, sorely embittered by the world as he has known it; and he writes much as a Tory bishop of the present time, with disestablishment impending, might write from an Irish see. His maxims and reflections are addressed chiefly to one Cyrnus, and the progress of the popular triumph at Megara may be traced in these sad or rather atrabilious lines. Theognis denounces the Megara Reform Bill, objects to have the taxes rectified, objects to everything which has happened, in point of fact. Even the women of the city fall under his lash; and if he has painted his fair fellow *citoyennes* accurately, Megara in 550 B.C. must have been but too much like Belgravia in the present year of grace. He writes :—

οὐδὲ γυνὴ κακοῦ ἀνδρὸς ἀναίνεται εἶναι ἄκοιτις
πλουσίου, ἀλλ' ἀφνεὸν βούλεται ἀντ' ἀγαθοῦ.
χρήματα γὰρ τιμῶσι, καὶ ἐκ κακοῦ ἐσθλὸς ἔγημεν
καὶ κακὸς ἐξ ἀγαθοῦ· πλοῦτος ἔμιξε γένος.

No maid declines to be a bad man's wife.
Is he but rich? riches will make him good;
Of wealth alone they think; foul marries fair,
Fair, foul; God Plutus pairs the greedy brood.

Theognis, it will be seen, had much of the easy flow and finish of his time; and there are passages of his work extant where he is not quite so moody and ill-tempered. Yet there is nothing that can be called lofty in thought or fine in style among the relics of this oligarch, who presents himself to us in fancy as a Megarean Horace Walpole, fallen upon times very distasteful to his habits and disagreeable for his pocket. In the following lines he gives Megara and the world up altogether, with a faint reservation in favour of what a Tory now-a-days would call some future "Conservative reaction:"—

Ἐλπὶς ἐν ἀνθρώποισι μόνη θεὸς ἐσθλὴ ἔνεστιν,
ἄλλοι δ' Οὔλυμπόνδ' ἐκπρολιπόντες ἔβαν.
ᾤχετο μὲν Πίστις μεγάλη θεός, ᾤχετο δ' ἀνδρῶν
Σωφροσύνη, Χάριτές τ', ὦ φίλε, γῆν ἔλιπον.
ὅρκοι δ' οὐκέτι πιστοὶ ἐν ἀνθρώποισι δίκαιοι,
οὐδὲ θεοὺς οὐδεὶς ἅζεται ἀθανάτους.

Hope is the only god or goddess left,
The others are gone up Olympus' side.
Faith, holiest of all, is fled; bereft
Is Modesty; the Graces terrified
Have quitted earth; oaths are observed no more,
And no man any longer fears great heaven:

εὐσεβέων δ' ἀνδρῶν γένος ἔφθιτο, οὐδὲ θέμιστας
οὐκέτι γιγνώσκουσ' οὐδὲ μὲν εὐσεβίας.

The age of piety is past and o'er,
And righteousness to all the winds is given.

But we may trust that Megara was not altogether so bad as this. It produced some good men in after years, when Theognis had cooled his indignation and settled prosaically down at Thebes.

HIPPONAX AND ANANIUS.

THESE unknown celebrities, whose names have survived their fame, invented, or were amongst the very first to employ, the *choliambus*, or "halting iambic," a measure which, in its rhythm and character, goes very well to satire, and was used for satirical verse. Hipponax was an Ionian of Ephesus, living in the latter half of the sixth century before Christ. He led a worried and unlucky existence, as did Theognis, and died in exile—circumstances which tended to sour the milk of his kindness. He lashed the vices of his age with much consequent severity, especially its prodigality and luxury. He lashed the vicious also. Bupalus and Athenis, two worthless sculptors of Chios, made a caricature in marble of this stern moralist of Ephesus, unkindly exaggerating every point of his thin and awkward figure. The poet paid them back in their own bitter way; he flayed them alive with his choliambics—drove them up and down Ionia with stinging epigrams and ingenious epithets, which burned like Greek fire; till at last, according to the legend, the hapless artists hanged themselves, after the fashion of Lycambes, and found refuge in death from this terrible satiric muse.

His contemporary and imitator, Ananius, is *nominis umbra*—a name, and nothing more; but the two poets must have a place together upon the roll of Hellenic art for a still better reason than the invention of the "choliambics." They conceived, or first perfected, that great weapon of wit and humour, the *Parody.* Hipponax has the credit of having earliest discovered how to "sap a solemn creed with solemn sneer," to prolong a huge and organised jest, to make serious fun of seriousness, and render gravity ridiculous with grave words. The oldest and still the best example of this potent instrument of mockery is the "Batrachomyomachia," or "Battle of the Frogs and the Mice." There is a foolish tradition that Homer himself composed this parody. It is, indeed, almost lively and close enough to deserve the compliment, but Homer would never thus have travestied himself. The "Batrachomyomachia" is a bright, clever, witty parody of the Iliad, in which the heroics of Greeks and Trojans are mocked in the most amusing style, under cover of an imaginary battle between the frogs and the mice. Epithet, phrase, metre, imagery, "pride, pomp, circumstance of glorious war," are all hit off after the Homeric method with a perfectly captivating art; and this well-sustained *jeu d'esprit* remains as fresh in interest and rich mirth as when it was first written down on parchment or palm-leaf by its ancient author. Even in the translation of Parnell, the comic force and "inextinguishable laughter" of the excellent poem is very fully seen. The author, whoever he be, had learned his lesson from Hipponax, the first parodist; and to Hipponax every clever travesty must pay the tribute of gratitude; while it is scarcely too much to say that the *riant* spirit provoked by this mocking-bird muse had as direct a share in producing the Greek Comedy, as Homer's majestic verses in the outcoming of Greek Tragedy.

THE LYRICAL POETS OF ÆOLIA.

LESBOS, soft in name, is pleasant and beautiful to behold. It lies like a green and purple cloud upon the Ægean sea, as the traveller sails down the winding Gulf of Smyrna; and as he opens the Kara-Ras, or Black Cape, the cloud grows up into a glorious island, whose very brambles are wild vines, and its underwood myrtles and jasmine—among which the white and red houses of the towns and villages shine, at a distance, like flowers. The women are still the fairest in the Archipelago, the air the finest, the soil the richest; and, until the earthquake lately ravaged this smiling scene, it was the happiest and wealthiest of the Ottoman Turk's sea-possessions. But what makes the wandering scholar love it, and hasten towards its emerald shores, to land upon them with eager delight, is the memory of its lyric glories. Alcæus and Sappho, Erinna and Arion were islanders of lovely Lesbos. Here was born that softer music of the Grecian muse, which seems to lisp, as it were, in its open Æolic vowels—fierce as it knew how to be in war-songs, and passionate in the frenzies of love or hate.

TERPANDER.

LESBOS was Æolian, and consecrated, from the earliest poetic age, by no meaner relics than the head and the lyre of Orpheus. When the Mænads tore him to pieces, and threw his mutilated body into the Hebrus, the river bore it to the sea, and the sea washed it up upon the Lesbian coast. The Lesbians preserved the sacred head at Antissa, in a shrine of marble, and suspended the lyre above it; and it was always believed that not only the poets and poetesses of the island derived a sweeter science from the trophy, but that the very nightingales had certain delicious notes in their song unknown to birds in any other woods in Greece. Terpander was one of those who must often have lingered at this hallowed tomb, to hear the Ægean winds setting a-thrill the chords of the lyre of Orpheus as it hung. But Terpander's great fame in the Temple of Greek poetic art is due to the fact that he improved that lyre; he added three strings to the four of Orpheus, and by that innovation not merely invented the phorminx—and Greek music with it—but we may also say, the harmonic music of the western world. As a poet, Terpander cannot now be fairly judged, for the remnants of his writings are very few, and found chiefly in quotations. It is as a musician, the forerunner of the lyrists, that Terpander was greatest. This is not the place to discuss the very interesting question of Greek musical art; but it may be safely believed that, side by side with a poesy so noble and varied as the choruses of the Tragedians and the odes and dithyrambs of all the later lyric singers, a sister science must have marched, not unworthy of such stately company. The fact that Greek music was divided so distinctly into "modes" and "gnomes," shows how far it stood from being a mere barbaric accompaniment. There was the Dorian, the Lydian, and the Phrygian "mode." The Dorian was simple, grave, "Gregorian" in character; the Lydian was lighter, livelier, more tender and gay; fit for feast-days and holidays, wine-cups and flower-crowns, and it went best, say the classics, to flutes and feminine voices. The Phrygian mode was wild, excited, "Wagner-like" in its vague, aspiring strains, for both the Phrygian and Lydian, as their names show, were semi-Asiatic. Terpander seems to have taken these existing "modes," and blending them together, to have constructed a system of melody and harmony which passed into Greece, and gave to poetry—already richly and variously developed—a music rich and various enough, albeit still undeveloped, to be worthy of setting to the words of such writers as Alcman and Sappho, Pindar and Sophocles.

ALCÆUS.

ALREADY it has been seen, by incidental remarks, how Hellas was throughout divided into the aristocratic and democratic elements. In point of fact, its political history is a recital of the struggle between these principles, which are never absent from any human story of civilisation, and which make the staple of all civil annals alike in Greece between Ionians and Dorians, in Rome between plebeians and patricians, in England between Conservatives and Radicals. Alcæus was an oligarch like Theognis of Megara, and a busy, fierce, embittered, political personage. It is not necessary to recite the events of his stormy career; but fair as Lesbos was, its face was often ravaged by civil and foreign warfare, and to give the poet his just place in the temple of fame, the influences of his time and society must be duly allowed for. Alcæus used the gift of poetry for a weapon in the intestine contests of Mitylene. Those odes which Horace borrows so freely from this Lesbian singer, were wet with blood at least as often as with wine. The "*Oh navis te referent*" is taken nearly word for word from a Greek ode of Alcæus; but the original was a wild and furious diatribe against the popular constitution towards which Myrsilus was conducting the islanders. The "*Nunc est bibendum*," again, which is a favourite bacchanalian quotation for modern as it was for Roman revellers, stands really, in the verses of the aristocratic poet, as a death-song, savage like a Red Indian's, inhuman as a cannibal's, composed upon the occasion of the murder of Myrsilus, the democratic chief of Mitylene. Alcæus flung his musical anger abroad upon the heads of his enemies, with all the prejudice of a Greek Tory, and all the polished and fastidious scorn of an English patrician. One has to keep in mind his real poetic gift, and the nobility of some of his writings, to give him therefore his unquestionable place in the sacred procession of poets. This he claims and must have, for his faults were due to the breeding and the morality of his time—his generous and lofty instincts were his own. He it was who wrote the noble sentence that "The best ramparts of a city are the manly breasts within it." He fought bravely for his opinions; and the story that he threw away his shield at the battle of Sigæum is probably not true. There is bitterness and there is rancour in Alcæus, but no trace of cowardice; his odes, on the contrary, are full of warlike fire, which the life of the poet reflected. Nor, in truth, did war and politics wholly fill the heart of the Æolian—he wrote songs for the banquet and the festival, which Horace has copied by whole stanzas together; as well as religious hymns and choruses, after the ancient manner as far as epithet and ideas go, but in his own new lyric strain. This strain—the Alcaic verse—he is thought to have invented, and Horace calls him its inventor. It is not one which has found many imitators in any other tongues except the Greek and Latin, but it has a singular neatness, energy, and march in those classical languages, with a power of sustained music which the sweeter Sapphic verse cannot boast. Here is an Alcæan stanza, one of the many stolen by the Roman lyrist, the metre of which is preserved in the translation :—

κάββαλλε τὸν χειμῶν' ἐπὶ μὲν τιθεὶς
πῦρ, ἐν δὲ κίρναις οἶνον ἀφειδέως
μελιχρόν, αὐτὰρ ἀμφὶ κόρσᾳ
μαλθακὸν ἀμφιβαλὼν γνάφαλλον.

Drive out the winter, piling up plentiful
Fire-wood, and mingling cups of the honey-wine
Freely, while upon our foreheads
Sprays of the winter-green thus we fasten.

SAPPHO.

BUT the greatest distinction of Alcæus—at least, in the minds of all those who take delight in the Nine Muses—was that he was the lover of the "Tenth Muse." By this proud title the admiring Lesbians called that exquisite poetess, their countrywoman, whose genius among all feminine votaries of ancient singing stands incontestably highest. SAPPHO is the figure in all antiquity which rises to the mind of the scholar as the purest impersonation of the art of lyric song. Her name is musical and gentle; the verse to which she has given that name for ever is a soft and musical measure of melodious and perfect flow, while about her story there hangs a mystery revealing enough for sympathy, enough for imagination, enough for the heart to work with, in order to embody a delicate, but yet sufficient image of the Lesbian as she lived. All that we possess of her delicious singing (each line a precious thing) sheds upon her brow the light of a real and divine poetic inspiration; stamps her a Singer of the Singers—a true and undoubted poetess. Her name has grown famous in all the earth; the Ægean and the Adriatic Seas have been visited for her sake by travellers, who ask where Sappho lived, and whence Sappho sprang into the billows, now that nearly twenty-five centuries are passed since her time. The islands of those seas have seemed richer for the treasure of her fame, their waves shine brighter with the light of it; and whether the voyager, sailing past

Lesbos and Leucate, conjures up in his mind a Sappho of his own creation, or recalls that beautiful figure which the French sculptor Pradier has graved of her, the air, the water, the land, the spirit of these spots are full of the grace and sorrow of the Lesbian lady. A young English poet, perhaps the only one who could translate Sappho worthily—if he had at his disposal all the lost wealth of her poems—although he stoops to repeat the untrue and unnatural scandal against her sweet name which gossiping generations have invented—does brilliant justice to her deathless genius, and speaks unquestionable truth in these lines from his "Anactoria."

"These hath God made, and me as these, and wrought
Song, and hath lit it at my lips ; and me
Earth shall not gather, though she feed on thee.

* * * * *

Albeit they hide me in the deep dear sea,
And cover me with cool wave foam, and ease
This soul of mine as any soul of these,
And give me water, and great sweet waves, and make
The very sea's name lordlier for my sake,
The whole sea sweeter—albeit I die indeed,
And hide myself, and sleep, and no man heed,
Of me the high God hath not all his will !
Blossom of branches, and on each high hill
Clear air, and wind, and under, in clamorous vales,
Fierce noises of the fiery nightingales,
Buds burning in the sudden spring like fire,
The wave-washed sand, and the wave's vain desire ;
Sails seen like blown white flowers at sea, and words
That bring tears swiftest, and long notes of birds
Violently singing, till the whole world sings—
I, Sappho, shall be one with all these things,
With all high things for ever ; and my face
Seen once, my songs once heard in a strange place
Cleave to men's lives, and waste the days thereof
With gladness and strange sadness and with love."

Swinburne's "Poems and Ballads."

Such, and so blended with all that is passionate and lovely on the lyric lyre of Greece, is the memory of Sappho to the scholar. Let not that memory be ungratefully and unjustly sullied by those who should defend it! Sappho the poetess never burned with an unnatural fire, as is alleged; nor corrupted the maidens of Lesbos; nor did nor said nor thought the things which are attributed to her by unkind or blundering critics. Nay, and though romance may complain, and a lovely scene of land and water may lose one of its charms for the traveller, Sappho the poetess never leaped from the rock of Leucate, and never, in spite of the mellifluous verses of Ovid, sighed for, nor even saw *Phaon.* One, the most shameful of these calumnies, has sprung from the simple fact that she taught the love and the art of her perfect song to a circle of Lesbian women. Herodotus mentions Sappho, but says nothing about Phaon, nor does Hermesianax either, or Antipater of Sidon, who, indeed, on the contrary, relates that she died peacefully in her own island. Furthermore, in the Bibliotheca of Photius, an extract is given from a work of Ptolemy, the son of Hephæstion, in which there is a catalogue of all the despairing lovers who had leaped from the Leucadian steep, and therein there is no allusion at all to the Lesbian poetess. The Sappho who *did* leap into the Ionian waves was "Sappho of Eresus," also a native of the island of Lesbos—and this personage may, perhaps, have deserved all that the unpleasant scandal of the ages has heaped upon the noble and pure singer. Let, then, such slanders die, and let the laurels upon the brow of Sappho gleam free of canker or blight. Is the verse which she addressed to Alcæus such as a "light o' love" would have written? The poet had sent her this line:—

> Θέλω τι εἰπῆν, ἀλλά με κωλύει
> αιδώς.
>
> Something I would say, but that shame prevents me.

And Sappho replied with the following poetical rebuke:—

> Αἰ δ' ἶκέ σ' ἐσθλῶν ἵμερος ἠ καλῶν
> καὶ μή τι εἰπῆν γλῶσσ' ἐκύκα κακόν,
> αἰδώς κέ σευ οὐκ εἶχεν ὄππατ',
> ἀλλ' ἔλεγες περὶ τῶ δικαίω.
>
> If thou wert longing for right things or fair things,
> If thy lips trembled with nothing that was sinful,
> Shame had not held thee from speaking out thy meaning;
> Silence had not so chained thy tongue.

An answer like this could not come, one would say, from any but a good and honourable spirit; it ought of itself to silence the absurd accusations which people have not been ashamed to heap upon the gentle head of the Sappho of Mitylene. Besides, when Sappho's brother Charaxus brought from Egypt, where he had purchased her, a beautiful woman called Rhodopis, of the same ill trade with the Sappho of Eresus—the really profligate Sappho—this one, our poetess, upbraided him in very severe verses; and when she wrote them, be it remarked, she must have been far past the usual age of romance or of suicide on account of passion, since Amasis was King of Egypt when Rhodopis lived there; and as that monarch did not begin to reign till B.C. 570, Sappho the poetess must have been even then fifty years old, peacefully and purely living, as these facts go to show, with her daughter Cleis, the child of her husband Cercolas. Equally untrue appears the statement that Anacreon was a lover of the Lesbian singer: although Alcæus, as has been seen, paid court to her; nor indeed is it likely that she was not sought by many in Lesbos, since the islanders regarded her with absolute enthusiasm, and stamped her face upon their coins, where they were wont to impress the effigies of the gods only. There are other lines of Alcæus extant, breathing towards her a very tender and respectful sentiment. "Violet-crowned" he calls her, "modest and sweetly-smiling;" and this again is not the language in which a courtesan or corrupter of the girls of Lesbos would be addressed by a lover like Alcæus. No doubt, we must not try the manners and morals of the island by the standards of later ages; it is not to be supposed that Sappho was a cold or insensible person, who wrote a few songs, lived an altogether ordinary life, and died "as the leaves do." Enough if the ungenerous calumny has been repelled which loads her nature with cruel injustice, and her name with unnatural disgrace—enough if these brief remarks permit us to hear the music of her exquisite and tender lyre, without the painful feeling that the song is sweet, but the singer evil.

Too few, alas! for art, for music, for all those ears which know the subtle sound of perfect poetry, are the echoes that still survive of her delicious singing. Love is the burden of the greater part of them—love, passionate, burning, intense; but such as pure and noble hearts will and may feel, though few have set the sighs of it to words so eloquent as these :—

Ποικιλόθρον' ἀθάνατ' Ἀφροδίτα,
παῖ Διὸς δολόπλοκε, λίσσομαί σε,
μή μ' ἄσαισι μηδ' ἀνίαισι δάμνα,
πότνια, θυμόν.
ἀλλὰ τυίδ' ἔλθ', αἴ ποτα κἀτέρωτα,
τᾶς ἐμᾶς αὔδας ἀΐοισα· πολλὰ δ'
ἔκλυες, πατρὸς δὲ δόμον λιποῖσα
χρύσεον ἦλθες
ἄρμ' ὑποζεύξασα· καλοὶ δέ σ' ἆγον
ὠκέες στρουθοὶ πτέρυγ ς μελαίνας
πυκνὰ διννῆντες περάτων ἀπ' αἰθέ-
ρος διὰ μέσσω·
αἶψα δ' ἐξίκοντο· τὺ δ', ὦ μάκαιρα,
μειδιάσαισ' ἀθανάτῳ προσώπῳ,
ἤρε' ὄττι δηὖτε πέπονθα, κὄττι
δηὖτε κάλημι,

Splendour-throned Queen ! immortal Aphrodite !
Daughter of Jove—Enchantress ! I implore thee
Vex not my soul with agonies and anguish ;
Slay me not, Goddess !
Come in thy pity—come, if I have prayed thee ;
Come at the cry of my sorrow ; in the old times
Oft thou hast heard and left thy father's heaven,
Left the gold houses,
Yoking thy chariot. Swiftly did the doves fly,
Swiftly they brought thee, waving plumes of wonder—
Waving their dark plumes all across the æther,
All down the azure !
Very soon they lighted. Then didst thou, Divine one,
Laugh a bright laugh from lips and eyes immortal,
Ask me, " What ailed me—wherefore out of heaven
" Thus I had called thee ?

κὄττι ἐμῷ μάλιστα θέλω γενέσθαι
μαινόλᾳ θυμῷ, τίνα δηὖτε πείθω
καὶ σαγηνάεσσαν φιλότατ', ὄτις σ', ὦ
Ψάπφ', ἀδικήῃ.
καὶ γὰρ αἰ φεύγει, ταχέως διώξει,
αἰ δὲ δῶρα μὴ δέκετ', ἀλλὰ δώσει,
αἰ δὲ μὴ φιλεῖ, ταχέως φιλήσει
κοὐκ ἐθέλοισαν.
ἔλθέ μοι καὶ νῦν, χαλεπᾶν δὲ λῦσον
ἐκ μεριμνᾶν, ὄσσα δέ μοι τελέσσαι
θυμὸς ἰμέῤῥει τέλεσον, σὺ δ' αὐτὰ
σύμμαχος ἔσσο.

"What it was made me madden in my heart so?"
Question me, smiling—say to me, "My Sappho,
"Who is it wrongs thee? tell me who refuses
"Thee, vainly sighing."
"Be it who it may be, he that flies shall follow;
"He that rejects gifts, he shall bring thee many;
"He that hates now shall love thee dearly, madly—
"Ay, though thou wouldst not."
So once again come, Mistress; and, releasing
Me from my sadness, give me what I sue for,
Grant me my prayer, and be as heretofore now
Friend and protectress!

The translation here given seems, in truth, to the translator, as much as it possibly can to any one else, to lack the tender earnest Æolic melody of the original; while phrases or words which in that original have a Sapphic sweetness, a sense and fervour utterly peculiar and original, are quite lost as the lovely Greek passes forth into English. As it passes, indeed, into *any* tongue; for see how poorly even Catullus deals with the first two stanzas of the best known of all the poems of Sappho:—

φαίνετάι μοι κῆνος ἴσος θεοῖσιν
ἔμμεν ὠνήρ, ὅστις ἐναντίος τοι,
ἰζάνει καὶ πλησίον ἀδὺ φωνεύ-
σας ὑπακούει
καὶ γελαίσας ἱμερόεν· τό μοι τὰν
καρδιάν ἐν στηθεσιν επτόασεν·
ὡς ἴδω γὰρ σε βροχέ', ὥς με φωνᾶς
ὀυδὲν ἔτ' ἴκει.

This the Roman poet turns into Latin as follows:—

Ille mî par esse deo videtur,
Ille, si fas est, superare divos
Qui sedens adversus identidem te
Spectat et audit.
Dulce ridentem, misero quod omnis
Eripit sensus mihi; nam simul te
Lesbia adspexi nihil est super mî.
(Voce relictum.)

This version of Catullus, ingenious as it is, halts clumsily over the *ἴσος θεοῖσιν*, and expands the two words into a line and a half, with the foolish *si fas est* interpolated; while in other respects it serves but to show how airy and evanescent is the charm of Sappho. The familiar lines are far better—

Blest as the immortal gods is he,
The youth who fondly sits by thee;
And hears and sees thee all the while
Softly speak and sweetly smile.

But her verse is like the plant mentioned by Milton, which bore its "bright golden flower" only in its "own soil." It is like the white Lesbian roses which are said to lose their strange scent of honey when they are transplanted elsewhere.

One fragment of her music, sounding like a few soft notes of an Æolian harp, is this :—

῞Εσπερε πάντα φέρεις, ὅσα φαινόλις ἐσκέδασ' αὔως·
φέρεις ὄϊν, φέρεις ἆιγα, φέρεις ματέρι παῖδα.

Hesperus brings all things back
Which the day-light made us lack,
Brings the sheep and goats to rest,
Brings the baby to the breast.

It breathes of the calm island evenings, when Lesbos lay shadowed upon the sleeping sea ; the star of dusk gleaming upon her quiet villages, the vineyard-gates just closed ; the flocks returning, the families gathering for the homely meal and the happy sleep.

Another different echo from these long-silent strings is the following, addressed to some Lesbian woman—a rival, perhaps—ignorant of the joys of the Muses, dull and vain. Over the grave of such an one Sappho has inscribed this contemptuous epitaph :—

Κατθανοῖσα δὲ κείσεαι, οὐδέ ποτε μναμοσύνα σέθεν
ἔσσετ' οὔτε τότ' οὔτ' ὕστερον· οὐ γὰρ πεδέχεις βρόδων
τῶν ἐκ Πιερίας, ἀλλ' ἀφανὴς κἠν 'Αΐδα δόμοις
φοιτάσεις πεδ' ἀμαυρῶν νεκύων ἐκπεποταμένα.

Thou liest dead, and there will be no memory left behind
Of thee or thine in all the earth, for never didst thou bind
The roses of Pierian streams upon thy brow ; thy doom
Is writ to flit with unknown ghosts in cold and nameless gloom.

The subjoined might well describe her own eminence among the poets and poetesses of Lesbos :—

'Αστέρες μὲν ἀμφὶ καλὰν σελάναν
ἂψ ἀποκρύπτοισι φαεννὸν εἶδος,
ὀππότ' ἂν πλήθοισα μάλιστα λάμπῃ
γᾶν [ἔπι πᾶσαν]
ἀργυρέα.

The stars about the lovely moon
Fade back and vanish very soon,
When, round and full, her silver face
Swims into sight, and lights all space.

On many such a moonlight night she had wandered along the sea by Mitylene; looking up the lovely gulf to the Ionic hills, upon the far-off mainland of Asia. And not alone, doubtless; for though Sappho was, as we have maintained, a true woman, she was no cold worshipper of the Graces and the Loves. She loved, and loved more than once, and loved to the point of desperate sorrow; though it did not come to the mad and fatal leap from Leucate, as the unnecessary legend pretends. There are, nevertheless, worse steeps than Leucate down which the heart may fall; and colder seas of despair than the Adriatic in which to engulf it. We know not whether the passion was prosperous or hopeless, serious or slight, which is faintly chronicled thus :—

ἠράμαν μέν ἐγὼ σέθεν, 'Ατθὶ, πάλαι πότε.

I loved thee, Atthis, dearly,
A long while ago.

And thus again—

Ἔρος δηὖτέ μ' ὁ λυσιμελὴς δονεῖ,
γλυκύπικρον ἀμάχανον ὄρπετον.

Love torments me once again,
Sweetly-bitter, sadly-dear,
Binds me with a rosy chain,
Hard to break, and hard to bear.

While these tender words, which paint a picture of two lives, come, doubtless, out from the same ancient heart-ache—

Γλυκεῖα μᾶτερ, οὔτοι δύναμαι κρέκην τὸν ἰστὸν,
πόθῳ δαμεῖσα παιδὸς βραδινὰν δὶ ’Αφροδίταν.

I cannot, sweet my mother,
Throw shuttle any more;
My heart is full of longing,
My spirit troubled sore,
All for a love of yesterday,
A boy not seen before.

It seems that the Lesbian poetess excelled especially in Epithalamia or Marriage Hymns, which Catullus imitated in his "Peleus and Thetis," and other well-known pieces. It would be hard, perhaps, to make such a sacrifice, but if we could have the Greek of Sappho back, who would not gladly surrender to oblivion the Latin of the Roman for it! Into these compositions she seems to have thrown all her rich and passionate soul, her love of nature, her finest delicacy in phrase, her tenderest sense of music, her indefinable and, so to speak, "lady-like" grace of thought. Thus she speaks, in one fragment, about the untouched beauty of the bride:—

Οἶον τὸ γλυκύμαλον ἐρεύθεται ἄκρῳ ἐπ' ὄσδῳ
ἄκρον ἐπ' ἀκροτάτῳ· λελάθοντο δὲ μαλοδροπῆες,
οὐ μὰν ἐκλελάθοντ', ἀλλ' οὐκ ἐδύναντ' ἐφικέσθαι.

Grown to her rosy grace like the rose-apple, high on the branches,
Hanging highest of all—so high that the canker-worms miss it—
Nay, not "miss it," in truth, but cannot in any way reach it.

And again, in a little piece of broken sweetness, Sappho thus speaks of the unhappy one whose life is lived in loneliness and loveless solitude :—

Οἴαν τὰν ὑάκινθον ἐν οὔρεσι ποιμένες ἄνδρες
ποσσὶ καταστείβοισι, χαμαὶ δέ τε πορφύρον ἄνθος.

Pines she like to the hyacinth out on the path by the hill-top ;
Shepherds tread it aside, and its purples lie lost on the herbage.

Then there are slighter echoes, fragmentary refrains of gayer or more careless singing, such as this, directed again at a rival :—

Τίς τοι ἀγροιῶτις ἀγροιῶτιν ἐπεμμένα
στόλαν . . . θέλγει νόον, ...
οὐκ ἐπισταμένα τὰ βράκε' ἕλκην ἐπὶ τῶν σφυρῶν ;

What country damsel charms thee
With country smock and face?
Who knows not how to fasten,
A stole, nor step with grace.

And what a Greek love of life, what a "longing lingering" thought of the "warm precincts" of that pleasant island is audible in these half satirical words :—

'Αποθνάσκειν κακόν· οἱ θεοὶ γὰρ οὕτω κεκρίκασιν·
ἀπέθνασκον γὰρ ἄν, αἴπερ ἦν καλὸν ἀποθνάσκειν.

To die must needs be sad, the gods do know it ;
For were death sweet, they'd die, and straightway show it.

Such are a few specimens of the singing which remain to us from this unrivalled singer—the truest genius of all the Greek lyric schools, whether Ionian, Dorian, or Æolian. It may seem extravagant praise to say this of a poetess, whose longest surviving work is but an ode or two of a few verses in each; while the rest of her musical work has all vanished except detached lines, phrases, names, and words. But the fragrance and the splendid tints of a rose-garden can be guessed at by detached petals; and he that has the scholar's knowledge and the poet's ear and heart, will never deny to Sappho the admiration which we know she received from her countrymen and country-women. There is nothing, let it be repeated, in the often passionate expressions of her muse to justify the calumny of those ancient critics. There is fire, there is fervour, there is burning love; but these are not crimes, nor monstrosities. The same ugly and ignorant slander which has branded an evil word upon the brow of Sappho, might as well dare to do the same to Shakespeare because of his sonnets, or to Tennyson on account of his solemn "In Memoriam." Emphatically we repudiate the charge, and repeat the assertion that Sappho was true to her art and true to her womanhood. And if romance complains to find that she never leaped at all from the fatal promontory, and never wrote the elegant letter to Phaon which Ovid has composed for her, there still remains, we think, an image as stately, as graceful, as passionate, as enchanting, and more noble in the Sappho which these verses and this broken music recall, than in that sadder fictitious Sappho whom poets or sculptors have pictured, bending among the myrtles with her broken lyre at her foot, before she sprang to her death in the blue grave of the Saronic sea.

THE IONIAN LYRISTS.

ANACREON.

If all that glitters with the name of Anacreon were real Anacreontic gold, a great space would have to be devoted to the poet of Teos. But his genius and style have been made to stand godfathers to very many odes and poems which were never written by him. The metres that he invented or popularised are so simple and easily managed, and his usual themes are so much within the compass of ordinary inspiration, that a large volume of spurious Greek verse has crystallised about the very small nucleus of genuine Anacreontics. He is said to have written five books of songs, of which sixty-eight are presented to us as veritable remains of the poet. Very few of these could pass the barrier of stern comparative criticism. Some of them may be the production of imitators almost as brilliant as the master; some may have resulted from the not very secular labours of the monks, who in the middle ages gave much attention to the classical authors. But there are a few, obviously from the master's hand, which convict the false pretenders by their greater grace and skill of versification, for Anacreon was certainly a lyrist of the first order. There is enough of his singing still extant to prove that his reputation among the Greeks, and the friendship entertained towards him by Polycrates, was well deserved. There is something extremely graceful, bright, and original in the versicules of the Teian bard; yet with their airy sweetness there mingles also an occasional pathos—the soft shadow of the glad sunshine of his spirit. In the translations of Moore the English reader has this spirit very aptly transmitted, for the genius of the Ionian and Irish singers was almost identical. The praise of love, of music, and of feasting engaged each; and each had that subtle-sweet power of sensuous language which seems to sparkle with the colour of the wine, and to glow with the warmth of the passion. The subjoined is as tender and pretty as a plaque of Watteau painted on a Rose du Barri jar of Sèvres china:—

Ἔρως ποτ' ἐν ῥόδοισι
κοιμωμένην μέλιτταν
οὐκ εἶδεν, ἀλλ' ἐτρώθη
τὸν δάκτυλον. παταχθεὶς
τὰς χεῖρας ὠλόλυξεν·
δραμὼν δὲ καὶ πετασθεὶς
πρὸς τὴν καλὴν Κυθήρην,

Love once among the roses
Perceived a bee reposing,
And wondered what the beast was,
And touched it, so it stung him.
Sorely his finger smarted,
And bitterly he greeted,
And wrung his hands together ;
And half he ran, half fluttered
Unto Cythera's bosom,
Unto his fair, sweet mother.

ὄλωλα, μῆτερ, εἶπεν,
ὄλωλα κἀποθνήσκω.
ὄφις μ' ἔτυψε μικρὸς
πτερωτός, ὃν καλοῦσιν
μέλιτταν οἱ γεωργοί.
ἁ δ' εἶπεν· εἰ τὸ κέντρον
πονεῖ τὸ τᾶς μελίττας,
πόσον δοκεῖς πονοῦσιν,
Ἔρως, ὅσους σὺ βάλλεις;

Loud sobbed he, "Ai! ai! mother!
Olola! I am murdered!
Olola! it has killed me!
A small brown snake with winglets,
That men the bumble-bee call,
Has bit me." But Cythera
Said, laughing, "Ah, my baby,
If bees' stings hurt so sorely,
Bethink thee what the smart is
Of those, Love, that thou piercest."

It seems that Anacreon generally, though by no means always, wrote in this light and swift little measure—admirably adapted to the banquet and the dance—but so easily composed by a practical verse-maker, that it must have bubbled from the lips of the old Teian like Cyprus wine from a grey amphora. Here is just such a *chansonette* as may have thus sprung into existence at a moment's inspiration, within some Samian festal-hall; on some night, perhaps, when Polycrates unbent his brow from toils of state, and called upon his Ionian laureate for a defence of drinking:—

Ἡ γῆ μέλαινα πίνει,
πίνει δὲ δένδρε' αὐτήν,

πίνει θάλασσ' ἀναύρους,
ὁ δ' ἥλιος θάλασσαν,
τὸν δ' ἥλιον σελήνη.
τί μοι μάχεσθ', ἑταῖροι,
καὐτῷ θέλοντι πίνειν;

The black earth tipples rain,
The earth is sucked by trees,
The seas the rivers drain,
The sun drinks up the seas;
And the moon drinks the sun;
Why, then, will any one
Contend with me, who think
That all the world should drink?

It is said that this votary of the wine-cup died at the age of eighty-five, choked by a grape-stone. That mode of dissolution seemed almost too *apropos* to be true; but he certainly lived to a great age, chirping out his light-hearted *Lieder*, amid the turmoil of the revolt of Histiæus, and all kinds of other national and civic troubles. Remark how merrily he bears the snows of approaching senility!—

Λέγουσιν αἱ γυναῖκες,
Ανακρέων, γέρων εἶ.
λαβὼν ἔσοπτρον ἄθρει
κόμας μὲν οὐκέτ' οὔσας,
ψιλὸν δέ σευ μέτωπον.
ἐγὼ δὲ τὰς κόμας μέν,

The women to me say,
"Anacreon, you grow grey!
Look in your glass, and see
Your hairs, how scantily
They flow—your brows are bare."
Then I: "As for the hair,

εἴτ' εἰσὶν εἴτ' ἀπῆλθον,
οὐκ οἶδα· τοῦτο δ' οἶδα,
ὡς τῷ γέροντι μᾶλλον
πρέπει τὸ τερπνὰ παίζειν,
ὅσῳ πέλας τὰ Μοίρης.

That may be, or may not,
I reck it not a jot;
But this I know, indeed,
If I grow old, more need
To have my fling of laughter,
The sooner Fate comes after."

And if a grape-stone choked him, as is alleged, it must have been because he tried, indomitable to the last in his Greek gaiety, to sing while he was drinking.

SIMONIDES OF CEOS.

GRAVE and learned, discreet and nice, Simonides of Ceos, of the same school and time with Anacreon, is his exact contrast in literature. He was, like the Teian, a friend of kings and rulers, but not because he sang to them at their banquet-hours. He had Hipparchus at Athens for his patron, and lived long enough to be intimate with Themistocles and Pausanias. He reconciled the two Sicilian monarchs, Hiero of Syracuse and Theron of Agrigentum, at the moment when their armies were opposed in battle array. Finally, Plato calls him emphatically "a wise man," and Cicero writes of Simonides, "Non enim poeta solum mavis, verum etiam cæteroquin doctus sapiensque traditur." He was a teacher of his art to Pindar, and his somewhat *triste* and contemplative genius gave to the word ἔλεγος that funereal signification which "elegy" has ever since possessed. He invented, it is declared, four letters of the Greek alphabet; but his chief reputation arose from his epitaphs, which are sometimes remarkably elegant and ingenious. He appears to have enjoyed a quite unrivalled reputation for the couplets or verses which the Greeks were wont to carve upon their trophies and monuments. The fashion was to inscribe metrical legends, generally a hexameter and pentameter; and Simonides is said to have carried the garland away from Æschylus himself in a competition for the verses to be placed over the dead Greeks who fell in battle against the Persians at Thermopylæ. It is said that the subjoined couplet was that which gained so great a distinction :—

Ὦ ξεῖν', ἀγγέλλειν Λακεδαιμονίοις ὅτι τᾷδε
κείμεθα τοῖς κείνων ῥήμασι πειθόμενοι.

Go, stranger! tell the Spartans here we lie,
Faithful to death, because they bade us die.

This which follows was dedicated to the Athenians who died at Marathon :—

Ἑλλήνων προμαχοῦντες Ἀθηναῖοι Μαραθῶνι
χρυσοφόρων Μήδων ἐστόρεσαν δύναμιν.

Athens at Marathon, in front of Greece,
Met the proud Mede, and made his boasting cease.

And this is one of another group of epitaphs, written for the monumental erections with which the states of Hellas commemorated the glorious repulse of the barbarian :—

Μυριάσιν ποτὲ τᾷδε τριακοσίαις ἐμάχοντο
ἐκ Πελοποννάσου χιλιάδες τέτορες.

Here, with three hundred myriad Persians, fought
Four thousand Greeks from Peloponnesus brought.

These also were composed upon the same great event of mingled sadness and gladness in Grecian history :—

Εἰ τὸ καλῶς θνήσκειν ἀρετῆς μέρος ἐστὶ μέγιστον,
ἡμῖν ἐκ πάντων τοῦτ' ἐπένειμε τύχη·
Ελλάδι γὰρ σπεύδοντες ἐλευθερίην περιθεῖναι
κείμεθ' ἀγηράντῳ χρώμενοι εὐλογίῃ.

If a fair end be Virtue's chiefest glory,
To us of all men Fortune that gift gave,
Who, dying here, won an undying story,
Saving our dear land from the name of "slave."

Ασβεστον κλέος οἵδε φίλῃ περὶ πατρίδι θέντες
κυάνεον θανάτου ἀμφεβάλοντο νέφος,
οὐδὲ τεθνᾶσι θανόντες, ἐπεί σφ' ἀρετὴ καθύπερθε
κυδαίνουσ' ἀνάγει δώματος ἐξ 'Αΐδεω.

Here, giving all for Greece, her bravest children
Wrapped themselves from us in the dark death-wreath;
Yet these dead are not dead, their virtue leads them
In glory upward from the place beneath.

Εὐκλέας αἶα κέκευθε, Λεωνίδα, οἳ μετὰ σεῖο
τῇδ' ἔθανον, Σπάρτης εὐρυχόρου βασιλεῦ,
πλείστων δὴ τόξων τε καὶ ὠκυπόδων σθένος ἵππων
Μηδείων ἀνδρῶν δεξάμενοι πολέμῳ.

Glorious the soil that holds these Spartan men
Who died, Leonidas, for Greece with thee,
Not caring for the storm of javelins,
Nor all the thundering Persian cavalry.

Simonides was one of the most prolific writers known, and the relics of his prodigious fertility are still numerous, but for the most part not very remarkable. He had, however, a vein of pathos and melancholy eloquence which might be illustrated by more than one specimen of his remains; but his fame as the epitaph-maker of Greece bears sufficient testimony to this sombre trait in his genius. He could write stinging satire, too, upon a tombstone; witness the distich which he dedicated to the hapless memory of Timocreon of Rhodes, a sour poetaster, who was greedy and scurrilous :—

Πολλὰ πιὼν καὶ πολλὰ φαγὼν καὶ πολλὰ κάκ' εἰπὼν
ἀνθρώπους κεῖμαι Τιμοκρέων 'Ρόδιος.

With drink, meat, slander, fuddled fat and foul,
Timocreon of Rhodes lies in this hole.

It is said that Simonides grew avaricious and mercenary towards the close of his life; but the spirit of the poet, refined and contemplative, does not seem to warrant this; and antiquity is sometimes, as Sappho's instance proves, an arrant slander-monger. It was he who gave the famous answer about "the nature of God." Hiero, King of Syracuse, asked him his opinion upon this problem, and Simonides demanded a day to reply, then another, and another, and so put the king off till his patience was worn out, when the poet explained himself by saying, "The longer I think upon it, the farther off appears the possibility of any true reply." This may remind Sanskrit scholars of the definition which the Veda gives of BRAHM, viz., "OM"—that is to say, *spoken silence*, the sound that the lips make in closing to say "nothing."

BACCHYLIDES.

OF Ceos also, and the nephew of Simonides, this poet had something of the grace and finish of his uncle, and acquired reputation enough at the court of Hiero of Syracuse to move the envy of Pindar himself. A Dorian manner pervades his writings, although his extraction was Ionian. Something of the melancholy also which is visible in his uncle's writings colours the verses of Bacchylides: he is constantly repeating the despondent sentiment of these lines:—

> *Θνατοῖσι μὴ φῦναι φέριστον,*
> *μηδ' ἀελίου προσιδεῖν φέγγος·*
> *ὄλβιος δ' οὐδεὶς βροτῶν πάντα χρόνον.*

> 'Twere best never to be,
> Never sunlight to see,
> For no man lives whose happiness endures.

One may see in such complaining music how the child-like inclination of these early Greeks to live and love and be happy within the delicious limits of their climate and land, chafed at the grim interruptions of wars and troubles, disease and death. The soft Ægean and Sicilian airs, the fertility of Ceos, and the graceful ease of Hiero's court, made this world very pleasant to Bacchylides but for the shadow of such things. He loves to sing, like Anacreon, of wine and roses; and if he could he would have placid joys and gentle music always embellishing life. Here is a piece of his verse, as charming in sentiment and picturesque in detail as Landseer's lovely parable in colours of "Peace," where the little children play upon the grass on the cliff, and the lamb nibbles daisies from the muzzle of the rusted cannon. "Ah, sweet peace!" sings Bacchylides:—

> Τίκτει δέ τε θνατοῖσιν Εἰράνα μεγάλα
> πλοῦτον μελιγλώσσων τ' ἀοιδᾶν ἄνθεα,
> δαιδαλέων τ' ἐπὶ βωμῶν θεοῖσιν αἴθεσθαι βοῶν
> ξανθᾷ φλογὶ μῆρα τανυτρίχων τε μήλων,
> γυμνασίων τε νέοις αὐλῶν τε καὶ κώμων μέλειν.
> ἐν δὲ σιδαροδέτοις πόρπαξιν αἰθᾶν
> ἀραχνᾶν ἱστοὶ πέλονται·
> ἔγχεά τε λογχωτὰ ξίφεά τ' ἀμφάκε' εὐρὼς δάμναται·
> χαλκεᾶν δ' οὐκέτι σαλπίγγων κτύπος.

> Peace, potent Peace! gives all good gifts to men,
> The wealth of soft words, and the flower of song;
> The smoking on the ancient altar-tops
> Of sheep in yellow flame of sacrifice;
> And in the towns and villages the shout
> Of happy youth at play and exercise:
> While helms and bucklers hang, and spiders weave
> Their nets across the iron hollows of 'em;
> And the rust eats the sword-edge and the spear,
> And horrid trumpets hush.

MESOMEDES.

ONE name must be included, somewhat by anticipation, in the catalogue of writers of lyric verse—that of Mesomedes the Cretan—for the sake of the wonderful, the almost terrible poem which bears his authorship. Of the poet nothing more is known than that he was a freedman of Hadrian, and therefore of a very late age in Greek literature. Two of his epigrams only are extant, with an invocation to Nemesis, the Goddess of Divine Equity and Final Restitution. This latter piece paints that dread deity—she who, in Greek belief, "wronged the wronger, till he rendered right"—as no other passage in Greek literature does. It runs as follows:—

Νέμεσι πτερόεσσα, βίου ῥοπὰ,
κυανῶπι θεά, θύγατερ Δίκας,
ἃ κοῦφα φρυάγματα θνατῶν
ἐπέχεις ἀδάμαντι χαλινῷ,
ἔχθουσά θ' ὕβριν ὀλοὰν βροτῶν
μέλανα φθόνον ἐκτὸς ἐλαύνεις.

Daughter of Justice, wingèd Nemesis;
Thou of the awful eyes,
Whose silent sentence judgeth mortal life!
Thou with thy curb of steel,
Which proudest jaws must feel,
Stayest the snort and champ of human strife;
And, hating miserable pride of men,
Dost tame fierce hearts, and turn them meek agen.

Ὑπὸ σὸν τρόχον ἄστατον, ἀστιβῆ
χαροπὰ μερόπων στρέφεται τύχα,
    λήθουσα δὲ πὰρ πόδα βαίνεις,
    γαυρούμενον αὐχένα κλίνεις·
ὑπὸ πῆχυν ἀεὶ βίοτον μετρεῖς
    ζυγίον μετὰ χεῖρα κρατοῦσα.

Under thy wheel, unresting, trackless, all
    Our joys and griefs befall;
In thy full sight our secret things go on;
    Stop after step thy wrath
    Follows the caitiff's path,
And in his triumph breaks his vile neck-bone.
To all alike thou metest out their due,
Cubit for cubit, inch for inch—stern—true.

THE "SKOLIA."

DIAGORAS, Praxilla, and Pythermas, are some out of many others which, being mere names, belong to the catalogue of Hellenic poets, rather than to any critical sketch of their style and works. But there arose a class of composition at this date which deserves allusion. It was an elegant custom of the Greeks, at their festal repasts, especially in the time of Pericles, to pass round the table from hand to hand, after the serious business of the banquet was over, a lyre or a branch of myrtle. Each person to whom it came was expected to recite or sing, or to express at least some agreeable sentiment, clothed in the language of the Muses. Terpander is thought to have introduced the fashion, which is first mentioned, however—at least of the authors known to us—by Pindar and Aristophanes. The word σκολιός means "crooked," and might have been applied to these *vers de societé* either because the metre was dithyrambic and uneven for the most part (as might well be the case, when unpractised guests were called upon to improvise in rhythmic language), or else because the manner was to pass the myrtle-branch *irregularly* from one hand to the other; part of the gaiety being, doubtless, to surprise an unready guest, and thus enjoy his confusion at being suddenly "knocked down" for something brilliant in Doric or Ionic Greek. Sometimes, however, great poets seized these occasions to produce something really fine; and many of such "impromptus" —perhaps not always made without a little previous preparation—are carefully preserved. A collection of them, complete and fragmentary, has been made by the Prussian critic, Ilgen, whereby the curious may fully study this "literature of the Greek salon." For those who can be contented with a few examples, we proceed to quote the celebrated *σκόλιον* of CALLISTRATUS, in honour of the slayers of Hipparchus; a song which was the *Marseillaise* of Athens, and the very anthem of Revolution and Liberty. It must have been at a circle of fiery young Republicans, on some night of wild and patriotic talk, that such a hymn as this answered to the challenge of the myrtle-branch :—

Εν μύρτου κλαδὶ τὸ ξίφος φορήσω,
ὥσπερ Ἁρμόδιος κ' Ἀριστογείτων,
ὅτε τὸν τύραννον κτανέτην
ἰσονόμους τ' Ἀθήνας ἐποιησάτην.

Φίλταθ' Ἁρμόδι', οὔ τί που τέθνηκας,
νήσοις δ' ἐν μακάρων σέ φασιν εἶναι,
ἵνα περ ποδώκης Ἀχιλεὺς,
Τυδεΐδην τέ φασιν Διομήδεα.

My sword I wreathe in a myrtle-spray,
Aristogeiton's and Harmodius' way;
When they the king had valorously slain,
And made our Athens free and great again.

Ah, dear Harmodius! but thou art not dead;
Unto the Blessed Islands thou art sped;
Where, as they say, swift-limbed Achilles is,
And Tydeus' son, the happy Diomed.

Ἐν μύρτου κλαδὶ τὸ ξίφος φορήσω,
ὥσπερ Ἁρμόδιος κ' Ἀριστογείτων,
ὅτ' Ἀθηναίης ἐν θυσίαις
ἄνδρα τύραννον Ἵππαρχον ἐκαινέτην.

Ἀεὶ σφῷν κλέος ἔσσεται κατ' αἶαν,
φίλταθ' Ἁρμόδιος κ' Ἀριστογείτων,
ὅτι τὸν τύραννον κτανέτην,
ἰσονόμους τ' Ἀθήνας ἐποιησάτην.

My sword I wreathe in the myrtle-spray,
Aristogeiton's and Harmodius' way;
When at the feast of Pallas those brave youths
The King Hipparchus gloriously did slay.

Ever and everywhere their fame shall be,
Aristogeiton and Harmodius!
Because they killed the wicked king for us,
All to make this our Athens great and free.

The second *σκόλιον* best worthy citing is a soldier's catch—rough, insolent, audacious, yet with music in it of rare and masculine sort—such a song, in fact, as a Cretan swash-buckler like its author HYBRIAS might well have struck off at heat, when the "rosy wine had done its deed." The good steel sword is my wealth! he sings:—

Στροφή.

Ἔστι μοι πλοῦτος μέγας δόρυ καὶ ξίφος,
καὶ τὸ καλὸν λαισήϊον πρόβλημα χρωτός·

The wealth I have is my sword and spear,
And the fence I fight with, my buckler fair;
With these, the lord of all, I go,
With these I plough, with these I sow;

τούτῳ γὰρ ἀρῶ, τούτῳ θερίζω,
τούτῳ πατέω τὸν ἁδὺν οἶνον ἀπ' ἀμπέλω·
τούτῳ δεσπότας μνωΐας κέκλημαι.

Ἀντιστροφή.

Τοὶ δὲ μὴ τολμῶντ' ἔχειν δόρυ καὶ ξίφος
καὶ τὸ καλὸν λαισήϊον, πρόβλημα χρωτὸς,
πάντες γόνυ πεπτηῶτες ἀμὸν
κυνεῦντι τε δεσπόταν
καὶ μεγαν βασιλῆα φωνέοντες.

With these I tread the sweet red wine
From grapes and vats that never were mine ;
With these, albeit no varlets I fee,
Wherever I come, men lackey me.

For the knaves are afeard of sword and spear,
And the fence I fight with, my buckler fair ;
And so at my knees they humbly fall,
Bringing me all and giving me all ;
And they fawn upon me because of my sword,
And because of my spear they call me lord ;
For wealth unbounded is sword and spear,
And the fence that I fight with, my buckler fair.

Here is a specimen of these table songs, which might have been produced when philosophers sate together at a light and learned feast :—

Εἴθ' ἐξῆν ὁποῖός τις ἦν ἕκαστος
τὸ στῆθος διελόντ', ἔπειτα τὸν νοῦν
ἐσιδόντα, κλείσαντα πάλιν,
ἄνδρα φίλον νομίζειν ἀδόλῳ φρενί.

If it only were right, how delightful 'twould be,
  To open the breast of a friend ;
And peep at his heart, and replace it again,
  And believe in him then without end.

And here another, which Alcibiades might have murmured into the ear of Aspasia when philosophers were far away:—

Σύν μοι πῖνε, συνήβα, συνέρα, συστεφανηφόρει,
σύν μοι μαινομένῳ μαίνεο, σὺν σώφρονι σωφρόνει.

Drink from my cup, Dear! live my life—be still
Young with my youth! have one heart, word, and will,
One love for both; let one wreath shade our eyes;
Be mad when I am—wise when I am wise.

ERINNA.

THE wearer of this famous and melodious name was the pupil and the friend of Sappho. She was one of those Lesbian maidens who learned the secrets of song from the great poetess, and the little by which we can judge of her genius, together with the praise which her mistress gave her, and the admiration with which she is mentioned by the critics of antiquity, combine to make it seem that she might have been in time a rival of the renowned Lesbian. But she left the harsh weather of this lower life at eighteen, before the flower of her genius was full-blown. A tender epitaph, which her hand inscribed upon the funeral urn of a fellow learner in the school of Sappho, is a becoming memorial of herself, and musical as her sweet name. A sad fragrance lingers about it, like that of a dead violet, blown in the brief sunshine, and killed by the first wind of March :—

Νύμφας Βαυκίδος ἐμμί· πολυκλαύταν δὲ παρέρπων
στάλαν, τῷ κατὰ γᾶς τοῦτο λέγοις 'Αΐδᾳ·
" Βάσκανος ἔσσ', 'Αΐδα·" τὰ δέ τοι καλὰ σάμαθ' ὁρῶντι
ὠμοτάταν Βαυκοῦς ἀγγελέοντι τύχαν,

I am the urn of Baucis ! Look down low,
Past urn and stone, and say to Death thereunder,
"Thou art a cheat, O, Death !" Then turn and know
From these fair griefs inscribed what horrid wonder

ὡς τὰν παῖδ', Ὑμέναιος ἐφ' αἷς ἀείδετο πεύκαις,
ταῖσδ' ἐπὶ καδευτὰς ἔφλεγε πυρκαϊᾷ·
καὶ σὺ μὲν, ὦ Ὑμέναιε, γάμων μολπαῖαν ἀοιδὰν
ἐς θρηνῶν γοερῶν φθέγμα μεθαρμόσαο.

The juggler wrought : how, when the lamps were lighted
For marriage, he did turn the bed to bier,
Lit it therewith, and made Hymen, affrighted,
Change bridal songs to sound of sob and tear.

ARION.

HERODOTUS tells a story of this poet, which makes him the very Jonah of literature. He was thrown overboard by sailors, like that prophet; but a dolphin, charmed by his exquisite music, took him upon its back, and carried him safely to shore. Modern interpreters think that the "whale" of the Biblical story was but a Phœnician ship, called by such a name, and "bound outward" from Tyre or Sidon, which picked up Jonah, a derelict, at sea; and possibly the legend of Arion on the dolphin's back would come to this—if we knew the truth—that a vessel of Sicily gave him a free passage, on condition, as is often done now-a-days, that he should supply the crew with music on the voyage. Thus the poet would emerge from the fog of fable which obscures him now, and we might recognise in him no mythical bestrider of fishes, but a simple citizen of Methymna, uncommonly skilful in lyre-playing, and especially remarkable for the development which he gave to the dithyramb. This, in its ancient form, was probably a wild chant in praise of the Indian Bacchus—a loud, excited, and half-articulate succession of cries, like the "hymn" of the Mohurrum among the Islamites, or the monotonous shouts of the dancing dervishes. Arion reduced the short phrenetic measure to ordered music, keeping its characteristics of swift emotion, but supplying graces of art and language to the altered dithyramb, which he employed to narrate the adventures of the various gods. The verses which he thus composed were sung by dancers, who held hands, and paced or whirled round the altars of the temples at Corinth, where the inventor's skill had made him the favourite of Periander, the ruler of the City of Two Seas. The following fragment of such a choral song—chanted many a time, doubtless, by the Saronic Gulf in praise of Poseidon—may serve to represent the manner of Arion :—

> *Ὕψιστε θεῶν ποντιε,*
> *χρυσοτρίαινε Πόσειδον,*
> *γαιήοχε, κυμονάρχα.*
> *βράγχιοι περὶ δὲ σὲ πλωτοὶ θῆρες*
> *χορεύουσιν ἐν κύκλῳ,*
> *κούφοισι ποδῶν ῥίμμασιν*
> *ἐλαφρὰ ἀναπαλλόμενοι·*
> *σιμοί, φριξαυχένες,*
> *ὠκυδρόμοι σκύλακες,*
> *φιλόμουσοι δελφῖνες,*
> *ἔναλα θρέμματα κουρᾶν*

> Mighty Master of the ocean !
> Neptune of the golden trident !
> Oh, Earth-shaker ! oh, Storm-maker !
> Gilled things, snorting, slimy, strident,
> Glide about thee in a ring
> Winnowing fins with rapid motion ;
> Fish with beaks and fish with backs
> Bristly, and the dog-fish packs ;

Νηρηίδων θεᾶν,
ἃς ἐγείνατο 'Αμφιτρίτα.

Silvery dolphins dear to song,
With the salt-sea maids that throng,
Scale-tailed Nereids, one with other,
Whereof Amphitrite was mother.

THE DORIAN LYRISTS.

ALCMAN.

THE Dorian genius and dialect did not lend themselves readily to the softer muses, but these brilliant schools of Æolic and Ionic singers had rivals, nevertheless, of no mean merit in the cities and islands which looked to Sparta as their centre. Yet it is notable that the greatest master of the Doric lyre was a Lydian, and probably a slave. Alcman was born at Sardis, about 680 B.C., and was a Lacedæmonian only by residence at Sparta in the house of his master Agesidas. His talent procured him freedom at a time when the Dorian races were in a state of peace—very rare with them—and therefore at leisure to listen to the notes of this Asiatic bird which they had caught and tamed. It is observable that many of the artistic celebrities of antiquity were originally slaves, a fact which probably arose from the use which their owners made of them as amanuenses, singers, musicians, and the like. Alcman never forgot the Eastern home which he had left; but he was proud of his Spartan reputation notwithstanding. Thus he sings:—

Σάρδιες, ἀρχαῖος πατέρων νομός, εἰ μὲν ἐν ὑμῖν
ἐτρεφόμαν, κερνᾶς ἦν τις ἂν ἢ βακέλας

χρυσοφόρος, ῥήσσων καλὰ τύμπανα· νῦν δέ μοι 'Αλκμὰν
οὔνομα καὶ Σπάρτας εἰμὶ πολυτρίποδος,
καὶ Μούσας ἐδάην 'Ελικωνίδας, αἵ με τυράννων
θῆκαν Δασκύλεω μείζονα καὶ Γύγεω.

Sardis, my father's city! had my fate
So willed, by this time I were priest in thee,
Gold-robed, beating the drum; now I am great
As ALCMAN, and a Spartan known and free,
And Heliconian Muses make my name
Higher than Gyges of Dascylium.

In truth, the Oriental airs of Alcman and the stern character of Doric speech and manners were strange things to be mingled. His ardent love songs and soft passages of lyric verse grew upon the trunk of Spartan history much like the leaves and berries of the mistletoe upon oak. So far as we can judge of Alcman, he was a genuine poet, inspired by a love of nature remarkable amid his race and time—a thinker, a moralist, and, in an Eastern minstrel's way, even a philosopher. Among the numerous but very fragmentary relics of the Slave of Agesidas, the subjoined is one which shows a poet's sense of the awful calm of nature during some still and moonless midnight:—

Εὕδουσιν δ' ὀρέων κορυφαί τε καὶ φάραγγες
πρώονές τε καὶ χαράδραι,
φῦλα τε ἑρπετά θ' ὅσσα τρέφει μέλαινα γαῖα,
θῆρές τ' ὀρεσκῷοι

The mountain brows, the rocks, the peaks are sleeping,
Uplands and gorges hush!
The thousand moorland things are stillness keeping;
The beasts under each bush

καὶ γένος μελισσᾶν
καὶ κνώδαλα ἐν βένθεσι πορφυρᾶς ἁλός.
εὕδουσιν δ' οἰωνῶν φῦλα τανυπτερύγων.

Crouch, and the hivèd bees
Rest in their honied ease;
I' the purple sea fish lie as they were dead,
And each bird folds his wing over his head.

It is disputed whether, in a certain fragment, this writer has called Memory (*Μνάμα*) "back-glancing" (*παλί δορκος*), or (*φρασί δορκος*), the "eye of the mind." Either epithet would show the dawn of that reflective and metaphysical poesy which we shall have to notice hereafter. A large portion of the songs of Alcman were classed and called "Parthenia," or "Songs for Maidens;" but only a few incoherent phrases or lines survive of these famous compositions, which were once recited in all the Dorian temples, and which certainly must have been tender and charming, coming from the heart and lips of this accomplished lyrist.

STESICHORUS.

STESICHORUS was the contemporary of Alcman; but born at Himera, in Sicily, a lovely southern city half Dorian and half Ionian, which produced many singers, and two of this name. His original cognomen appears to have been Tisias, and that of Stesichorus, which means "Choir Leader," or "Choir Stayer," may have been conferred because he seems to have introduced the "Epode," a verse of the choral song chanted about the altars, in which the dancers or worshippers stayed their movements for awhile instead of passing round to right or left. Pindar and the Tragedians adopted the innovation, so that it must not be regarded as unimportant. Stesichorus also wrote *epithalamia*, and lyric poems, into which ancient legends were worked; imitated, probably, by Pindar in his fourth "Pythian," where the adventures of the Argonauts are recited. We have many titles of these productions, but very little of the texts. His "Europiad," which detailed the voyages and deeds of Cadmus, would be a welcome *trouvaille* of antiquity—if anybody could light upon it under the lily roots at Himera—for the sake of poesy less perhaps than of its legendary lore. Quintilian, indeed, speaks with enthusiasm of the artistic power of Stesichorus, but blames him for diffuseness and excess of imagery. Only scanty material survives to us for a review of the critic's decision; and, as the Himera singer has himself written—

ἀτελέστατα δη, καὶ ἀμάχανα τοὺς θανόντας κλαίειν.

It is idle and helpless to sigh for the dead.

IBYCUS.

IBYCUS of Rhegium is remembered more for his death than his life. He was a poet who loved Nature, and the natural objects which make life gay and populous; but cruel men waylaid the singer upon one of his lonely wanderings, and murdered him. As he bled to death, without any hope of the detection and punishment of his assassins, a flock of cranes passed overhead, and bent their flight near to him. "Be my witnesses, birds," the dying poet cried, "and make known these wicked murderers." Some time afterward the villains were at Corinth together, where Ibycus was daily expected. The poet did not come, but a certain man, one of his friends, heard one assassin whisper to another, when a flight of cranes settled near to them, "Ah! here are the witnesses of Ibycus!" They were arrested, put to the torture, and, upon confession, punished for their crime with death. This story, true or not, was as familiar to Dorian boys and girls as the tale of Robin Redbreast is with ours. It has given to the Rhegian singer more enduring fame than his verses could, for very few of them exist. Yet, in the following example, there is not only richness of epithet, but the apparent effort at a new style of song writing, in which *rhyme* was to play its part—a striking innovation:—

Τοῦ μὲν πετάλοισιν ἐπ' ἀκροτάτοισιν
ξανθαὶ ποικίλαι αἰολόδειροι
πανέλοπές θ' ἁλιπορφυρίδες τε καὶ
ἀλκύονες τανυσίπτεροι.

On the topmost height of the tree a flight
Of painted finches did sit and sing,
With sea-birds and land-birds in plumage bright,
And halcyons azure, and long of wing.

It describes either a piece of jeweller's work, or a real tree or plant; but there is an "assonant rhyme" about the lines which seems to foreshadow the monkish style of later ages, such as, for instance, that Latin song—

"Ave, cujus calcem clare
Nec centenni commendare
Sciret Seraph studio."

However, if Ibycus had it in his soul to invent the new beauty of rhymed verse, the highwaymen spoiled his design; and his own sad words are very true:—

οὐκ ἔστιν ἀποφθιμενόις ζωᾶς ἔτι φάρμακον εὑρεῖν.

The dead are done with care and cure.

LASUS.

ONLY two lines remain from Lasus the dithyrambic poet of Hermione in Argolis, but he must be mentioned with some respect, if it be true, as alleged, that he helped to teach Pindar the art of verse, and was the first who won the crown at the Olympic Games for dithyrambs. His two surviving lines have a peculiar claim to be quoted, as they are specimens of the dislike which Lasus had for the letter sigma—the Greek S.

Δάματρα μέλπω Κόραν τε Κλυμένοιο ἄλοχον Μελίβοιαν,
ὕμνων ἀνάγων Αἰολίδ' ἅμα βαρύβρομον ἁρμονίαν.

CORINNA.

THIS poetess was a native of Tanagra in Bœotia, and she must have been no mean singer, if it be true, as is alleged, that she four times wrested the prize of song from the great Pindar himself. There is nothing extant to account for this high triumph, or only a few incoherent fragments, quoted here and there by Apollonius, Hephæstio, and others. Thus it is at least possible, as certain mischievous authors report, that the beauty of Corinna had more effect upon the mind of her judges than her verses.

TELESILLA.

Of this daughter of the Muses also there is next to nothing remaining; but she deserves to be remembered as a singer for her virtues as a woman. When the Lacedæmonians killed their Argive prisoners in the temple, and advanced to the city to take it and put the inhabitants to the sword, Telesilla summoned her countrywomen to resistance, and, placing an Argive's helmet upon her long black hair, she led forth the girls and matrons of the place against the enemy. The Spartans, seeing this extraordinary host, halted, and finding that Telesilla was seriously bent on fighting, they turned round and marched back to their camp, considering it—so says Pausanias—a desperate thing to fight with an army of females, since to vanquish them would be no honour, while to be vanquished would seem an intolerable disgrace. The only echo which survives of this heroic Argive poetess is a fragment of what seems to have been a hymn in honour of Diana:—

Ἀ δ' Ἄρτεμις ὦ κόραι
φευγόισα τὸν Ἀλφέον.

Diana—listen, girls!
Flying from Alpheus' love.

It is fitting that, as the one deed reported of her was noble, so the one verse should be in praise of purity.

They made her a statue in the Temple of Venus, but Argos should have known better: her fair face beneath the plumed helmet, her figure with the lyre in one hand and the brazen spear in the other, belonged rather to the shrine of Pallas, or of her white mistress Diana.

PINDAR.

"THE great Emathian conqueror," as Milton writes, "bid spare" the house of Pindar at Thebes; and Time, which conquers conquerors, has not been less lenient to the fame of the most celebrated of Greek lyrical poets. Enough remains of his voluminous compositions to make us comprehend, and in great part confirm, the enthusiastic judgment which Greece passed upon the laureate of her national games. The life of Pindar passed as an ideal poetic life. He was the cherished singer of his time, the "Master of Music," welcome in every city and court. Great kings, like Arcesilas of Cyrene and Amyntas of Macedonia, were glad to be his friends; states voted him public receptions; rich citizens implored the honour of his visits; Athens made him *proxenus*, or "public guest;" and Ceos, though well supplied with her own poets, paid him sumptuously for a choral prayer written on the occasion of an island festival. His long and honoured career was one continuous fête; he passed from town to town, paying for everything with his rich gift of song; and when he died at a ripe age, wearied with fame and admiration, his descendants at Thebes were allowed many privileges simply because they bore his name; while the much-prized crowns of the games ceased to be so highly valued when Pindar's rapid and resonant verses no longer made the laurel-leaves immortal.

Such a career could not have fallen to any but a remarkable man; for kings cannot make poets by patronage, and Greece, besides, was critical. Yet the judgment of Horace upon Pindar sounds high-flown and extravagant, for he vows the Theban poet to be "unapproachable—a Dircean swan singing and soaring out of sight in the clouds." It is true that the Roman does not base this appreciation of the Greek upon the poems we now possess. The "Epinicia," or "songs of victory," which have come down to us, are precisely those compositions which Horace puts in the background; while he speaks with boundless enthusiasm of the Pæans, Dithyrambs, and Parthenia of the lyrist.

Nor is it reasonable to believe that Pindar's muse is best represented in these congratulatory odes. His fiery and vivid spirit found a rare delight, doubtless, in the themes suggested by the contests of the Olympic, Isthmian, Nemean, and Pythian games, and there are many passages where the anapæsts of Pindar truly fly with the flash of the chariot-wheels, and are full of all the life and splendour that stirring thoughts and burning energy can impart to speech. But, on the other hand, these odes were written "to order" by him as the laureate of the Greek games, and we know that genius cannot play the courtier without loss. No doubt we owe their preservation, where so much is lost, to the pride of those families that boasted any hero commemorated by the poet. Greeks descended from a victor upon whose head Pindar had laid the leaves of coronal would obviously preserve the verses written by him as sacred family archives. Thus a hundred lips would be familiar with such odes, while the statelier and more solid pieces have disappeared.

Still, in these "official" singings there is nothing venal or unworthy. Pindar always, or nearly always, writes like a poet, full of the dignity of his calling. He does not fear to reprove monarchs for tyranny or injustice, and he extracts from nearly every flower of mythology which he weaves into his verse the honey of the moral that virtue is the only good. His countrymen, to their shame, had taken part with the Persians in the recent invasion of Hellas. He never extenuates this treason, but ardently praises those who fought and fell at Salamis and Platæa.

As for the rhythm, the music, of these renowned triumphal chants, let it be frankly said that there is none at all, at least for modern eyes and ears. Pindar is printed according to the fancy of his editor; for, excepting the divisions of strophe and antistrophe, and a certain vague sort of recurring cadence now and then recognisable, nobody can tell where the lines should begin and end. Had we the Lydian or Dorian measures extant to which such odes were sung at the festival, some light might fall upon the versification of the poet; but as it is, the stanzas of Mr. Walt Whitman, the American dithyrambist, are not more wild and apparently lawless than Pindar's. As for the plan of these "Epinicia," it is for the most part simple and uniform. There comes first a eulogy of the particular victor in the games; next honorific allusions to his family; then praise of his place of birth; and lastly, pious allusions to the gods and goddesses who preside over the festivities. Pindar diversifies the method of this quadrupartite encomium with legends and traditions, counsels and maxims—sometimes with personal allusions and deliverances. In these it must be avowed that the inattentive student becomes here and there hopelessly lost; there is a wild Olympic dust raised now and then by the rush of his fancy, wherein the meaning grows utterly obscure. His rapid course takes him sometimes flying, as it were, away from the goal, instead of neatly rounding it, as his victors were trained to do. Thus Pindar is decidedly "hard reading," and unattractive to many; although, when the winding channel of his verse is faithfully followed, exquisite expressions and rich beauties of style and thought reward the scholar, who will never doubt that Pindar was of the first order of lyrical singers, when he has once mastered the peculiar manner and caught the poetic "aroma" of the man.

It is next to impossible to translate Pindar; the perfume of his genius evaporates in handling. There is a charm completely *sui generis* about his diction which disappears in the act of exhibition like the stars and patterns of melting snow-flakes. Perhaps Heber succeeded as well as any in this dangerous task, and the subjoined "Olympian," with his version of it, may convey something of the character of the famous Theban's style. It is the triumphal hymn to Psaumis of Camarina, conqueror in the chariot race:—

'Ελατὴρ ὑπέρτατε βρον- στρ.
τᾶς ἀκαμαντόποδος,
Ζεῦ· τεαὶ γὰρ Ὧραι
ὑπὸ ποικιλοφόρμιγγος ἀοι-
δᾶς ἑλισσόμεναί μ' ἔπεμψαν,
ὑψηλοτάτων μάρτυρ' ἀέθλων·
ξείνων δ' εὖ πρασσόντων, ἔσα-
ναν αὐτίκ' ἀγγελίαν
ποτὶ γλυκεῖαν ἐσλοί·
ἀλλ', ὦ Κρόνου παῖ, ὃς Αἴτναν ἔχεις,
ἶπον ἠνεμόεσσαν ἑκατογκεφάλα
Τυφῶνος ὀμβρίμου,
Οὐλυμπιονίκαν δέκευ
Χαρίτων ἕκατι τόνδε κῶμον,
χρονιώτατον φάος εὐ- ἀντ.
ρυσθενέων ἀρετᾶν.

Oh, urging on the tireless speed
Of Thunder's elemental steed,
Lord of the world, Almighty Jove!
Since these thine hours have sent me forth
The witness of thy champions' worth,
And prophet of thine olive grove;
And since the Good thy poet hear,
And hold his tuneful message dear;
Saturnian Lord of Etna hill!
Whose storm-cemented rocks encage
The hundred-headed rebel's rage;
Accept with favourable will
The Muses' gift of harmony;
The dance, the song, whose numbers high
Forbid the hero's name to die,
A crown of life abiding still!

Hark, round the car of victory,
Where noble Psaumis sits on high,
The cheering notes resound;

Ψαύμιος γὰρ ἵκει
ὀχέων· ὅς, ἐλαίᾳ στεφανω-
θεὶς Πισάτιδι, κῦδος ὄρσαι
σπεύδει Καμαρίνᾳ. θεὸς εὔφρων
εἴη λοιπαῖς εὐχαῖς· ἐπεί
μιν αἰνέω, μάλα μὲν
τροφαῖς ἑτοῖμον ἵππων,
χαίροντά τε ξενίαις πανδόκοις,
καὶ πρὸς ἁσυχίαν φιλόπολιν καθαρᾷ
γνώμᾳ τετραμμένον.
οὐ ψευδεῖ τέγξω λόγον.
διάπειρά τοι βροτῶν ἔλεγχος·
ἅπερ Κλυμένοιο παῖδα ἐπ.
Λαμνιάδων γυναικῶν
ἔλυσεν ἐξ ἀτιμίας.
χαλκέοισι δ' ἐν ἔντεσι νικῶν δρόμον,

Who vows to swell with added fame
His Camarina's ancient name;
With Pisan olive crown'd.
And thou, oh father, hear his prayer!
For much I praise the knightly care
That trains the warrior steed:
Nor less the hospitable hall
Whose open doors the stranger call;
Yet, praise I Psaumis most of all
For wise and peaceful rede,
And patriot love of liberty.
What? do we weave the glozing lie?
Then whoso list my truth to try,
The proof be in the deed!
To Lemnos' laughing dames of yore,
Such was the proof Ernicus bore,
When, matchless in his speed,
All brazen-arm'd the racer hoar,
Victorious on the applauding shore,
Sprang to the proffer'd meed;

ἔειπεν Ὑψιπυλείᾳ, μετὰ στέφανον ἰών·
οὗτος ἐγὼ ταχυτᾶτι·
χεῖρες δὲ καὶ ἦτορ ἴσον.
φύονται δὲ καὶ νέοις
ἐν ἀνδράσιν πολιαὶ
θαμά, καὶ παρὰ τὸν ἁλικίας
ἐοικότα χρόνον.

Bow'd to the queen his wreathed head :
" Thou seest my limbs are light," he said ;
" And, lady, mayst thou know,
That every joint is firmly strung,
And hand and heart alike are young ;
Though treacherous time my locks among
Have strew'd a summer snow !"

Heber's Poems.

THE LATER ORPHIC POETS.

WHILE the epic strains of Homer and Hesiod had melted off into these many elegiac and lyric echoes, the mystical poems of Orpheus and his followers found their later imitators. Under the name of "Orphic verses" are now grouped many fragmentary productions of various Greek sages, loftier in inspiration than most of the slight pieces hitherto quoted. CERCOPS and ONOMACRITUS were two of these Orphic singers. The former developed the principle of Orpheus in a poem called "Sacred Legends;" the latter, a friend of Pisistratus, made, at the statesman's request, a collection of the oracular sayings of Musæus. Following these in a long and serious *stemma* came the philosophic poets Xenophanes, Empedocles, Parmenides, and the Pythagoreans. The examination of the remains of these writers would lead the present conspectus away from its purpose of naming, estimating, and lightly acquainting the reader with the poets of Greece in their poetic rather than philosophic character. The pen would be tempted, by the great themes opened by such fragments, to wander into those metaphysical regions where the horizon is infinity. That these poets had boldness may be judged by the lines in which XENOPHANES derides even the honours of the Olympian games in comparison with wisdom. Not even the victory of *παγκράτιον,* he says, is to be compared to philosophy.

ῥώμης γαρ ἀμείνων
ἄνδρων ἠδ' ἵππων ἡμετέρη σοφίη.

Our lore
Than strength of athlete and of steed is more.

This poet blames the Colophonians, his countrymen, for their luxury and effeminate manners with severity and fearless freedom, as well as a certain sarcastic humour. One of his elegiac relics is a curious expression of the belief of Pythagoras in transmigration :—

Καὶ ποτέ μιν στυφελιζομένου σκύλακος παριόντα
φασὶν ἐποικτεῖραι καὶ τόδε φάσθαι ἔπος·
Παῦσαι μηδὲ ῥάπιζ', ἐπειὴ φίλου ἀνέρος ἐστὶ
ψυχή, τὴν ἔγνων φθεγξαμένης ἀΐων.

Going abroad, he saw one day a hound was beaten sore,
Whereat his heart grew pitiful : "Now beat the hound no more!
Give o'er thy cruel blows," he cried ; "a man's soul verily
Is lodged in that same crouching beast—I know him by the cry."

PARMENIDES, the disciple and philosophic heir of Xenophanes, set pantheistic metaphysics to verse in a poem entitled περὶ φύσεως. Lucretius has borrowed from him, and might do so without blushing at the mention of his creditor, for the poetry of the Elean was of a high order. His name is rendered immortal by the dialogue which Plato has consecrated to it, and that which we know of him helps to prove that he deserved the honour of figuring in those stately pages as the "philosophic poet" *par excellence.*

EMPEDOCLES was another and the greatest of these later "Orphics;" philosopher, poet, and historian in one;

the pride of Agrigentum; and, if the tale be true that he perished in the eruption of Etna, doubtless an over-ardent natural philosopher to boot. Indeed, we know that he was a man of science, for he drained marsh-lands, practised medicine, cured madness and passion by music, and was even said to have restored a dead woman to life. Such attributions disclose the experimentalist, whose achievements the vulgar take in early days for miracles. He seems, if one can judge from fragmentary poetic relics, to have encouraged that popular superstition which greeted him almost as a god whenever he appeared abroad; and perhaps those very verses have given rise to the absurd idea that he precipitated himself into the crater of the volcano, in order that his death might be unknown. He was a Pythagorean in belief, admitted the metempsychosis, and gave out that he had been in turn a girl, a boy, a shrub, a bird, a fish, and Empedocles. But lest this order should strike modern ideas of development as too ludicrously inconsequent, it should be added that he maintained the organic majesty and latent divinity in man; and looked upon him after the Buddhist's idea, as separated by accident, not essence, from the Supreme. He was brave, humane, virtuous, and so simple-minded that he refused the crown of his native country. His extant writings show a grave and gifted mind: his style is rich, nervous, and vital with thought; so that profound respect must be felt for the name which Greek critics coupled with Homer's, and which Lucretius declared to be the greatest glory of Sicily.

THE GREEK THEATRE.

THE scope of this review does not include the great tragic poets of Hellas, ÆSCHYLUS, SOPHOCLES, and EURIPIDES; nor the ancient master of comedy, ARISTOPHANES; nor yet the writers of the Middle and New Comic Drama of Greece; nor even those whose reputation largely depends upon dramatic verse, like ANTIPHANES and ALEXIS, PHILEMON and MENANDER. The perfect genius of the three great tragedians, the wit and force of Aristophanes, and the vast merits of Menander, among many others, demand a graver tribute than the brief examination which could be here bestowed. Referring to these illustrious names, therefore, in due order of the poetic succession; our survey passes on to the declining hours of Greek poesy, to witness the light of Greek song dying down from Athens and the home cities of Hellas, to flicker a little at Alexandria with reflected beams, and in Sicily with the sunset colours of Theocritus, Bion, and Moschus; before it sinks—not destitute of a last sad lustre—with Proclus.

OTHER POETS OF AND AFTER THE AGE OF PERICLES.

THERE are certain singers of the Grecian *moyen-âge* who deserve to be briefly mentioned as stars of the second and third magnitude, shining in the same sky with the great tragic writers, here reluctantly overpassed. PANYASIS, the uncle of the historian Herodotus, composed an epic poem upon the adventures of Hercules, which came to be held a classic by the Alexandrian critics. ANTIMACHUS, called the Colophonian, attained in the estimation of the same judges the next place after Homer for his poem "The Thebaid;" and Quintilian praises him excessively. It is not possible to quote anything which could justify these high eulogies. Time has been severer with Antimachus than his Greek and Egyptian reviewers. CRITIAS, one of the thirty tyrants of Athens, also left some elegant but laboured verses, among them an encomium upon the Spartan customs at table, from which the subjoined lines in praise of temperate drinking may be worth presenting :—

οἱ Λακεδαιμονίων δὲ κόροι πίνουσι τοσοῦτον
ὥςτε φρέν' εἰς ἱλαρὰν ἀσπίδα πάντ' ἀπάγειν
εἴς τε φιλοφροσύνην γλῶτταν μέτριόν τε γέλωτα.
τοιαύτη δὲ πόσις σώματί τ' ὠφέλιμος

At Spartan feasts they drink no more
Than takes the cloud from off the mind,
Makes the tongue merry, wrinkles melt
In sober laughter, hearts feel kind :

γνώμῃ τε κτήσει τε, καλῶς δ' εἰς ἔργ' Ἀφροδίτης
πρός θ' ὕπνον ἥρμοσται, τὸν καμάτων λιμένα,
πρὸς τὴν τερπνοτάτην τε θεῶν θνητοῖς Ὑγίειαν.
καὶ τὴν Εὐσεβίης γείτονα Σωφροσύνην.

And this is good for flesh and blood,
Pricks wit, helps thrift, makes lusty youth;
Brings restful sleep, wins heavenly health,
And pleases Prudence, sib of Truth.

CHŒRILUS of Samos earned a certain fame by writing a poem upon the invasion of Xerxes, wherein the Athenians were profusely lauded; and on that account, rather than because of his poetic merits, a law was passed that extracts from it should be read in public every year, at the festival of the Panathenæa. It was a namesake of this writer, CHŒRILUS of Iasus, who made the perilous contract to write a panegyric on Alexander the Great, for every good line of which he was to receive a piece of gold, and for every bad one a blow with a scourge. The rash minstrel, alas! earned only seven "staters," and then all but died under the critical lash..

CLEANTHES of Assos, the "Well-drawer," as he was called at Athens, though rather a philosopher than a poet, merits a niche in the gallery of Grecian singers. His love of the Muses was so passionate that he came to Zeno with only four drachmæ in his pouch in order to study. The citizens, observing him to be hale and hearty, although a philosopher and a poet, and not practising any visible trade, cited him to the Areopagus, to account for his mode of living. The young poet produced a gardener for whom he drew water by night, and also a woman for whom he ground meal, explaining that he paid his academic fees and got his modest livelihood in that way. He was so poorly provided for the climbing of Helicon, that he used to write down the heads of his master's lectures about poetry and art upon bones and potsherds. This humble and devoted servant of the Muses has left a fairly-written "Hymn to Jupiter," and rose from his obscurity to such fame that the Roman Senate voted him a statue at Assos, in Lydia, his native city.

With these names the poetic roll of Ionia closes. Athens, the chief Ionian city, in the generations following that age of Pericles which was made so brilliant with the glory of arms abroad and the grandeur of art at home, abruptly declined from political life. She remained a school of philosophy; a foster-nurse of foreign poets and poetasters, but she was mother of no more chief minstrels—her myrtles lived, but blossomed no longer.

THE ALEXANDRIANS.

WHILE Greece, in the third century before Christ, thus suffered decay and trouble, the traditions of her arts were established in many countries which her genius had conquered. Sicily, as will be seen, caught the mantle of poesy from her, all purple and perfect; and Egypt, while the Ptolemies were ruling and attracting a brilliant court of philosophers and scholars, re-succeeded in some measure to the studies and skill which had come, in the first place, from the Nile to the Ilissus. The libraries of Alexandria grew to be the richest in the world; there the famous "Seventy" translated the Hebrew Scriptures; there Manetho made his archæological researches; Euclid, the geometer, created the science of plane geometry, and a crowd of "poets," more or less worthy of that high title, wrote in the dying Attic tongue. In philosophy the Alexandrian age is of the first importance, in poetry it makes a certain mark. A few of its leading names must here claim attention, more for their reputation than any great foundation for it.

LYCOPHRON composed a poem called the "Alexandra," which Joseph Scaliger and a few others have claimed to comprehend and admire. It is cumbrous, turgid, and obscure, and the most notable point is, perhaps, that Lycophron puts Hercules into the belly of a whale, like Jonah, where he utters piteous lamentations.

The work was nick-named *τὸ σκοτεινὸν ποίημα*, "The Dark Poem;" it is written in iambics, smooth and neat enough sometimes, and is a mixture of prophetic allusions uttered by Cassandra during the Trojan war.

CALLIMACHUS was a master of the Alexandrian schools, much regarded by the Romans. He wrote enormously, but the value of his works is well summed up by Ovid—

"Ingenio non valet, arte valet."

He was more of a pedant than a poet, and his "Ibis," directed against an ungrateful pupil, was a miracle of book-worming. If we could have back his "Settling of Islands and Founding of Cities," it might be worth more to the Royal Geographical Society than all his poesy to the Muses. Yet one line of Callimachus ought to be cited, from the hymn to the "Washing of Pallas," as it is excessively neat, and may point many a modern lover's compliment with an ancient turn. "Bring no myrrh nor alabaster unguent-boxes for Minerva," he says:—

οἴσετε μηδὲ κάτοπτρον· ἀεὶ καλὸν ὄμμα τὸ τήνας.

Nor hold a tiring-glass to her; her face is always fair.

APOLLONIUS wrote a very excellent poem upon the expedition of the Argonauts, which was badly received by the Alexandrians, and its ill success drove the writer in chagrin to Rhodes. The work has come down to us in four books, and has a steady, praiseworthy march, not without touches of tenderness and descriptive beauty. Longinus calls the author *ἄπτωτος*, or the "unstumbling," which gives very justly the idea of his easy but sure poetic paces. Varro Atacinus, among the Latins, translated the "Argonautica," and Virgil, in the fourth Æneid, has imitated it; indeed, the poet lived to become fashionable again in the city of the Ptolemies, where he was made librarian in the great Bibliotheca. He was perhaps the best of the Alexandrine poets—no vast distinction among the names of Philiscus, Sositheus, Sosiphanes, and the like—though, as has been remarked, Alexandria was so rich in philosophers, scholars, and commentators.

THE SICILIANS.

THEOCRITUS.

HERE at length is a high and veritable poet, a name to rank with the foremost of Greek minstrels. Sicily possessed famous singers before this date, whose renown has received homage in this procession of laurelled musicians. The gift of Greek verse fell, therefore, naturally to the beautiful island when Hellas was given over to decay and slavery; nevertheless the Muse, in emigrating from the slopes of snowy Parnassus to flowery Himera and the southern languor of Syracuse, underwent a certain change. Her fair cheeks were bronzed to a country russet, her stately braids grew a little dishevelled, and her sweet voice broadened into the Dorian of the Trinacrian people. Theocritus was nevertheless the most perfect, because the most sincere, of pastoral poets. Many have borne that title whose pictures of the country appear no more rural than the brocaded figures of Watteau, or the bepatched beauties of Lely and Kneller. Theocritus painted the bucolic life that was actually lived around him; the lovely Sicily days led in the soft weather, under smiling skies, amid scenes of exquisite beauty, by a race cultured enough to enjoy existence to the lees, yet not so cultured as to speculate upon and spoil it. His delicious lines are sweet with all which was sweet in paganism, and graceful with the polish of the finest poetic art, albeit so simple and easy. Were one called upon to name the four truest poets of Hellas, the vote should be given for Homer, Sappho, Euripides, and Theocritus, with many a pang to do such apparent irreverence to the great names omitted, yet with no hesitation at all about the right of the Sicilian to that place of honour, at least so long as—

> "They shall be accounted poet kings,
> Who simply tell the most heart-easing things."

Little is known of the history of Theocritus. He was a Syracusan, the pupil of Philetas and friend of that Aratus whose name will by-and-by have to be mentioned. It seems that he spent part of his life in Alexandria—where Ptolemy Philadelphus was his patron —and the remainder in Sicily, where some think he was put to death by Hiero the Second, whom he had offended, it is said, by a satirical epigram. The supposition rests, however, upon a passing expression of Ovid, which may mean anything; and certainly he who can have murdered such a poet must have been a ferocious and "unmusical" tyrant indeed. There is an eulogy written by him upon this very Syracusan ruler, which would surely outweigh any conceivable satire. But, in truth, the tradition is a groundless one; we may believe that Theocritus died at an old age, honoured and happy, except for the fact that he must have witnessed, before he ceased to live and sing, the siege and capture of his native city by the Romans.

Of his elegies, hymns, and iambics, none but the merest fragments remain; some epigrams survive, more or less certainly attributed to him; but the idylls, about thirty in number, are those which embalm his fame, and form one of the most delightful volumes of verse which literature possesses. A doubt, indeed, hangs over more than two of these charming poems; but if the suspected flowers be not from the asphodel meadows of Theocritus, such fair blossoms of poetry were surely grown from the same seed, and the doubt need not greatly vex the mind of the reader. The poems bear the name of idylls, which does not signify that they are all pastoral in subject. This one is an epic piece, that wholly lyrical; the other a comedy in exquisite hexameters, and yet another is an epithalamium. But there are enough of a purely rural character to have stamped upon the word "Idyll," which merely means "sketch," or "fugitive piece," its now traditional signification of a bucolic composition. Almost all the thirty are written in Dorian, and in the hexametric line, which, under the magical skill of Theocritus, bends and plays with the burden of its meaning like a Sicilian stream laden with lilies. His Greek is the softest ever spoken or written—so musical that the turns and phrases of his exquisite lines cling to the ear, and fix themselves by their melody. All is simple and natural with him—sometimes too natural, perhaps—for he makes his shepherds and shepherdesses say very plain things occasionally; but the grace, the freshness, the country music, the fragrance of his flowery valleys; the light of his bright noons, the myrtle thickets and clear Greek rivers which shine through his pastoral landscapes; and in the others his rich relish of human life, his tenderness, his grace, his pagan contentment with the beautiful world, are all fascinating, and never to be forgotten by one who has caught the spirit of this Sicilian. "Contentment!" have we said? Nay, indeed!—among these very Sicilians, gay as *cicadæ*, light as vine-leaves, musical with summer joy as rivulets, the saddest verses in the region of verse-making are to be found. MOSCHUS writes—

> *αἴ, αἴ, ταὶ μαλάχαι μὲν ἐπὰν κατὰ κᾶπον ὄλωνται,*
> *ἢ τὰ χλωρὰ σέλινα, τό τ' εὐθαλὲς οὖλον ἄνηθον,*
> *ὕστερον αὖ ζώοντι καὶ εἰς ἔτος ἄλλο φύοντι·*
> *ἄμμες δ', οἱ μεγάλοι καὶ καρτεροὶ ἢ σοφοὶ ἄνδρες,*
> *ὁππότε πρᾶτα θάνωμες, ἀνάκοοι ἐν χθονὶ κοίλᾳ*
> *εὕδομες εὖ μάλα μακρὸν ἀτέρμονα νήγρετον ὕπνον.*

> Alas! alas! when mallows die, when winter tempests kill
> The light-leaved humble parsley, or the curly tufted dill,
> They live again, and come to leaf and seed each opening year;
> But we that are the lords of all—we men of wisdom clear,
> So strong and great and crafty, in dying once die out,
> And lie for ever in the ground, stark, quiet, wrapped about
> With sleep that has no waking up;—

For them, in truth, the earth was almost too fair; life was so sweet that death seemed too dreadful to think about; but they hid the thought of it away under amaranth flowers, and chirped like summer crickets heeding little of winter. Thus begins the first idyll of Theocritus; the pine music and the bubble of the fountain whisper and tinkle through its lines :—

ΘΥΡΣΙΣ.

Ἁδύ τι τὸ ψιθύρισμα καὶ ἁ πίτυς, αἰπόλε, τήνα,
ἁ ποτὶ ταῖς παγαῖσι, μελίσδεται· ἁδὺ δὲ καὶ τὺ
συρίσδες· μετὰ Πᾶνα τὸ δεύτερον ἆθλον ἀποισῇ.
αἴκα τῆνος ἕλῃ κεραὸν τράγον, αἶγα τὺ λαψῇ·
αἴκα δ' αἶγα λάβῃ τῆνος γέρας, ἐς τὲ καταῤῥεῖ
ἁ χίμαρος· χιμάρω δὲ καλὸν κρῆς, ἔστε κ' ἀμέλξῃς.

THYRSIS.

Softly the sway of the pine-branches murmurs a melody, Shepherd !
Down by the rim of the fountain, and softly dost thou, on the Pan-pipes,
Pipe to the pines : next to Pan thou bearest the bell for rare music.
Say that he wins a great-horn'd goat, then thine is a she-goat ;
Say that the she-goat is his, but thine is the kid, then ; and tender
Savours the meat of a kid—till she comes to the bearing and milking.

ΑΙΠΟΛΟΣ.

Ἅδιον, ὦ ποιμάν, τὸ τεὸν μέλος, ἢ τὸ καταχὲς
τῆν' ἀπὸ τᾶς πέτρας καταλείβεται ὑψόθεν ὕδωρ.
αἴκα ταὶ Μῶσαι τὰν οἴϊδα δῶρον ἄγωνται,
ἄρνα τὺ σακίταν λαψῇ γέρας· αἰ δέ κ' ἀρέσκῃ
τήναις ἄρνα λαβεῖν, τὺ δὲ τὰν ὄϊν ὕστερον ἀξῇ.

GOATHERD.

Sweeter I call thy strain than the tinkle of water that trickles,
Tinkling, and trickling, and rippling adown the green shelves of the mountain.
If we must grant the high Muses their prize from the pick of the wethers,
Certainly thine is a ewe : or if a ewe pleases their fancy,
Then at the least a lamb comes to thee—to drive to thy sheep-folds.

ΘΥΡΣΙΣ.

Λῇς, ποτὶ τᾶν Νυμφᾶν, λῇς, αἰπόλε, τᾷδε καθίξας,
ὡς τὸ κάταντες τοῦτο γεώλοφον αἵ τε μυρῖκαι,
Συρίσδεν; τὰς δ' αἶγας ἐγὼν ἐν τῷδε νομευσῶ.

THYRSIS.

Sit thee adown, good friend—sit down, and pipe to us, Shepherd !
Here where the side of the hill slopes fair, and the myrtles are thickest,
Blow the fine music out : the yearlings can pasture around us !

ΑΙΠΟΛΟΣ.

Οὐ θέμις, ὦ ποιμάν, τὸ μεσαμβρινόν, οὐ θέμις ἄμμιν
συρίσδεν· τὸν Πᾶνα δεδοίκαμες· ἦ γὰρ ἀπ' ἄγρας
τανίκα κεκμακὼς ἀμπαύεται· ἐντὶ δὲ πικρός,
καί οἱ ἀεὶ δριμεῖα χολὰ ποτὶ ῥινὶ κάθηται.
ἀλλὰ (τὺ γὰρ δή, Θύρσι, τὰ Δάφνιδος ἄλγεα εἶδες,
καὶ τᾶς βωκολικᾶς ἐπὶ τὸ πλέον ἵκεο μώσας),
δεῦρ', ὑπὸ τὰν πτελέαν ἑσδώμεθα, τῶ τε Πριήπω
καὶ τᾶν Κρανιάδων κατεναντίον, ᾇπερ ὁ θῶκος
τῆνος ὁ ποιμενικὸς καὶ ταὶ δρύες. αἰ δέ κ' ἀείσῃς,
ὥς ποκα τὸν Λιβύαθε ποτὶ Χρόμιν ᾆσας ἐρίσδων,
αἶγά τέ τοι δωσῶ διδυματόκον ἐς τρὶς ἀμέλξαι,
ἅ, δύ' ἔχοισ' ἐρίφως, ποταμέλξεται ἐς δύο πέλλας,
καὶ βαθὺ κισσύβιον, κεκλυσμένον ἁδέϊ καρῷ,
ἀμφῶες, νεοτευχές, ἔτι γλυφάνοιο ποτόσδον·

GOATHERD.

Nay ! 'twere a sin, 'twere a sin—the sun's at his highest, my Thyrsis ;
Pan would be anger'd to hear me—just now, he breaks off from hunting,
Stretches his hairy limbs in the shade, and puffs his great nostrils,
Panting, and surly for lack of breath, and longing for slumber.
You now, Thyrsis, might sing ! you know the ballad of Daphnis :
None of our woodside singers have half such a trick at the measure.
Couch we here under these elms, on the grass at the foot of the stone-god,
Facing the fountain, and looking right on to the mountains and meadows,
Over the tops of the oaks ; and if you sing but as deftly
As you did once on the day when Chromis the African dared you,
Look ! I'll give you yon she-goat ; the dam of a couplet of weanlings ;
Udder she carries for both, and then to fill two of thy milk-bowls.
Her, and a cup cut in beech, two-handled and polished with beeswax,
Clean and new, with the smell of the chisel and fresh wood about it ;

τῶ περὶ μὲν χείλη μαρύεται ὑψόθι κισσός,
κισσὸς ἑλιχρύσῳ κεκονισμένος· ἁ δὲ κατ' αὐτὸν
καρπῷ ἕλιξ εἱλεῖται ἀγαλλομένα κροκόεντι.
ἔντοσθεν δὲ γυνά, τὶ θεῶν δαίδαλμα, τέτυκται,
ἀσκητὰ πέπλῳ τε καὶ ἄμπυκι· πὰρ δέ οἱ ἄνδρες
καλὸν ἐθειράζοντες ἁμοιβαδὶς ἄλλοθεν ἄλλος
νεικείουσ' ἐπέεσσι· τὰ δ' οὐ φρενὸς ἅπτεται αὐτᾶς·
ἀλλ' ὁκὰ μὲν τῆνον ποτιδέρκεται ἄνδρα γελεῦσα,
ἄλλοκα δ' αὖ ποτὶ τὸν ῥιπτεῖ νόον. οἱ δ' ὑπ' ἔρωτος
δηθὰ κυλοιδιόωντες ἐτώσια μοχθίζοντι.
τοῖς δὲ μέτα γριπεύς τε γέρων, πέτρα τε τέτυκται
λεπράς, ἐφ' ᾇ σπεύδων μέγα δίκτυον ἐς βόλον ἕλκει
ὁ πρέσβυς, κάμνοντι τὸ καρτερὸν ἀνδρὶ ἐοικώς.
φαίης κεν γυίων νιν ὅσον σθένος ἐλλοπιεύειν·
ὧδέ οἱ ᾠδήκαντι κατ' αὐχένα πάντοθεν ἶνες,
καὶ πολιῷ περ ἐόντι· τὸ δὲ σθένος ἄξιον ἅβας.
τυτθὸν δ' ὅσσον ἄπωθεν ἁλιτρύτοιο γέροντος
πυρναίαις σταφυλαῖσι καλὸν βέβριθεν ἀλωά·

All round its rim, on the top, there creeps a string of ground ivy,
Twisted and tangled with woodbine, while here and there, in the circle,
Tendrils curl and clasp—with bunches of berries among them.
Outside a damsel is carved—so fair the gods might have wrought her !
Neat and trim, with her mantle and net—and—this hand and that hand—
Two youths—both long-hair'd—both comely—contend for her favours
Angrily—never a jot cares my pretty jade for their anger !
Sometimes she flings a smile to one, and frowns to his fellow,
Sometimes she softens to t'other—and there they stand in the beechwood,
Laugh'd at, but mad with love—half-teased, half-pleased at the wanton.
Next a fisherman comes, cut out on a rock, and its ledges
Jut up rough and stark—the old boy, done to a marvel,
Staggers and sweats at his work—just like a fisherman hauling ;
Looking upon it you'd swear the work was alive, and no picture :
So do the veins knot up and swell in his neck and his shoulders,
For, though he's wrinkled and grey, there's stuff left yet in the ancient.
Next to this old sea-dog you see a vine, with its branches

τὰν ὀλίγος τις κῶρος ἐφ' αἱμασιαῖσι φυλάσσει
ἥμενος· ἀμφὶ δέ μιν δύ' ἀλώπεκες, ἁ μὲν ἀν' ὄρχως
φοιτῇ σινομένα τὰν τρώξιμον, ἁ δ' ἐπὶ πήραν
πάντα δόλον τεύχοισα, τὸ παιδίον οὐ πρὶν ἀνήσειν
φατὶ, πρὶν ἢ ἀκράτιστον ἐπὶ ξηροῖσι καθίξῃ.
αὐτὰρ ὄγ' ἀνθερίκεσσι καλὰν πλέκει ἀκριδοθήραν,
σχοίνῳ ἐφαρμόσδων· μέλεται δέ οἱ οὔτε τι πήρας,
οὔτε φυτῶν τοσσῆνον, ὅσον περὶ πλέγματι γαθεῖ.
παντᾶ δ' ἀμφὶ δέπας περιπέπταται ὑγρὸς ἄκανθος,
Αἰολικόν τι θάημα· τέρας κέ τυ θυμὸν ἀτύξαι.
τῶ μὲν ἐγὼ πορθμεῖ Καλυδωνίῳ αἶγά τ' ἔδωκα
ὦνον, καὶ τυρῶντα μέγαν λευκοῖο γάλακτος·
οὐδέ τί πα ποτὶ χεῖλος ἐμὸν θίγεν, ἀλλ' ἔτι κεῖται
ἄχραντον. τῷ κέν τυ μάλα πρόφρων ἀρεσαίμαν,
αἴκεν μοι τὺ φίλος τὸν ἐφίμερον ὕμνον ἀείσῃς.
κοὔ τοι τὶ φθονέω. πόταγ', ὦ 'γαθέ· τὰν γὰρ ἀοιδὰν
οὔτι πα εἰς Αΐδαν γε τὸν ἐκλελάθοντα φυλαξεῖς.

Heavy with globing grapes—a little lad sits by a thicket
Guarding the grapes, but close at hand two foxes come creeping,
One in the vineyard munches the clusters—one's after the wallet :
Gods ! you can see his scheme—he'll keep his eye on the youngster,
Till that he finds a chance, and leaves him dinnerless. Blind one !
Why do you sit there weaving with grasses a cage for your crickets,
Plaiting the grasses, and wholly forgetting your wallet and dinner,
Wholly forgetting your grapes—wrapped up in those grasshopper-engines ?
All the work in this cup's filled in with leaves of acanthus ;
'Tis an Æolic thing—and sooth, of a wonderful fancy,
Sirs ! it cost me to buy of the Calydon sailor, a big cheese
Made of snow-white curds, and a she-goat into the bargain ;
Yet it has touch'd no lip, but lies this while in my cottage.
See now ! I mean it for you ! 'tis yours, if you sing us that ditty
Half so well as you sang it before to the Himera shepherds.
No thanks ! do but sing !—there's no more sunshine nor singing
Under the grass—in the realm of the dead—where all is forgotten !

This is the pastoral vein of the great poet of Trinacria; the second idyll is a good specimen of his picturesque and passionate manner, and of the exquisite melody of his line. It is a love piece, tender and fierce alternately, as were the dark eyes of the island girls. The English version given below of this remarkable poem is a paraphrase in part, rather than an exact translation; but there are passages in the "Pharmakeutria" which go almost beyond the grace of English. In this idyll Simœtha, a Syracusan girl, deserted by her lover Delphis, performs, to bring him back to her, the "Incantation of the Bird;" wherein the bird called the wryneck was bound to a wheel, and whirled round, while prayers were made to the Moon and the deities of the Night. The sweet Greek runs thus:—

Πᾷ μοι ταὶ δάφναι; φέρε, Θέστυλι· πᾷ δὲ τὰ φίλτρα;
στέψον τὰν κελέβαν φοινικέῳ οἰὸς ἀώτῳ,
ὡς τὸν ἐμὸν βαρὺν εὖντα φίλον καταθύσομαι ἄνδρα,
ὅς μοι δωδεκαταῖος ἀφ' ᾧ τάλας οὐδέποθ' ἥκει,
οὐδ' ἔγνω, πότερον τεθνάκαμες ἢ ζοοὶ εἰμές,
οὐδὲ θύρας ἄραξεν ἀνάρσιος· ἦ ῥά οἱ ἄλλᾳ
ᾤχετ' ἔχων ὅ τ' Ἔρως ταχινὰς φρένας, ἅ τ' Ἀφροδίτα.
βασεῦμαι ποτὶ τὰν Τιμαγήτοιο παλαίστραν

Thestylis! where are the laurel-leaves? Quick, girl! bring me the love-spells!
Fasten the scarlet thread in and out round the brim of the beaker!
Quick! for I mean to charm my lover, my false-hearted lover.
Twelve long days are passed, and he never has once come to see me,
Knows not if I be living or dead—never sends me a message,
No! not even a word at my door! Has he gone to some new love,
Light as the wings of Eros, and fleeting as Queen Aphrodite?
Down to the town I will hasten to-morrow, and see him, and ask him

αὔριον, ὥς νιν ἴδω· καὶ μέμψομαι, οἷά με ποιεῖ.
νῦν δέ νιν ἐκ θυέων καταθύσομαι. ἀλλά, Σελάνα,
φαῖνε καλόν· τὶν γὰρ ποταείσομαι ἅσυχα, δαῖμον,
τᾷ χθονίᾳ θ' Ἑκάτᾳ, τὰν χαὶ σκύλακες τρομέοντι,
ἐρχομέναν νεκύων ἀνά τ' ἠρία καὶ μέλαν αἷμα.
χαῖρ', Ἑκάτα δασπλῆτι, καὶ ἐς τέλος ἄμμιν ὀπάδει,
φάρμακα ταῦθ' ἕρδοισα χερείονα μήτε τι Κίρκας,
μήτε τι Μηδείας, μήτε ξανθᾶς Περιμήδας.
    Ἶυγξ, ἕλκε τὺ τῆνον ἐμὸν ποτὶ δῶμα τὸν ἄνδρα.
ἄλφιτά τοι πρᾶτον πυρὶ τάκεται· ἀλλ' ἐπίπασσε,
Θέστυλι· δειλαία, πᾷ τὰς φρένας ἐκπεπότασαι;
ἦ ῥά γέ τοι μυσαρὰ καὶ τὶν ἐπίχαρμα τέτυγμαι;
πάσσ' ἅμα καὶ λέγε ταῦτα· τὰ Δέλφιδος ὀστέα πάσσω.
    Ἶυγξ, ἕλκε τὺ τῆνον ἐμὸν ποτὶ δῶμα τὸν ἄνδρα.
Δέλφις ἔμ' ἀνίασεν· ἐγὼ δ' ἐπὶ Δέλφιδι δάφναν
αἴθω· χ' ὡς αὐτὰ λακεῖ μέγα καππυρίσασα,

Face to face, why he treats me so coldly: but Thestylis! thou now
Help me to try him with charms, and oh Moon! glitter thy brightest!
Shine, pale Moon! for thee I invoke, and thy sister and shadow
Hecate—the under-world Moon, whom even the little dogs howl at
When she goes forth o'er the graves, and all her footmarks are bloody:
Make my magic to-night as strong as ever was Circe's,
Potent as white Perimede's, and mighty as Colchian Medea's!

Little bird! whirl and scream, and whirl, and bring me my lover!
Turn wheel, turn! and burn, cake, burn! Ah! Thestylis, sprinkle!
What are you doing to tremble so? sprinkle the salt on the brazier!
Where are your wits gone, girl! or is it that you too must vex me?
Sprinkle the salt, and say, "Flesh and blood of Delphis I scatter!"

    Little bird! scream, and whirl, and scream, and bring me my lover!

        Delphis grieves me—in my turn
        I will grieve him. Laurel, burn!
        As thy bright leaves curl and crack,
        Smoke and blaze and vanish black,

κὴξαπίνας ἅφθη, κοὐδὲ σποδὸν εἴδομες αὐτᾶς·
οὕτω τοι καὶ Δέλφις ἐνὶ φλογὶ σάρκ᾽ ἀμαθύνοι.
"Ιϋγξ, ἕλκε τὺ τῆνον ἐμὸν ποτὶ δῶμα τὸν ἄνδρα.
ὡς τοῦτον τὸν καρὸν ἐγὼ σὺν δαίμονι τάκω,
ὣς τάκοιθ᾽ ὑπ᾽ ἔρωτος ὁ Μύνδιος αὐτίκα Δέλφις·
χ᾽ ὡς δινεῖθ᾽ ὅδε ῥόμβος ὁ χάλκεος, ἐξ 'Αφροδίτας
ὣς κεῖνος δινοῖτο ποθ᾽ ἁμετέρῃσι θύρῃσιν.
"Ιϋγξ, ἕλκε τὺ τῆνον ἐμὸν ποτὶ δῶμα τὸν ἄνδρα.
νῦν θυσῶ τὰ πίτυρα, τὺ δ᾽, "Αρτεμι, καὶ τὸν ἐν ᾄδᾳ
κινήσαις ἀδάμαντα, καὶ εἴτι περ ἀσφαλὲς ἄλλο.
Θέστυλι, ταὶ κύνες ἄμμιν ἀνὰ πτόλιν ὠρύονται.
ἁ θεὸς ἐν τριόδοισι· τὸ χαλκίον ὡς τάχος ἄχει.
"Ιϋγξ, ἕλκε τὺ τῆνον ἐμὸν ποτὶ δῶμα τὸν ἄνδρα.
ἠνίδε σιγᾷ μὲν πόντος, σιγῶντι δ᾽ ἆηται·

Leaving not a leaf to see :
May his heart love-scorchèd be !

Little bird ! whirl, and scream, little bird ! and bring me my lover !

As I melt this waxen ball
May the great gods hear me call,
And Delphis melt with love for me !
And as this wheel turns rapidly
So may Queen Venus speed the charms
And bring him quickly to my arms !

Little bird, whirl, whirl, whirl ! scream ! scream ! and bring me my lover !

Now I scatter on the flame
Bran. Oh ! Artemis ! thy name
Moves the Judge of Hell to fear,
Rhadamanth himself ! Then hear !
Hear ! oh, hear me ! Thestylis,
Did the dogs bark ? Yes, it is !
'Tis the goddess in the street !
Beat the cymbals ! quick, girl ! beat !

Little bird, scream—scream louder ' and bring me my false-hearted lover !

ἁ δ' ἐμὰ οὐ σιγᾷ στέρνων ἔντοσθεν ἀνία,
ἀλλ' ἐπὶ τήνῳ πᾶσα καταίθομαι, ὅς με τάλαιναν
ἀντὶ γυναικὸς ἔθηκε κακὰν καὶ ἀπάρθενον ἦμεν.
Ἴϋγξ, ἕλκε τὺ τῆνον ἐμὸν ποτὶ δῶμα τὸν ἄνδρα.
ἐς τρὶς ἀποσπένδω, καὶ τρὶς τάδε, πότνια, φωνῶ·
εἴτε γυνὰ τήνῳ παρακέκλιται, εἴτε καὶ ἀνήρ,
τόσσον ἔχοι λάθας, ὅσσον ποκὰ Θασέα φαντὶ
ἐν Δίᾳ λασθῆμεν ἐϋπλοκάμω Ἀριάδνας.
Ἴϋγξ, ἕλκε τὺ τῆνον ἐμὸν ποτὶ δῶμα τὸν ἄνδρα.
ἱππομανὲς φυτόν ἐστι παρ' Ἀρκάσι· τῷ δ' ἔπι πᾶσαι
καὶ πῶλοι μαίνονται ἀν' ὤρεα καὶ θοαὶ ἵπποι.
ὣς καὶ Δέλφιν ἴδοιμι· καὶ ἐς τόδε δῶμα περάσαι
μαινομένῳ ἴκελος, λιπαρᾶς ἔκτοσθε παλαίστρας.
Ἴϋγξ, ἕλκε τὺ τῆνον ἐμὸν ποτὶ δῶμα τὸν ἄνδρα.
τοῦτ' ἀπὸ τᾶς χλαίνας τὸ κράσπεδον ὤλεσε Δέλφις,
ὠγὼ νῦν τίλλοισα κατ' ἀγρίῳ ἐν πυρὶ βάλλω.

Look ! the restless sea is sleeping,
Milk-white ripples curling, creeping !
Listen ! all the winds are quiet,
Folded up from rage and riot !
Only in my heart the pain
Wakes, and will not sleep again !
Bitter pain the sport to be
Of him who hath unmaidened me.

Little bird, whirl—whirl fast ! scream sharp—scream ! call me my lover !

Thrice libations due I pay
Thrice, great goddess ! this I say :
Whom he loves now I know not,
But let her come to be forgot !
Clean forgot from head to feet
As Ariadne was of Crete.

Scream, little bird ! more—more ! and whirl, and fetch me my lover !

In Arcady there grows a flower,
Stings the herds with subtle power,

αἶ αἴ, ἔρως ἀνιαρέ, τί μευ μέλαν ἐκ χροὸς αἷμα
ἐμφὺς ὡς λιμνᾶτις ἅπαν ἐκ βδέλλα πέπωκας;
"Ιϋγξ, ἕλκε τὺ τῆνον ἐμὸν ποτὶ δῶμα τὸν ἄνδρα.
σαύραν τοι τρίψασα, κακὸν ποτὸν αὔριον οἰσῶ.
Θέστυλι, νῦν δὲ λαβοῖσα τὺ τὰ θρόνα ταῦθ' ὑπόμαξον
τᾶς τήνω φλιᾶς καθυπέρτερον, ἇς ἔτι καὶ νῦν
ἐκ θυμῶ δέδεμαι· ὁ δέ μευ λόγον οὐδένα ποιεῖ·
καὶ λέγ' ἐπιφθύζοισα· τὰ Δέλφιδος ὀστέα μάσσω.
"Ιϋγξ, ἕλκε τὺ τῆνον ἐμὸν ποτὶ δῶμα τὸν ἄνδρα.
νῦν δὴ μούνη ἐοῖσα πόθεν τὸν ἔρωτα δακρυσῶ;
ἐκ τίνος ἀρξεῦμαι; τίς μοι κακὸν ἄγαγε τοῦτο;
ἦνθ' ἁ τῶ' υβούλοιο καναφόρος ἄμμιν 'Αναξὼ
ἄλσος ἐς 'Αρτέμιδος· τᾷ δὴ τόκα πολλὰ μὲν ἄλλα
θηρία πομπεύεσκε περισταδόν, ἐν δὲ λέαινα.

Drives them mad on vale and height:
Would I had that flower to-night!
Delphis should come quick to me,
Come, whate'er his company!

Scream for me still, little bird! scream once, and call me my lover!

Delphis left this gift with me:
In the fire I fling it. See!
Burn it red and burn it black,
Angry hissing flames! Alack!
It leaps away—he'll not return!
It only burneth as I burn,
And now 'tis ashes, pale and grey,
As pale as I grow day by day.

Scream ere you die, little bird! one cry to call me my lover!

Lizards green and gold I take
(Mighty magic this will make);
Slit them down from chin to tail,
Squeeze their cold blood, cold and pale.
Thestylis, take this to-morrow
(It can work him bliss or sorrow),

Φράζεό μευ τὸν ἔρωθ', ὅθεν ἵκετο, πότνα Σελάνα.
καί μ' ἁ Θευχαρίλα, Θρᾷσσα τροφὸς ἁ μακαρῖτις,
ἀγχίθυρος ναίοισα, κατεύξατο, καὶ λιτάνευσε
τὰν πομπὰν θάσασθαι· ἐγὼ δέ οἱ ἁ μεγάλοιτος
ὡμάρτευν, βύσσοιο καλὸν σύροισα χιτῶνα,
κἀμφιστειλαμένα τὰν ξυστίδα τὰν Κλεαρίστας.
Φράζεό μευ τὸν ἔρωθ', ὅθεν ἵκετο, πότνα Σελάνα.
ἤδη δ' εὖσα μέσαν κατ' ἀμαξιτόν, ᾇ τὰ Λύκωνος,
εἶδον Δέλφιν ὁμοῦ τε καὶ Εὐδάμιππον ἰόντας.
τοῖς δ' ἦν ξανθοτέρα μὲν ἑλιχρύσοιο γενειάς,
στήθεα δὲ στίλβοντα πολὺ πλέον, ἢ τύ, Σελάνα,
ὡς ἀπὸ γυμνασίοιο καλὸν πόνον ἄρτι λιποῦσι.

Lay it on his threshold stone,
Spit to the left, and say alone,
"She whose heart you tread on here
Charms you, Delphis! Love or Fear!"

Dead are you, poor little fool! and you could not bring me my lover!

Ah, me! what shall I do? Alone, alone!—
I'll think the story over of my love,
How it began—what made the sweet pain come.
It was the day Anaxo was to walk
Bearing the basket for great Artemis,
With striped and spotted beasts in the procession.
Oh!—and you recollect—a lioness!

Lady Moon! listen and pity! and help me, bringing my lover!

And my old Thracian nurse, Theucharila
Came—you remember—teasing, tempting me
To go and see them pass, and so I went.
O fool! I went wearing the yellow bodice,
And Clearista's purple train from Tyre.

Lady Moon! listen and pity, and say where tarries my lover!

And when we came hard by where Lycon lives
Upon the paved way, there I saw him first,
Delphis, with Eudamippus—oh, you know!

Φράζεό μευ τὸν ἔρωθ', ὅθεν ἵκετο, πότνα Σελάνα.
χὠς ἴδον, ὡς ἐμάνην, ὥς μευ περὶ θυμὸς ἰάφθη
δειλαίας· τὸ δὲ κάλλος ἐτάκετο, κοὐδέ τι πομπᾶς
τήνας ἐφρασάμαν, οὐδ' ὡς πάλιν οἴκαδ' ἀπῆνθον
ἔγνων· ἀλλά μέ τις καπυρὰ νόσος ἐξαλάπαξε·
κείμαν δ' ἐν κλιντῆρι δέκ' ἄματα καὶ δέκα νύκτας.
Φράζεό μευ τὸν ἔρωθ', ὅθεν ἵκετο, πότνα Σελάνα.
καί μευ χρὼς μὲν ὁμοῖος ἐγίνετο πολλάκι θάψῳ·
ἔῤῥευν δ' ἐκ κεφαλᾶς πᾶσαι τρίχες· αὐτὰ δὲ λοιπὰ
ὀστέ' ἔτ' ἦς καὶ δέρμα· καὶ ἐς τίνος οὐκ ἐπέρασα
ἢ ποίας ἔλιπον γραίας δόμον, ἅτις ἐπᾷδεν;
ἀλλ' ἦς οὐδὲν ἐλαφρόν· ὁ δὲ χρόνος ἄνυτο φεύγων.
Φράζεό μευ τὸν ἔρωθ', ὅθεν ἵκετο, πότνα Σελάνα.
χ' οὕτω τᾷ δώλᾳ τὸν ἀλαθέα μῦθον ἔλεξα·

His hair danced back from off his brow, like sprays
Of bright amaracus, when the west blows,
And all his neck, flushed with the heat of the games,
Shone as thou shinest, Moon! but rosier pearl!

Lady Moon! Lady Moon, listen, and pity, and bring me my lover;

I saw him—looked! loved! oh, my foolish eyes!
Oh me! the coward colour of my cheeks!
Oh, heart that straight went mad! I did not mark
Those tame beasts any more; how I came home
I cannot call to mind; you know I lay
Ten days and nights indoors, and never rose.

Lady Moon, sweet pale Moon! have mercy, and bring me this lover!

I grew as pale—as white as thapsus-wood!
Say if I braided up my hair, or sang?
Say if I grew not to a ghost, with thinking?
When was the day you sought not who he was,
Where was the crone we did not plague for charms
To bring him? All in vain; he never came!

Oh, Moon! hide not thy face. Oh, white Moon! listen and pity!

So I grew sick with waiting, and I said,

εἰ δ' ἄγε Θέστυλί μοι χαλεπᾶς νόσω εὑρέ τι μᾶχος.
πᾶσαν ἔχει με τάλαιναν ὁ Μύνδιος. ἀλλὰ μολοῖσα
τήρησον ποτὶ τὰν Τιμαγήτοιο παλαίστραν·
τηνεὶ γὰρ φοιτῇ, τηνεὶ δέ οἱ ἁδὺ καθῆσθαι.

Φράζεό μευ τὸν ἔρωθ', ὅθεν ἵκετο, πότνα Σελάνα.

κἠπεί κά νιν ἐόντα μάθῃς μόνον, ἅσυχα νεῦσον,
κἠφ', ὅτι Σιμαίθα τὺ καλεῖ, καὶ ὑφάγεο τᾷδε.
ὣς ἐφάμαν· ἁ δ' ἦνθε, καὶ ἄγαγε τὸν λιπαρόχρων
εἰς ἐμὰ δώματα Δέλφιν· ἐγὼ δέ μιν ὡς ἐνόησα
ἄρτι θύρας ὑπὲρ οὐδὸν ἀμειβόμενον ποδὶ κούφῳ,

Φράζεό μευ τὸν ἔρωθ', ὅθεν ἵκετο, πότνα Σελάνα,

πᾶσα μὲν ἐψύχθην χιόνος πλέον, ἐκ δὲ μετώπω
ἱδρώς μευ κοχύδεσκεν ἴσον νοτίαισιν ἐέρσαις,
οὐδέ τι φωνᾶσαι δυνάμαν, οὐδ' ὅσσον ἐν ὕπνῳ
κνυζεῦνται φωνεῦντα φίλαν ποτὶ ματέρα τέκνα·
ἀλλ' ἐμάγην δαγῦδι καλὸν χρόα πάντοθεν ἶσα.

"Oh, Thestylis, help !—heal me, or I die !
"This Greek boy hath bewitched me. Go, my friend !
"Watch at the gateway of the wrestling-school.
"He cometh there, I think, to play or sit.

Silver-faced Queen of the stars, thou know'st we are not as immortals !

"And when he is alone, whisper full soft
"And say, 'Simœtha bids thee come,' and then
"If he will, bring him !" So you went and came
Bringing my love to me. But when I heard
His sandals on the step, and saw his face—

Lady Moon ! hear this now, and pity, and shine while I tell you !

And saw his face, I turned as cold as snow,
And tears—I wot not why—sprang to my lids,
And how to speak I knew not ; not so much
As little children startled in the night,
That sob and know it is all well—but sob,
And will not stint even for their mother's voice.
I was as dumb as dead things, Thestylis.

Φράζεό μευ τὸν ἔρωθ', ὅθεν ἵκετο, πότνα Σελάνα.
καί μ' ἐσιδὼν ὥστοργος, ἐπὶ χθονὸς ὄμματα πήξας,
ἕζετ' ἐπὶ κλιντῆρι, καὶ ἑζόμενος φάτο μῦθον·
ἦ ῥά με, Σιμαίθα, τόσον ἔφθασας, ὅσσον ἐγώ θην
πράν ποκα τὸν χαρίεντα τρέχων ἔφθαξα Φιλῖνον,
ἐς τὸ τεὸν καλέσασα τόδε στέγος, ἤ με παρῆμεν.
Φράζεό μευ τὸν ἔρωθ', ὅθεν ἵκετο, πότνα Σελάνα.
ἦνθον γὰρ κἠγών, ναὶ τὸν γλυκύν, ἦνθον, ἔρωτα,
ἢ τρίτος ἠὲ τέταρτος ἐὼν φίλος, αὐτίκα νυκτός,
μᾶλα μὲν ἐν κόλποισι Διωνύσοιο φυλάσσων,
κρατὶ δ' ἔχων λεύκαν, Ἡρακλέος ἱερὸν ἔρνος,
πάντοσε πορφυρέῃσι περιζώστρῃσιν ἑλικτάν.
Φράζεό μευ τὸν ἔρωθ', ὅθεν ἵκετο, πότνα Σελάνα.
καί μ' εἰ μέν κ' ἐδέχεσθε, τάδ' ἦς φίλα· καὶ γὰρ ἐλαφρὸς
καὶ καλὸς πάντεσσι μετ' ἠϊθέοισι καλεῦμαι.

Queen of the planets and stars! forgive, and listen, and pity!
For he with a bright gladness—not too bold—
Entered; and looked hard once and then looked down!
And sat against my feet; and sitting, said,
"Only so little, sweet Simœtha! thou
"Hast been the first to speak—as I was first
"Against Philinus in the race to-day,—

White-sandalled Mistress of Night! have patience, and hear me and help me.*
"I should have come, I swear it by my head!
"To-morrow at the dusk. I meant to bring
"Some choice rose-apples in my breast. Mayhap
"You love them; and a crown of poplar leaves
"Twisted with myrtle-buds and tied with red;

Lady Moon, where is he now? so soft, so gentle, so fickle!
"And if you had seemed kind I should have spoke.
"I was not hopeless, for I won the prize
"At running, and the maidens call me fair.
"The one prize I have longed for since the feast
"Was once to touch the goal of those dear lips;

εὗδον δ', αἴ κε μόνον τὸ καλὸν στόμα τεῦς ἐφίλασα,
εἰ δ' ἄλλᾳ μ' ὠθεῖτε, καὶ ἁ θύρα εἴχετο μοχλῷ,
πάντως καὶ πελέκεις καὶ λαμπάδες ἦνθον ἐφ' ὑμέας.
Φράζεό μευ τὸν ἔρωθ', ὅθεν ἵκετο, πότνα Σελάνα.
νῦν δὲ χάριν μὲν ἔφαν τᾷ Κύπριδι πρᾶτον ὀφείλειν,
καὶ μετὰ τὰν Κύπριν τύ με δευτέρα ἐκ πυρὸς εἵλευ,
ὦ γύναι, ἐσκαλέσασα τεὸν ποτὶ τοῦτο μέλαθρον,
αὔτως ἡμίφλεκτον· Ἔρως δ' ἄρα καὶ Λιπαραίου
πολλάκις Ἁφαίστοιο σέλας φλογερώτερον αἴθει.
Φράζεό μευ τὸν ἔρωθ', ὅθεν ἵκετο, πότνα Σελάνα.
συν δὲ κακαῖς μανίαις καὶ παρθένον ἐκ θαλάμοιο
καὶ νύμφαν ἐφόβησ', ἔτι δέμνια θερμὰ λιποῖσαν
ἀνέρος· ὣς ὁ μὲν εἶπεν· ἐγὼ δέ οἱ ἁ ταχυπειθὴς
χειρὸς ἐφαψαμένα μαλακῶν ἔκλιν' ἐπὶ λέκτρων·
καὶ ταχὺ χρὼς ἐπὶ χρωτὶ πεπαίνετο, καὶ τὰ πρόσωπα
θερμότερ' ἧς ἢ πρόσθε· καὶ ἐψιθυρίσδομες ἁδύ.

"Then I could rest—not else! But had you frowned,
"And bade me go, and barred your door on me,
"Oh, Sweet! I think I should have come with lamps,
"And axes, and have stolen you like gold!

Lady Moon, where is he now? so gentle, so earnest, so winning!

"How shall I," he went on, "thank the gods first,
"And next you—you! the queen and life of me!
"My kindest love—who badst me hither come
"When I did burn for leave—yea! for I think
"Hephæstus hath no flame like Eros knows!"

Lady Moon, look out of heaven, and find him, and bring him for pity.

So he spake, low and fair, and I, alas!
What could I do, but reach my hand to him,
And let him take it, and take me, and have
The kiss he sued for, and another such?
My cheeks were white no more, nor my heart sad,
Nor any trouble left; but we sat close,

χὤς κά τοι μὴ μακρά, φίλα, θρυλέωμι, Σελάνα,
ἐπράχθη τὰ μέγιστα, καὶ ἐς πόθον ἤνθομες ἄμφω.
κοὔτε τι τῆνος ἐμὶν ἐπεμέμψατο μέσφα τοι ἐχθές,
οὔτ' ἐγὼ αὖ τήνῳ· ἀλλ' ἦνθέ μοι ἅ τε Φιλίστας
μάτηρ τᾶς γ' ἁμᾶς αὐλητρίδος, ἅ τε Μελιξοῦς,
σάμερον, ἁνίκα πέρ τε ποτ' οὐρανὸν ἔτρεχον ἵπποι,
ἀῶ τὰν ῥοδόπαχυν ἀπ' Ὠκεανοῖο φέροισαι·
κῆπέ μοι ἄλλα τε πολλά, καὶ ὡς ἄρα Δέλφις ἐρᾶται·
κἤτε μιν αὖτε γυναικὸς ἔχει πόθος, εἴτε καὶ ἀνδρός,
οὐκ ἔφατ' ἀτρεκὲς ἴδμεν, ἀτὰρ τόσον· αἰὲν ἔρωτος
ἀκράτω ἐπεχεῖτο, καὶ ἐς τέλος ᾤχετο φεύγων,
καὶ φάτο οἱ στεφάνοισι τὰ δώματα τῆνα πυκάσδεν.
ταῦτά μοι ἁ ξείνα μυθήσατο· ἔστι δ' ἀλαθής·
ἦ γάρ μοι καὶ τρὶς καὶ τετράκις ἄλλοτ' ἐφοίτη,
καὶ παρ' ἐμὶν ἐτίθει τὰν Δωρίδα πολλάκις ὄλπαν·
νῦν δέ τε δωδεκαταῖος ἀφ' ὧτέ νιν οὐδέποκ' εἶδον.

And the light talk bubbled from lip to lip
Like fountains in the roses. All that time,
And many a time we sat so : never once
He failed to keep his word, and never once
Left save with lingering foot. But one ill day
He did not come, and then it was I heard
Stories, that vexed me, of another love :
Melixa's mother, and the harp-player
Told me—and both are friends—he'd come no more,
And that his house was loud with pipes and songs,
And gay with crowns, not woven now for me.
Oh, Thestylis ! twelve days ago this was,
And never have I seen him since that day,
And never shall, unless my magic works :
Therefore blow up the flame, and whirl the wheel !

Lady Moon ! speed this spell ; and fetch me my false-hearted lover.

Speed this spell ! if it brings you,
Delphis, love shall live anew :

ἦ ῥ' οὐκ ἄλλο τι τερπνὸν ἔχει, ἁμῶν δὲ λέλασται ;
νῦν μὲν τοῖς φίλτροις καταθύσομαι· αἰ δ' ἔτι κἠμὲ
λυπῇ, τὰν Ἀΐδαο πύλαν, ναὶ Μοίρας, ἀραξεῖ.
τοῖά οἱ ἐν κίστᾳ κακὰ φάρμακα φαμὶ φυλάσσειν,
Ἀσσυρίω, δέσποινα, παρὰ ξείνοιο μαθοῖσα.
Ἀλλὰ τὺ μὲν χαίροισα ποτ' Ὠκεανὸν τρέπε πώλους,
πότνι'· ἐγὼ δ' οἰσῶ τὸν ἐμὸν πόνον, ὥσπερ ὑπέσταν.
χαῖρε, Σελαναία λιπαρόχροε· χαίρετε δ', ἄλλοι
ἀστέρες, εὐκήλοιο κατ' ἄντυγα νυκτὸς ὀπαδοί.

If in vain I watch and wait,
Delphis, love will turn to hate!
Subtle drugs I treasure here,
Drugs of awful force and fear:
A Syrian witch culled these for me
In lonely caverns by the sea.
Delphis, if I brew this drink
It will send you, as I think,
Down to Hades' gate, to seek
A sweeter lip, a fairer cheek.
Oh, Moon! spare me this at last!
Oh, Moon! speed it—if I must.
And now farewell! for one day more
I wait, and love him as before!
Farewell, pale Moon, and planets bright,
Watchers with me this silent night!

BION.

THERE are two Dorian writers who have obtained and deserved the glory of perpetual fellowship with Theocritus in the procession of Greek poets. In the third idyll of Moschus these names are all embalmed together, where the death of Bion is lamented by his fellow poet, and Theocritus is named as joining in the sorrow inspired by his early end. The three poets compose together a delicious chord of country music. Theocritus is far the most varied, skilful, and sustained; while time, which has dealt hardly by the gracious and finished verses of Bion, and the cameo-like poetic gems of Moschus, has spared enough of the Syracusan to survive as a full-blown classic. Much, indeed, of what is called "classical" might be freely —well-nigh contemptuously—given away for more of the soft melodies of Bion and Moschus. Little is known of the lives of these two friends of Theocritus. Bion was born, it seems, near Smyrna, but dwelt in Sicily, where he was poisoned, we know not how; though his death is recorded in many lovely lines by Moschus, of which these are four:—

Φάρμακον ἦλθε, Βίων, ποτὶ σὸν στόμα, φάρμακον ᾔδες·
τοιούτοις χείλεσσι ποτέδραμε, κοὐκ ἐγλυκάνθη;
τίς δὲ βροτὸς τοσσοῦτον ἀνάμερος, ἢ κεράσαι τοι,
ἢ δοῦναι λαλέοντι τὸ φάρμακον; ἔκφυγεν ᾠδάν.

Ah! Bion thou art poisoned—an ill drink hath brought thee low;
How could it pass such lips as thine, and not to honey grow?
And who in all the world could be so bad in heart and head,
To hear thee speak, then murder thee?—'tis Poesy that's dead.

His best extant work is the half-religious, half-erotic "Lament of Adonis," so splendidly plagiarised by Shelley in the "Adonais." It is too beautiful to withhold, though its conceits are of a later and less natural air than those which fill the verses of Theocritus with scents of myrtle and pine. Bion learned the art of Song in the Asiatic atmosphere, where lingered mystic traditions of Thammuz, and the Syrian fervour of this warm litany of love.

Αἰάζω τὸν Ἄδωνιν· ἀπώλετο καλὸς Ἄδωνις.
ὤλετο καλὸς Ἄδωνις, ἐπαιάζουσιν Ἔρωτες.
μηκέτι πορφυρέοις ἐνὶ φάρεσι, Κύπρι, κάθευδε·
ἔγρεο δειλαία κυανοστόλε, καὶ πλατάγησον
στάθεα, καὶ λέγε πᾶσιν· ἀπώλετο καλὸς Ἄδωνις.
Αἰάζω τὸν Ἄδωνιν· ἐπαιάζουσιν Ἔρωτες.
κεῖται καλὸς Ἄδωνις ἐπ' ὤρεσι, μηρὸν ὀδόντι
λευκῷ λευκὸν ὀδόντι τυπείς, καὶ Κύπριν ἀνιᾷ
λεπτὸν ἀποψύχων· τὸ δέ οἱ μέλαν εἴβεται αἷμα
χιονέας κατὰ σαρκός· ὑπ' ὀφρύσι δ' ὄμματα ναρκῇ,

Woe is me for Adonis! gone dead is the comely Adonis!
Dead is the god-like Adonis! the young Loves wail for him, ai! ai!
Sleep no more, wrapped in thy mantles of Tyrian, lady of Cyprus!
Rise, don thy raiment of azure, pale mourner, and beat on thy bosom!
Tell out thy sorrow to all—he is dead, thy darling Adonis.

Ai! ai! wail for Adonis!—the young Loves wail for him, ai! ai!
Hurt on the hill lies Adonis the beautiful; torn with the boar's tusk,
Torn on the ivory thigh with the ivory tusk, his low gasping
Anguishes Cypris' soul: the dark blood trickles in rivers

καὶ τὸ ῥόδον φεύγει τῶ χείλεος· ἀμφὶ δὲ τήνῳ
θνάσκει καὶ τὸ φίλαμα, τὸ μήποτε Κύπρις ἀφήσει.
Κύπριδι μὲν τὸ φίλαμα καὶ οὐ ζώοντος ἀρέσκει,
ἀλλ' οὐκ οἶδεν Ἄδωνις ὅ μιν θνάσκοντ' ἐφίλασεν.
Αἰάζω τὸν Ἄδωνιν· ἐπαιάζουσιν Ἔρωτες.
ἄγριον, ἄγριον ἕλκος ἔχει κατὰ μηρὸν Ἄδωνις·
μεῖζον δ' ἁ Κυθέρεια φέρει ποτικάρδιον ἕλκος.
κεῖνον μὲν περὶ παῖδα φίλοι κύνες ὠδύραντο,
καὶ Νύμφαι κλαίουσιν Ὀρειάδες. ἁ δ' Ἀφροδίτα,
λυσαμένα πλοκαμῖδας, ἀνὰ δρυμὼς ἀλάληται
πενθαλέα, νήπλεκτος, ἀσάνδαλος· αἱ δὲ βάτοι νιν
ἐρχομέναν κείροντι, καὶ ἱερὸν αἷμα δρέπονται·
ὀξὺ δὲ κωκύουσα δι' ἄγκεα μακρὰ φορεῖται,
Ἀσσύριον βοόωσα πόσιν, καὶ παῖδα καλεῦσα.
ἀμφὶ δέ μιν μέλαν αἷμα παρ' ὀμφαλὸν ᾐωρεῖτο,
στήθεα δ' ἐκ μηρῶν φοινίσσετο, οἱ δ' ὑπομαζοὶ
χιόνεοι τὸ πάροιθεν Ἀδώνιδι πορφύροντο.

Down from his snowy side—his eyes are dreamily dimming
Under their lids ; and the rose leaves his lip, and the kisses upon it
Fade, and wax fainter, and faintest, and die, before Cypris can snatch them ;
Dear to the Goddess his kiss, though it be not the kiss of the living ;
Dear—but Adonis wists none of the mouth that kissed him a-dying.

Ai ! ai ! wail for Adonis !—ai ! ai ! say the Loves for Adonis.
Cruel ! ah, cruel the wound on the thigh of the hunter Adonis,
Yet in her innermost heart a deeper wears Queen Cytheræa.
Round the fair dead boy his hounds pace, dismally howling ;
Round him the hill-spirits weep ; but chiefest of all Aphrodite,
Letting her bright hair loose, goes wild through the depths of the forest
Passionate, panting, unkempt ; with feet unsandalled whose beauty
Thorn-bushes tear as she passes, and drip with the blood of the Goddess.
Bitterly bitterly wailing, down all the long hollows she hurries,
Calling him Husband and Love—her Boy—her Syrian Hunter.
Meantime dead in his gore lieth he—from groin unto shoulder
Bloody ; from breast to thigh ; the fair young flank of Adonis,
Heretofore white as the snow, dull now, and dabbled with purple.

Αἲ αἲ τὰν Κυθέρειαν, ἐπαιάζουσιν Ἔρωτες.
ὤλεσε τὸν καλὸν ἄνδρα, συνώλεσεν ἱερὸν εἶδος.
Κύπριδι μὲν καλὸν εἶδος, ὅτε ζώεσκεν Ἄδωνις,
κάτθανε δ' ἁ μορφὰ σὺν Ἀδώνιδι Κύπριδος, αἲ αἴ.
ὤρεα πάντα λέγοντι, καὶ αἱ δρύες, Αἲ τὸν Ἄδωνιν.
καὶ ποταμοὶ κλαίοντι τὰ πένθεα τᾶς Ἀφροδίτας,
καὶ παγαὶ τὸν Ἄδωνιν ἐν ὤρεσι δακρύοντι,
ἄνθεα δ' ἐξ ὀδύνας ἐρυθαίνεται· ἁ δὲ Κυθήρα
πάντας ἀνὰ κναμώς, ἀνὰ πᾶν νάπος οἰκτρὸν ἀείδει.
Αἲ αἲ τὰν Κυθέρειαν, ἀπώλετο καλὸς Ἄδωνις.
ἀχὼ δ' ἀντεβόασεν, ἀπώλετο καλὸς Ἄδωνις.
Κύπριδος αἰνὸν ἔρωτα τίς οὐκ ἔκλαυσεν ἄν; αἲ αἴ.
ὡς ἴδεν, ὡς ἐνόησεν Ἀδώνιδος ἄσχετον ἕλκος,
ὡς ἴδε φοίνιον αἷμα μαραινομένῳ περὶ μηρῷ,
πάχεας ἀμπετάσασα, κινύρετο, Μεῖνον Ἄδωνι,
δύσποτμε μεῖνον Ἄδωνι, πανύστατον ὥς σε κιχείω,
ὥς σε περιπτύξω, καὶ χείλεα χείλεσι μίξω.

Ai! ai! woe for Adonis! the Loves say, "woe for Adonis!"
That which hath killed her sweet lover hath killed a grace which was god-like!
Perfect the grace seemed of Cypris so long as Adonis was living;
Gone is her beauty now—ai! ai! gone dead with Adonis:
All the hills echo it—all the oaks whisper it, "Ah, for Adonis!"
Even the river-waves ripple the sorrows of sad Aphrodite,
Even the springs on the hills drop tears for the hunter Adonis;
Yea, and the rose-leaves are redder for grief; for the grief Cytheræa
Tells in the hollow dells, and utters to townland and woodland.

Ai! ai! Lady of Cyprus, "Lo! dead is my darling Adonis!"
Echo answers thee back, "Oh! dead is thy darling Adonis."
Who, good sooth, but would say, Ai! ai! for her passionate story?
When that she saw and knew the wound of Adonis—the death-wound—
Saw the blood come red from the gash, and the white thigh a-waning,
Wide outraught she her arms, and cried, "Ah! stay, my Adonis!
Stay for me, ill-starred love!—stay! stay! till I take thee the last time,
Hold thee and fold thee, and lips meet lips, and mingle together.

ἔγρεο τυτθὸν Ἄδωνι, τὸ δ' αὖ πύματόν με φίλασον·
τοσσοῦτόν με φίλασον, ὅσον ζώει τὸ φίλαμα,
ἄχρις ἀπὸ ψυχῆς ἐς ἐμὸν στόμα κεἰς ἐμὸν ἧπαρ
πνεῦμα τεὸν ῥεύσῃ, τὸ δὲ σεῦ γλυκὺ φίλτρον ἀμέλξω,
ἐκ δὲ πίω τὸν ἔρωτα· φίλαμα δὲ τοῦτο φυλάξω,
ὡς αὐτὸν τὸν Ἄδωνιν· ἐπεὶ σύ με, δύσμορε, φεύγεις,
φεύγεις μακρόν, Ἄδωνι, καὶ ἔρχεαι εἰς Ἀχέροντα
καὶ στυγνὸν βασιλῆα καὶ ἄγριον· ἁ δὲ τάλαινα
ζώω, καὶ θεὸς ἐμμί, καὶ οὐ δύναμαί σε διώκειν.
λάμβανε, Περσεφόνα, τὸν ἐμὸν πόσιν· ἐσσὶ γὰρ αὐτά
πολλὸν ἐμεῦ κρέσσων· τὸ δὲ πᾶν καλὸν ἐς σὲ καταῤῥεῖ
εἰμὶ δ' ἐγὼ πανάποτμος, ἔχω δ' ἀκόρεστον ἀνίην,
καὶ κλαίω τὸν Ἄδωνιν, ὅ μοι θάνε, καὶ σὲ φοβεῦμαι.
θνάσκεις, ὦ τριπόθατε· πόθος δέ μοι ὡς ὄναρ ἔπτη.
χήρη δ' ἁ Κυθέρεια, κενοὶ δ' ἀνὰ δώματ' Ἔρωτες.
σοὶ δ' ἅμα κεστὸς ὄλωλε· τί γὰρ τολμηρὲ κυνάγεις ;
καλὸς ἐὼν τοσσοῦτον ἐμήναο θηρσὶ παλαίειν ;

Rouse thee—a little, Adonis ! kiss back for the last time, beloved !
Kiss me—kiss me—only so long as the life of a kiss is !
So I may suck from thy soul to my mouth, to my innermost heart-beat,
All the breath of thy life, and take the last of its love-spell
Unto the uttermost drop—one kiss ! I will tenderly keep it
As I did thee, my Adonis, sith thou dost leave me, Adonis !
Far thou dost go and for long—thou goest to the region of shadows,
Unto a hateful and pitiless Power, and I, the unhappy,
Live ! and alack ! am a goddess, and cannot die and go after ;
Take thou my spouse, dark Queen, have here my husband, as thou art
Stronger by far than I, and to thee goeth all that is goodly.
Utterly hapless my fate, and utterly hopeless my grief is,
Weeping my love who is dead, and hating the Fate that hath slain him.
Fled is my joy, like a dream ; thou art dead, thrice lovely and longed for !
Queen Cytheræa is widowed—the Loves in my bowers are idle—
Gone my charmed girdle with thee ; why, rash one, went'st thou a-hunting ?
Mad wert thou, being so fair, to match thee with beasts of the forest."

Ὧδ' ὀλοφύρατο Κύπρις· ἐπαιάζουσιν Ἔρωτες,
αἲ αἲ τὰν Κυθέρειαν, ἀπώλετο καλὸς Ἄδωνις.
δάκρυον ἁ Παφία τόσσον χέει, ὅσσον Ἄδωνις
αἷμα χέει· τὰ δὲ πάντα ποτὶ χθονὶ γίγνεται ἄνθη.
αἷμα ῥόδον τίκτει, τὰ δὲ δάκρυα τὰν ἀνεμώναν.

Αἰάζω τὸν Ἄδωνιν· ἀπώλετο καλὸς Ἄδωνις
μηκέτ' ἐνὶ δρυμοῖσι τὸν ἀνέρα μύρεο, Κύπρι.
ἔστ' ἀγαθὰ στιβάς, ἔστιν Ἀδώνιδι φυλλὰς ἑτοίμα·
λέκτρον ἔχει, Κυθέρεια, τὸ σὸν τόδε νεκρὸς Ἄδωνις
καὶ νέκυς ὢν καλός ἐστι, καλὸς νέκυς, οἷα καθεύδων.
κάτθεό νιν μαλακοῖς ἐνὶ φάρεσιν, οἷς ἐνίαυεν,
τοῖς μετὰ σεῦ ἀνὰ νύκτα τὸν ἱερὸν ὕπνον ἐμόχθει,
παγχρύσῳ κλιντῆρι· πόθει καὶ στυγνὸν Ἄδωνιν.
βάλλε δ' ἐνὶ στεφάνοισι, καὶ ἄνθεσι· πάντα σὺν αὐτῷ,
ὡς τῆνος τέθνακε, καὶ ἄνθεα πάντ' ἐμαράνθη.
ῥαῖνε δέ μιν καλοῖσιν ἀλείφασι, ῥαῖνε μύροισι.
ὀλλύσθω μύρα πάντα· τὸ σὸν μύρον ὤλετ' Ἄδωνις.
κέκλιται ἁβρὸς Ἄδωνις ἐν εἵμασι πορφυρέοισιν·

So grieved the Lady of Cyprus—the young Loves wept for her sorrow,
Saying, "Ai! ai! Cytheræa! gone dead is her darling Adonis."
Drop by drop as the hunter bleeds, the tears of the Goddess
Fall and blend with the blood, and both on the ground become flowers;
Rose-blossoms grow from the blood, and wind-lilies out of the tear-drops.

Ai! ai! comely Adonis—gone dead is the god-like Adonis;
Wander no longer bewailing in glade and in thicket, sad lady!
Fair is his bed of leaves, and fragrant the couch where the dead lies,
Dead, but as lovely as life—yea, dead—but as lovely as sleep is;
Lap him in mantles of silken—such robes as he once took delight in
When by thy side he passed in caresses the season of starbeams,
Lulled on a couch of gold—though dead, the raiments become him;
Heap on him garlands and blossoms and buds, entomb them together;
When that Adonis died, the flowers died too, and were withered!
Rain on him perfumes and odours, shed myrrh and spices upon him;
Let all delightful things die and go with him, for dead is the dearest.
So lies he lovely, in death-shroud of purple, the fair young Adonis;

ἀμφὶ δέ μιν κλαίοντες ἀναστενάχουσιν Ἔρωτες,
κειράμενοι χαίτας ἐπ' Ἀδώνιδι· χὼ μὲν ὀϊστώς,
ὃς δ' ἐπὶ τόξον ἔβαιν', ὃς δ' εὔπτερον ἆγε φαρέτραν·
χὼ μὲν ἔλυσε πέδιλον Ἀδώνιδος· ὃς δὲ λέβητι
χρυσείῳ φορέησιν ὕδωρ· ὁ δὲ μηρία λούει·
ὃς δ' ὄπιθεν πτερύγεσσιν ἀναψύχει τὸν Ἄδωνιν.

Αὐτὰν τὰν Κυθέρειαν ἐπαιάζουσιν Ἔρωτες.
ἔσβεσε λαμπάδα πᾶσαν ἐπὶ φλιαῖς Ὑμέναιος,
καὶ στέφος ἐξεπέτασσε γαμήλιον. οὐκ ἔτι δ' Ὑμάν,
Ὑμὰν οὐκ ἔτ' ἀειδόμενον μέλος ᾄδεται, αἶ αἴ,
αἶ αἴ· καὶ τὸν Ἄδωνιν ἔτι πλέον, ἢ Ὑμέναιος,
αἱ Χάριτες κλαίοντι, τὸν υἱέα τῶ Κινύραο,
ὤλετο καλὸς Ἄδωνις, ἐν ἀλλήλῃσι λέγοισαι·
καὶ Μοῖσαι τὸν Ἄδωνιν ἀνακλαίουσιν Ἄδωνιν,
καί μιν ἐπαείδουσιν· ὁ δὲ σφίσιν οὐκ ἐπακούει·
οὐ μὰν οὐκ ἐθέλει, Κώρα δέ μιν οὐκ ἀπολύει.

Λῆγε γόων, Κυθέρεια, τοσήμερον ἴσχεο κομμῶν·
δεῖ σε πάλιν κλαῦσαι, πάλιν εἰς ἔτος ἄλλο δακρῦσαι.

Round about his couch the Loves go piteously wailing,
Tearing their hair for Adonis; and one has charge of his arrows,
One of his polished bow, and one of his well-feathered quiver;
One unclasps his sandal, and one in a water-pot golden
Brings bright water to lave his limbs, and one at the bier-head
Fans with her pinions the forehead and eyes of the sleeping Adonis.

Ah! but for Cypris herself the young Loves sorrow the sorest;
Quenched are the marriage-lamps in the halls of the God Hymenæus,
Scattered his marriage crowns; no more he sings, "Hymen, oh! Hymen,"
"Hymen!" no more is the song he goes singing, but evermore ai! ai!
"Ah, for Adonis," he cries, and "Ah!" say the Graces, "Adonis!"
More than the marriage-god even, they weep for the Syrian huntsman,
One to the other still saying, "Dead—dead is the lovely Adonis!"
All the nine Muses bewail—but he hears no more music and singing,
Nay, not if that he would; Fate holds him fast and for ever.

Cease, Cytheræa, thy sobs; a little while rest from thine anguish,
Soon must thy tears flow again, and again comes the season of sorrow.

MOSCHUS.

Of the life of Moschus no details exist; it is doubtful where and when he lived, and the surest piece of history about him is the passage already quoted, wherein the poet speaks of Theocritus as his contemporary. In the long elegy which he has left upon Bion, he calls himself the "heir" of the second of the Sicilian Trio. Nor was he undeserving so proud a name, for his remaining verses are of the true Sicilian softness, as may be judged by the two extracts given. Let no one care too much for dates and dry particulars of such lives as these three Dorian poets must have led. Enough that the dying flower of Grecian poesy was nursed by them into such various but lovely colour in the rich Trinacrian air. Moschus, albeit the least and last of the three, hardly has his rival, nevertheless, for fineness of ear and nice taste in words; and this sonnet or little idyll of his has been famous ever since the poet made it, lying amid the asphodel by Arethusa:—

Τὰν ἅλα τὰν γλαυκὰν ὅταν ὥνεμος ἀτρέμα βάλλῃ,
τὰν φρένα τὰν δειλὰν ἐρεθίζομαι, οὐδ᾽ ἔτι μοι γᾶ
ἐντὶ φίλα, ποτάγει δὲ πολὺ πλέον ἄμμε γαλάνα.
ἀλλ᾽ ὅταν ἀχήσῃ πολιὸς βυθός, ἁ δὲ θάλασσα

When winds that move not its calm surface sweep
The azure sea, I love the land no more:
The smiles of the serene and tranquil deep
Tempt my unquiet mind. But when the roar

κυρτὸν ἐπαφρίζῃ, τὰ δὲ κύματα μακρὰ μεμήνῃ,
ἐς χθόνα παπταίνω καὶ δένδρεα, τὰν δ' ἅλα φεύγω·
γᾶ δέ μοι ἀσπαστά, χ' ἁ δάσκιος εὔαδεν ὕλα,
ἔνθα καί, ἢν πνεύσῃ πολὺς ὤνεμος, ἁ πίτυς ᾄδει.
ἦ κακὸν ὁ γριπεὺς ζώει βίον, ᾧ δόμος ἁ ναῦς,
καὶ πόνος ἐντὶ θάλασσα, καὶ ἰχθὺς ἁ πλάνος ἄγρα.
αὐτὰρ ἐμοὶ γλυκὺς ὕπνος ὑπὸ πλατάνῳ βαθυφύλλῳ,
καὶ παγᾶς φιλέοιμι τὸν ἐγγύθεν ἦχον ἀκούειν,
ἃ τέρπει ψοφέοισα τὸν ἄγριον, οὐχὶ ταράσσει.

Of ocean's grey abyss resounds, and foam
  Gathers upon the sea, and vast waves burst,
I turn from that drear aspect to the home
  Of earth and its deep woods, where, interspersed,
When winds blow loud pines make sweet melody;
Whose house is some lone bark, whose toil the sea,
Whose prey the wandering fish—an evil lot
Hath chosen. But I my languid limbs will fling
Beneath the plane, where the brook's murmuring
Moves the calm spirit, but disturbs it not. *Shelley.*

One more pretty, sparkling piece of Greek, and we have done with the sweetest trio of singers in all the Pan-Hellenic choir. Charming itself, it is rendered note for note throughout its playful music by the same delicate English voice. Moschus sings:—

Ἤρα Πὰν Ἀχῶς τᾶς γείτονος, ἤρατο δ' Ἀχὼ
σκιρτητᾶ Σατύρω, Σάτυρος δ' ἐπεμαίνετο Λύδᾳ.
ὡς Ἀχὼ τὸν Πᾶνα, τόσον Σάτυρος φλέγεν Ἀχῶ,
καὶ Λύδα Σατυρίσκον· ἔρως δ' ἐσμύχετ' ἀμοιβᾷ.
ὅσσον γὰρ τήνων τὶς ἐμίσεε τὸν φιλέοντα,
τόσσον ὁμῶς φιλέων ἐχθαίρετο, πάσχε δ' ἄποινα.
ταῦτα λέγω πᾶσιν τὰ διδάγματα τοῖς ἀνεράστοις·
στέργετε τοὺς φιλέοντας, ἵν', ἢν φιλέητε, φιλῆσθε.

Shelley's translation runs :—

Pan loved his neighbour Echo, but that child
  Of Earth and Air pined for the Satyr leaping ;
The Satyr loved with wasting madness blind
  The bright nymph Lyda—so the three went weeping.
As Pan loved Echo, Echo loved the Satyr,
  The Satyr Lyda—and so love consumed them.
And so to each, which was a woful matter,
  To bear what they inflicted Justice doomed them :
For inasmuch as each might hate the lover,
  Each loving, so was hated. Ye that love not
Be warned ; in thought turn this example over,
  That when ye love the like return ye prove not ! *Shelley.*

BABRIUS.

Babrius, or Gabrias, for his very name is disputed as well as his date, wrote fables in choliambic verse, which were called "Mythiambes." It is not long that the admirable little apologues of this author have been in the possession of scholars. The labours of Berges at Munich, and the lucky *trouvaille* of a MSS. in a convent at Mount Athos, containing one hundred and twenty three of the parables of Babrius, have restored one of the most ingenious and lively writers of the latest period of Greek art to his rights. No fabulist can well be original, for fables have been the work of the wit of mankind from the earliest days, and the "mythiambist" only collects and epigrammatises them. But the Greek of Babrius is clear and neat, and his style remarkable—the more so, if, as some think, he was a Roman living in the East, and no Greek or Byzantine.

RHIANUS.

AMONG the few writers who kept up elsewhere the fading traditions of Greek song during the third century before Christ, this one, native of Bena in Crete, is to be mentioned. Originally a slave in a gymnasium, he rose to considerable reputation as an epical and historical poet. He wrote the "Heracleid," "Thessalica," "Messeniaca," "Achaica," and "Eliaca," of which very scanty fragments are remaining; together with a few scattered epigrams.

ARATUS.

THIS astronomical versifier compiled a volume called "Appearances and Signs," which was held good enough to be translated into Latin verse by Cicero, Germanicus, and Avienus. It described the constellations, and discoursed upon the influences of the heavenly bodies. Virgil was under obligations to Aratus for passages in his "Georgics," and a world of grammarians and mathematicians have made the Cilician writer their subject. It is from Aratus that St. Paul quoted as "one of your own poets" to the Athenians, citing the words *τοῦ γὰρ καὶ γένος ἔσμεν*, in the 17th chapter of the Acts of the Apostles.

NICANDER.

POET, physician, and grammarian, Nicander was born at Claros, near Colophon, where he held the hereditary office of priest of Apollo. He was a man of high science for his time, and his researches and conclusions were embodied in two works called respectively *Theriaca*, treating of "Antidotes against the bites of venomous animals," and *Alexipharmaca*, or "Antidotes against poisons." Nicander, though a credulous and unreliable naturalist and savant, has some ingenious suggestions and valuable observations. He was the first to explain the mechanism of the serpent's poison-fang; and his remarks on many animals are full of the signs of close study. Still, we find him believing that wasps are produced from horseflesh in a putrid state; and in his treatise on mineral poisons he only knows, or seems to know, of whitelead and litharge. The Greek of these rhymed treatises upon medicine is extremely polished, and the general correctness and good sense of his physiological views such as to command admiration—regard being had to the age in which he lived.

LUCIAN, OPPIAN, WITH OTHERS.

HERMESIANAX, the writer of love-poems to the beautiful but profligate Leontium; and Meleager, the collector of epigrams under the title of *Στέφανος*, need not arrest this closing review; while Lucian, the witty, bitter, tasteful satirist of Samosata, belongs to the history of Greek prose, albeit he wrote certain agreeable verses of society. Yet, excepting Lucian's far-fetched epigrams, we scarcely find a voice perpetuating in Greek the culture of the Muses during the three centuries preceding Oppian and Proclus. Heliodorus, the author of the first real novel, wrote a poem on alchymy. Oppian, a native of Cilicia, preceded him, living in the time of Septimius Severus and Caracalla, and wrote upon subjects connected with field sports. His "Cynegetica," or treatise on hunting, was so much to the taste of the Emperor Caracalla, that a piece of gold was given to the fortunate poet for every line. He died of the plague at Anaxarbus, a town of Cilicia, in the thirtieth year of his age; and an epitaph declared upon his tomb that Oppian had been called to the society of the gods because he already excelled all mankind. Beside the "Cynegetica," Oppian—or another poet of the same name, as is maintained by some—composed "Halieutica," or a "Discourse on Fishing," and "Ixeutica," or a "Discourse on Fowling." The style of Oppian is animated and ornate; his descriptions are lively and just, and Buffon himself has not hesitated to draw upon the young naturalist for facts and particulars.

MUSÆUS.

THE date of this writer is much disputed, and has been variously fixed at terms between the third and thirteenth centuries after Christ—but the purity of diction, and the numberless graces of "the grammarian's" style, give to his poem upon "Hero and Leander" a claim to be quoted among the classics of Hellas, whatever its precise period. There are certainly signs about it of a very late age in Grecian composition, and some images and conceits are excessively modern in character. The story, however, is in itself so world-wide and tender, and Musæus narrates it with such liveliness and sympathy for the lovers, that it shall be cited freely enough to show all its best passages.

The poem thus opens:—

Εἰπὲ, θεὰ, κρυφίων ἐπιμάρτυρα λύχνον ἐρώτων,
καὶ νύχιον πλωτῆρα θαλασσοπόρων ὑμεναίων,
καὶ γάμον ἀχλυόεντα, τὸν οὐκ ἴδεν ἄφθιτος Ἠώς,
καὶ Σηστὸν καὶ Ἄβυδον, ὅπη γάμος ἔννυχος Ἡροῦς.
νηχόμενόν τε Λέανδρον ὁμοῦ καὶ λύχνον ἀκούω,
λύχνον ἀπαγγέλλοντα διακτορίην Ἀφροδίτης,

Sing, Muse, the beacon gleaming bright above,
That lit the nightly swimmer to his love;
The hidden meeting, and the midnight tide
Which bore the bridegroom to his watchful bride;
The marriage-robes sea-soaked, the moist embrace,
Abydos' town, and Sestos—Hero's place;

Ἡροῦς νυκτιγάμοιο γαμοστόλον ἀγγελιώτην,
λύχνον, ἔρωτος ἄγαλμα, τὸν ὤφελεν αἰθέριος Ζεὺς
ἐννύχιον μετ' ἄεθλον ἄγειν ἐς ὁμήγυριν ἄστρων,
καί μιν ἐπικλῆσαι νυμφοστόλον ἄστρον ἐρώτων,
ὅττι πέλεν συνέριθος ἐρωμανέων ὀδυνάων·
ἀγγελίην τ' ἐφύλαξεν ἀκοιμήτων ὑμεναίων,
πρὶν χαλεπὸν πνοιῇσιν ἀήμεναι ἐχθρὸν ἀήτην.
ἀλλ' ἄγε μοι μέλποντι μίαν συνάειδε τελευτὴν
λύχνου σβεννυμένοιο, καὶ ὀλλυμένοιο Λεάνδρου.
Σηστὸς ἔην καὶ Ἄβυδος ἐναντίον, ἐγγύθι πόντου,
γείτονές εἰσι πόληεσ· Ἔρως δ', ἀνὰ τόξα τιταίνων,
ἀμφοτέρῃς πτολίεσσιν ἕνα ξυνεηκεν ὀϊστὸν,
ἠΐθεον φλέξας καὶ παρθένον· οὔνομα δ' αὐτῶν
ἱμερόεις τε Λέανδρος ἔην, καὶ παρθένος Ἡρῶ.
ἡ μὲν Σηστὸν ἔναιεν, ὁ δὲ πτολίεθρον Ἀβύδου,
ἀμφοτέρων πολίων περικαλλέες ἀστέρες ἄμφω,

Longing Leander on the salt-wave's crest,
The lamp that led him to sweet Hero's breast;
Kind lamp—love's jewel— which the mighty Jove
Might well have taken to the orbs above,
And set it shining in the spangled sky
To be Love's star of all Heaven's company,
Seeing it was the planet of their bliss,
The glittering summons to the sleepless kiss,
Till the hard waves made end of him and this:
But help, high Muse! and teach me how to sing
Leander's death and lamp's extinguishing.

Sestos and white Abydos, cities twain,
Fronted each other upon Helle's main.
God Eros there, setting his shaft to string,
Wounded two bosoms with one shaft-shooting;
A maiden's and a youth's—Leander he,
And lovely Hero, Sestos' sweetest, she:
Each of each town the very best and boast,
A noble pair. If ever to that coast

εἴκελοι ἀλλήλοισι. σὺ δ', εἴ ποτε κεῖθι περήσεις,
δίζεό μοι τινὰ πύργον, ὅπῃ ποτὲ Σηστιὰς Ἡρὼ
ἵστατο, λύχνον ἔχουσα, καὶ ἡγεμόνευε Λεάνδρῳ·
δίζεο δ' ἀρχαίης ἁλιηχέα πορθμὸν Ἀβύδου,
εἰσέτι που κλαίοντα μόρον καὶ ἔρωτα Λεάνδρου.
ἀλλὰ πόθεν Λείανδρος, Ἀβυδόθι δώματα ναίων,
Ἡροῦς ἐς πόθον ἦλθε, πόθῳ δ' ἐνέδησε καὶ αὐτήν;
Ἡρὼ μὲν χαρίεσσα, διοτρεφὲς αἷμα λαχοῦσα,
Κύπριδος ἦν ἱέρεια, γάμων δ' ἀδίδακτος ἐοῦσα,
πύργον ἀπὸ προγόνων παρὰ γείτονι ναῖε θαλάσσῃ,
ἄλλη Κύπρις ἄνασσα· σαοφροσύνῃ δὲ καὶ αἰδοῖ
οὐδέποτ' ἀγρομένῃσι μεθωμίλησε γυναιξὶν,
οὐδὲ χορὸν χαρίεντα μετήλυθεν ἥλικος ἥβης,
μῶμον ἀλευομένη ζηλήμονα θηλυτεράων·
καὶ γὰρ ἐπ' ἀγλαΐῃ ζηλήμονές εἰσι γυναῖκες·
ἀλλ' αἰεὶ Κυθέρειαν ἱλασκομένη Ἀφροδίτην,
πολλάκι καὶ τὸν Ἔρωτα παρηγορέεσκε θυηλαῖς

Thou goest, inquire for Hero's tower, and roam
Where she Love's light-house nightly did illume.
Inquire for white Abydos, too, and muse
Where young Leander life and love did lose;
But now to tell how he fair Hero loved,
And how the maid to dote on him was moved.

Honey-sweet Hero, of a god-like race,
Was priestess to Queen Venus in that place;
And in her father's house by the sea set
Herself a Queen of Love, though virgin yet,
Dwelt; yet for modesty and beauty's shame
She never to the city-markets came,
Nor mingled with the feast-days or the dance,
Lest envious eyes upon her eyes should glance;
For those ill-favoured flout at fairer faces;
But ever in the holy temple-places
She worshipped rose-lipped Venus, queen above,

μητρὶ σὺν οὐρανίῃ, φλογερὴν τρομέουσα φαρέτρην.
ἀλλ' οὐδ' ὣς ἀλέεινε πυριπνείοντας ὀϊστούς.

And Eros eke, the tiny God of Love,
Beseeching that she might unscathèd go,
Yet not the more 'scaped she delicious woe.

Musæus then describes a festival which took place yearly in honour of Aphrodite, to which all the townsfolk of Sestos and Abydos, with those of the neighbouring cities, were wont to repair—and even the secluded Hero always bore part in this great day of her goddess. Not a maid or youth, indeed, lingered at home on such an occasion—though the poet archly hints that the maidens went more for the charming spectacle than anything religious, and the youths that they might behold the maidens. Among them, stateliest and loveliest, Hero appears—

Ἡ δὲ θεῆς ἀνὰ νηὸν ἐπῴχετο παρθένος Ἡρὼ,
μαρμαρυγὴν χαρίεντος ἀπαστράπτουσα προσώπου
υἱά τε λευκοπάρῃος ἐπαντέλλουσα σελήνη.
ἄκρα δὲ χιονέων φοινίσσετο κύκλα παρειῶν,
ὡς ῥόδον ἐκ καλύκων διδυμόχροον· ἦ τάχα φαίης
Ἡροῦς ἐν μελέεσσι ῥόδων λειμῶνα φανῆναι·
χροιὴν γὰρ μελέων ἐρυθαίνετο· νισσομένης δὲ
καὶ ῥόδα λευκοχίτωνος ὑπὸ σφυρὰ λάμπετο κούρης,

And Hero, too, went up unto the shrine,
The beauty of her fair face all a-shine,
Like the pure Moon's when first she swims the sky;
Her tender cheeks were touched with that soft dye
Which rosebuds show, when neither white nor red,
But crimson paled with milk. You would have said
She was all made of rose-leaf, she did show
So rose-bud pink under her thin robe's flow,

πολλαὶ δ' ἐκ μελέων Χάριτες ῥέον. οἱ δὲ παλαιοὶ
τρεῖς Χάριτας ψεύσαντο πεφυκέναι· εἷς δέ τις Ἡροῦς
ὀφθαλμὸς γελόων ἑκατὸν Χαρίτεσσι τεθήλει.

So roseate-necked, so rosy-footed. See !
Of old they said the Graces were but three,
But each bright eye of Hero, as it seemed,
With love-lights of a hundred Graces gleamed.

The forced fancy of these latter lines exemplifies how Greek poetry had declined from the stately simplicity of old models. The poet proceeds to narrate what ardent admiration Hero excited at the festival, and how Leander, suddenly encountering her there, fell instantly in love with the fair Sestian. Nor was she less struck with the young townsman of Abydos. Her beautiful eyes timidly return the messages of his; and Leander is emboldened, when the evening star breaks up the festival to steal behind her in the throng, and then,

ἠρέμα μὲν θλίβων ῥοδοειδέα δάκτυλα κούρης,
βυσσόθεν ἐστονάχιζεν ἀθέσφατον· ἡ δὲ σιωπῇ,
οἷα τε χωομένη, ῥοδέην ἐξέσπασε χεῖρα.
ὡς δ' ἐρατῆς ἐνόησε χαλίφρονα νεύματα κούρης,
θαρσαλέως παλάμῃ πολυδαίδαλον ἕλκε χιτῶνα,
ἔσχατα τιμήεντος ἄγων ἐπὶ κεύθεα νηοῦ.
ὀκναλέοις δὲ πόδεσσιν ἐφέσπετο παρθένος Ἡρώ,

Lightly he touched her soft and rosy hand,
Heaving a deep sigh, plain to understand ;
And she, as one an angered, drew it in,
But so that he might see 'twas no great sin.
Then bolder, by her stole he took the maid,
And prayed her turn one minute to the shade ;
Whereat with pretty frown and faltering feet

οἰάπερ οὐκ ἐθέλουσα, τόσην δ' ἀνενείκατο φωνὴν,
θηλυτέροις ἐπέεσσιν ἀπειλείουσα Λεάνδρῳ·
Ξεῖνε, τί μαργαίνεις; τί με, δύσμορε, παρθένον ἕλκεις;
ἄλλην δεῦρο κέλευθον· ἐμὸν δ' ἀπόλειπε χιτῶνα.

She turned and stayed, and said with chiding sweet—
"Sir! are you mad? How dare you hold me so?
"Leave plucking of my gown, and let me go,"

But it all ends, nevertheless, in the "old, old story." Leander pleads eloquently, and Hero is persuaded almost before she begins to listen. They exchange information as to each other's names and birth, and the minute grows to an hour during which they thus linger talking. Hero is in despair when she finds that the Hellespont flows between her lover's town and her own; but he passionately declares the Hellespont is nothing:—

Παρθένε, σὸν δι' ἔρωτα καὶ ἄγριον οἶδμα περήσω,
εἰ πυρὶ παφλάζοιτο, καὶ ἄπλοον ἔσσεται ὕδωρ.
οὐ τρομέω βαρὺ χεῦμα, τεὴν μετανεύμενος εὐνὴν,
οὐ βρόμον ἠχήεντα περιπτώσσοιμι θαλάσσης.
ἀλλ' αἰεὶ κατὰ νύκτα φορεύμενος ὑγρὸς ἀκοίτης,
νήξομαι Ἑλλήσποντον ἀγάρροον· οὐχ ἕκαθεν γὰρ
ἀντία σεῖο πόληος ἔχω πτολίεθρον Ἀβύδου.
μοῦνον ἐμοὶ ἕνα λύχνον ἀπ' ἠλιβάτου σέο πύργου

Sweet, for thy love the watery way I'd cleave,
Though foam were fire, and waves with flame did heave;
I fear not billows if they bear to thee,
Nor tremble at the hissing of the sea;
Do but one thing—set thine own lamp on high,
To shine at evening through the silent sky,
And I will be Love's ship, my pilot-star
That beam; whereto oaring my way afar,

ἐκ περάτης ἀνάφαινε κατὰ κνέφας· ὄφρα νοήσας
ἔσσομαι ὁλκὰς Ἔρωτος, ἔχων σέθεν ἀστέρα λύχνον.
καί μιν ὀπιπτεύων δύντ' ὄψομαι οὔτε Βοώτην,
οὐ θρασὺν Ὠρίωνα, καὶ ἄβροχον ὁλκὸν Ἁμάξης·
πατρίδος ἀντιπόροιο ποτὶ γλυκὺν ὅρμον ἱκοίμην.
ἀλλά, φίλη, πεφύλαξο βαρυπνείοντας ἀήτας,
μή μιν ἀποσβέσσωσι, καὶ αὐτίκα θυμὸν ὀλέσσω.

I shall not see Boötes, nor the Wain,
And bright Orion will be bright in vain.
Only take heed, dear, of the winds, and shield
The light, that when I toil, by waves concealed,
It be not quenched by any envious blast,
Lest I go down, a ship and venture lost.

Hero agrees to this arrangement, and the lovers part: she to her tower, and Leander to Abydos, where he counts the hours until the appointed night. Musæus then describes very charmingly how the youth watches for the gleam of the lamp, and how, beholding it, he casts himself into the sea-waves, after a prayer to Eros and the Deity of the Deep. Hero, on her side, has kindled the beacon, and stands shielding it against the breezes with the folds of her garment; while Leander

λαμπομένου δ' ἔσπευδεν ἀεὶ κατεναντία λύχνου
αὐτὸς ἐὼν ἐρέτης, αὐτόστολος, αὐτόματος νηῦς.

Steered with his face set hard where that ray shone,
Ship, pilot, rower, merchant, all in one.

He touches land at last, arrives beneath the tower, and Hero

Ἐκ δὲ θυράων
νυμφίον ἀσθμαίνοντα περιπτύξασα σιωπῇ,

ἀφροκόμους ῥαθάμιγγας ἔτι στάζοντα θαλάσσης,
ἤγαγε νυμφοκόμοιο μυχοὺς ἐπὶ παρθενεῶνος,
καὶ χρόα πάντα κάθηρε, δέμας δ᾽ ἔχριεν ἐλαίῳ
εὐόδμῳ, ῥοδέῳ, καὶ ἁλίπνοον ἔσβεσεν ὀδμήν.
εἰσέτι δ᾽ ἀσθμαίνοντα βαθυστρώτοις ἐνὶ λέκτροις
νυμφίον ἀμφιχυθεῖσα, φιλήνορας ἴαχε μύθους·
Νυμφίε, πολλὰ μογήσας, ἃ μὴ πάθε νυμφίος ἄλλος,
νυμφίε, πολλὰ μογήσας, ἅλις νύ τοι ἁλμυρὸν ὕδωρ,
ὀδμή τ᾽ ἰχθυόεσσα βαρυγδούποιο θαλάσσης·
δεῦρο, τεοὺς ἱδρῶτας ἐμοῖς ἐνικάτθεο κόλποις.

In gladness past all words her white arms flung
Round him, and on his panting bosom hung,
And led him from the cold and foamy beach
Up to her tower ; and when her room they reach,
She wiped his pearly body clean of brine,
And took the salt smell off with unguents fine,
In rose-leaves dyed and scented rich and rare ;
And then she clothed him with her own deep hair,
Yet panting from his voyage—while in his ear
She poured these tender accents :—
"Husband dear !
"Sore hast thou toiled, as never one save thee,
"Battling the horrid deep to come to me :
"Forget upon my lips the waves' harsh taste,
"The fierce sea-monsters and the roaring waste.
"The port is reached : anchor, dear ship, and have
"The goods you sailed for in your Hero's love."

Many such delicious times Leander makes the passage; but by-and-by the winter came, with wild storms in the Hellespont—and yet neither can Hero refuse to light her lamp, nor will her lover let the rough waves keep him away. The whole world knows the sequel of this ancient love story. One night, with more than "half a gale" blowing from the Sestos shores, the beacon gleams out, and the swimmer starts; but the storm blows the flame out when Leander is half-way, and, overwhelmed by the cruel billows, he is drowned, and flung ashore at the foot of the tower. Hero, when the morning breaks, beholds his corpse lying there, and flings herself down to perish by his side.

Enough has been cited of this little Greek epic to show that, whoever the author might be, it contains not only real poetry, but a deep and vivid sympathy and great power of narrative. Its faults are equally apparent, and separate it entirely from the majestic severity of ancient models, while they show how, under the subjective form of thinking characteristic of later times, the art of verse became transformed, and not a little corrupted.

PROCLUS.

OUR long list of poets, which began with the grand singing of Homer, and has faded away into such minor musicians as Callimachus and Rhianus, such mere rhyming professors as Nicander and Oppian, may end at least with a most noble name. Proclus was born at Constantinople in A.D. 412, and it is not too much to say that something eloquent from the greatest poet and something lofty from the greatest philosopher of Hellas—an inheritance at once of the melody of Homer and of the mind of Plato —fell upon this last of the Greek minstrels. It is for his philosophic works and career, no doubt, that Proclus is best known. His commentary on the "Timæus" of Plato was a masterpiece of erudition for the age. His mystic and religious writings are deeply interesting; and sublime in theory and aim, even where most extravagant. In his treatises on Providence, Fate, and Evil, he states with eloquent force the doctrine that all pain and sorrow spring from the limitation of human knowledge. In his "Eighteen Arguments against the Christians," he maintains the eternity of the world—a favourite thesis of the Platonists—and all these, as well as his other works, are saturated with the ardent and spiritual nature of a soul truly poetic and aspiring. A profound spirit characterises the six religious poems which Proclus has left; and it is interesting to notice how, retaining the form, the names, the mythological traditions of the hieratic and Orphic poets, this Neo-Platonic philosopher and singer bends all their old machinery to the needs of his time, teaching the high hopes and daring innovations of the Alexandrian school in the language of a religion which had really died four hundred years back, at the time when the Greek sailors heard that awful cry moaning round the islands of the Echinades, "*Great Pan is dead!*" These six hymns of Proclus close the long catalogue of Hellenic poesy with a solemn and tender strain. Take, for example, his "Prayer to the Muses," which breathes the spirit of an utterly new age, speaking though it does in the phrases used twenty centuries back. It is, in fact, an epitaph upon a buried religion, written in its own disused hieroglyphics; an elegy for Greek song, now at last ending for ever, along with its beautiful false fables and lovely intermingling of the lives of gods and men.

Ὑμνέομεν, μερόπων ἀναγώγιον ὑμνέομεν φῶς,
ἐννέα θυγατέρας μεγάλου Διὸς ἀγλαοφώνους,
αἳ ψυχὰς, κατὰ βένθος ἀλωομένας βιότοιο,
ἀχράντοις τελετῆσιν ἐγερσινόων ἀπὸ βίβλων

Glory and praise to those sweet lamps of earth,
  The nine fair Daughters of Almighty Jove,
Who all the passage dark to death from birth
  Lead wandering souls with their bright beams of love.

Through cares of mortal life, through pain and woe,
  The tender solace of their counsel saves;
The healing secrets of their songs forego
  Despair; and when we tremble at the waves

Of life's wild sea of murk incertitude,
  Their gentle touch upon the helm is pressed,
Their hand points out the beacon-star of good,
  Where we shall make our harbour, and have rest—

γηγενέων ῥύσαντο δυσαντήτων ὀδυνάων,
καὶ σπεύδειν ἐδίδαξαν ὑπὲρ βαθυχεύμονα λήθην
ἴχνος ἔχειν, καθαρὰς δὲ μολεῖν ποτὶ σύννομον ἄστρον,
ἔνθεν ἀπεπλάγχθησαν, ὅτ' εἰς γενεθλήϊον ἀκτὴν
κάππεσον, ὑλοτραφέσσι περὶ κλήροισι μανεῖσαι.
ἀλλὰ, θεαὶ, καὶ ἐμεῖο πολυπτοίητον ἐρωὴν
παύσατε, καὶ νοεροῖς με σοφῶν βακχεύσατε μύθοις·
μηδέ μ' ἀποπλάγξειεν δεισιθέων γένος ἀνδρῶν
ἀτραπιτοῦ ζαθέης, ἐριφεγγέος, ἀγλαοκάρπου·
αἰεὶ δ' ἐξ ὁμάδοιο πολυπλάγκτοιο γενέθλης
ἕλκετ' ἐμὴν ψυχὴν παναλήμονα πρὸς φάος ἁγνὸν,
ὑμετέρων βρίθουσαν ἀεξινόων ἀπὸ βίβλων,
καὶ κλέος εὐεπίης φρενοθελγέος αἰὲν ἔχουσαν.
κλῦτε θεοὶ σοφίης ἱερῆς οἴηκας ἔχοντες,
οἳ ψυχὰς μερόπων, ἀναγώγιον ἁψάμενοι πῦρ,

The planet of our home wherefrom we fell,
  Allured by this poor show of lower things,
Tempted among earth's dull deceits to dwell:
  But oh! great Sisters, hear his prayer who sings,

And calm the restless flutter of his breast,
  And fill him with the thirst for wisdom's stream;
Nor ever suffer thoughts or men unblest
  To turn his vision from the eternal beam.

Ever and ever higher, from the throng
  Lawless and witless, lead his feet aright
Life's perils and perplexities among,
  To the white centre of the sacred light.

Feed him with food of that rich fruit which grows
  On stems of splendid learning—dower him still
With gifts of eloquence to vanquish those
  Who err—let soft persuasion change their will.

Hear, heavenly Sisters, hear! oh, ye who know
  The winds of wisdom's sea, the course to steer;
Who light the flame that lightens all below,
  And bring the spirits of the perfect there

ἕλκετ' ἐς ἀθανάτους, σκότιον κευθμῶνα λιπούσας,
ὕμνων ἀῤῥήτοισι καθηράμενοι τελετῆσι·
κλῦτε σαωτῆρες μεγάλοι, ζαθέων δ' ἀπὸ βίβλων
νεύσατ' ἐμοὶ φάος ἁγνὸν, ἀποσκεδασαντες ὁμίχλην,
ὄφρα κεν εὖ γνώω θεὸν ἄμβροτον, ἠδὲ καὶ ἄνδρα.
μηδ' ἐμὲ ληθαίοις ὑπὸ χεύμασιν οὐλοὰ ῥέζων
δαίμων αἰὲν ἔχοι, μακάρων ἀπάνευθεν ἐόντα.
μη κρυερῆς γενέθλης ἐνὶ κύμασι πεπτωκυῖαν
ψυχὴν οὐκ ἐθέλουσαν ἐμὴν ἐπὶ δηρὸν ἀλᾶσθαι
Ποινή τις κρυόεσσα βίου δεσμοῖσι πεδήσῃ.
ἀλλὰ θεοὶ σοφίης ἐριλαμπέος ἡγεμονῆες,
κέκλυτ', ἐπειγομένῳ δὲ πρὸς ὑψιφόρητον ἀταρπὸν
ὄργια καὶ τελετὰς ἱερῶν ἀναφαίνετε μύθων.

Where the immortals are, when this life's fever
  Is left behind as a dread gulf o'erpassed ;
And souls, like mariners, escaped for ever,
  Throng on the happy foreland, saved at last.

So bring, high Muses ! open me the scroll
  Where Truth is writ in characters of fire ;
Roll from my eyes the mists of life—oh ! roll,
  That I may have my spirit's deep desire,

Discerning the divine in undivine,
  The god in man—the life of me in death ;
Nor let dire powers pluck this soul of mine
  From its most precious hope—to merge beneath

Deep floods of black oblivion, far from bliss,
  From light, from wisdom—never let their doom
Shut my lost soul in such despair as this,
  My soul that is so weary of the gloom !

But hear and help, ye wise and shining Nine !
  I yearn and strive towards your heavenly side ;
Teach me the secret of the mystic sign,
  Give me the lore that guards, the words that guide.

THE PRINCIPAL ERAS IN GREEK LITERATURE.

(FROM LIDDELL AND SCOTT.)

I. The Early Epic Period, comprising the Iliad and Odyssey, the Homeric Hymns, and the Poems of Hesiod.

II. From about 800 to 530 A.C., in which Literature chiefly flourished in Asia Minor and the Islands; the Period of the early Lyric, Elegiac, and Iambic Poets.

III. From 530 to 510 A.C., the Age of Peisistratus, &c.; the beginning of Tragedy at Athens.

IV. From 510 to 470 A.C., the Age of τὰ Περσικά, in which the Great Tragic Poets began to exhibit, and Simonides and Pindar brought Lyric Poetry to perfection.

V. From 470 to 431 A.C., the Age of Athenian Supremacy: perfection of Tragedy.

VI. From 431 to 403 A.C., the Age of the Peloponnesian War: perfection of the Old Comedy.

VII. From 403 to about 336, the Age of Spartan and Theban Supremacy, and of Philip: Middle Comedy.

VIII. From about 336 to the Roman Times: (1) Macedonian Age: New Comedy. (2) Alexandrian Age: later Epic and Elegiac writers, Callimachus, Theocritus, Apollonius Rhodius, &c.

IX. Roman Age: Epigrammatic Poets. The revived Atticism of Lucian, the Sophists, &c.

COMPLETE LIST OF GREEK POETS.

	Floruit A.C.	circa P.C.
Achæus, Tragicus	447	—
Æschylus, Tragicus (Date of first prize)	484	—
Agatho, Tragicus	416	—
Alcæus, Lyricus	610	—
——— Comicus (Vet.)	388	—
Alcman, Lyricus	650	—
Alexis, Comicus (Med.)	356	—
Alexander, Comicus (Incert.)	350?	—
Amipsias, Comicus (Vet.)	423	—
Amphis, Comicus (Med.)	350	—
Anacreon, Lyricus	559	—
Ananius, Iambographus	540?	—
Anaxandrides, Comicus (Med.)	376	—
Anaxilas, Comicus (Med.)	340	—
Anaxippus, Comicus (Nov.)	303	—
Antidotus, Comicus (Med.)	350	—
Antimachus, Elegiacus	405	—
Antipater Sidonius	127	—
——— Thessalonicensis	—	50
Antiphanes, Comicus (Med.)	388	—
Apollodorus (tres, Comici Nov.)	330 260	— —
——— Mythologus	140	—
Apollonius Rhodius, Epicus	194	—
Apollophanes, Comicus (Vet.)	407	—
Araros, Comicus (Med.)	375	—
Aratus, Poëta physicus	272	—
Archedicus, Comicus (Nov.)	302	—
Archilochus, Iambographus	690	—

		Floruit circa A.C.	P.C.
Archippus, Comicus (Vet.)		415	—
Aristagoras, Comicus (Vet.)		410	—
Aristias, Tragicus		450	—
Aristomenes, Comicus (Vet.)		425	—
Aristonymus, Comicus (Vet.)		420	—
Aristophanes, Comicus (Vet.)	(The Δαιταλεῖς)	427	—
Aristopho, Comicus (Med.)		350 ?	—
Asius, Elegiacus		700	—
Astydamas, Tragicus		398	—
Athenæus		—	200 ?
Athenio, Comicus (Incert.)		350 ?	—
Autocrates, Comicus (Vet.)		390	—
Axionicus, Comicus (Med.)		340	—
Babrius, Fabularum Scriptor		. . ?	—
Bacchylides, Lyricus		472	—
Bato, Comicus (Nov.)		260	—
Bion, Bucolicus		272	—
Callias, Comicus (Vet.)		424	—
Callicrates, Comicus (Med.)		350 ?	—
Callimachus, Epicus		256	—
Callinus, Elegiacus		730	—
Callippus, Comicus (Incert.)		. . ?	—
Cantharus, Comicus (Vet.)		420	—
Cephisodorus, Comicus (Vet.)		402	—
Chæremon, Tragicus		380	—
Chariclides, Comicus (Incert.)		. . ?	—
Chionides, Comicus (Vet.)		487	—
Chœrilus, Epicus		440	—
Chœrilus, Tragicus		480	—
Clearchus, Comicus (Incert.)		. . ?	—
Coluthus, Epicus		—	500 ?
Corinna, Lyrica		500	—
Crates, Comicus (Vet.)		450	—
Cratinus, Major, Comicus (Vet.)		454	—
——— Minor, Comicus (Med.)		350	—
Critias, Elegiacus et Tragicus		411	—
Crito, Comicus (Incert.)		. . ?	—
Crobylus, Comicus (Incert.)		335	—
Damoxenus, Comicus (Nov.)		345 ?	—

	Floruit circa A.C.	P.C.
Demetrius (duo, Comici)	400 299	— —
Demonicus, Comicus (Incert.)	..?	—
Dexicrates, Comicus (Incert.)	..?	—
Dinolochus, Comicus Doricus	487	—
Diocles, Comicus (Vet.)	470	—
Diodorus, Comicus (Med.)	354	—
Dionysius, Comicus (Med.)	350	—
Diophantus, Comicus (Vet.)	..?	—
Dioxippus, Comicus (Nov.)	..?	—
Diphilus, Comicus (Nov.)	320	—
Dromo, Comicus (Med.)	350?	—
Ecphantides, Comicus (Vet.)	460	—
Empedocles, Poëta philosophicus	444	—
Ephippus, Comicus (Med.)	368	—
Epicharmus, Comicus Syracusanus	500	—
Epicrates, Comicus (Med.)	376	—
Epigenes, Comicus (Med.)	378	—
Epilycus, Comicus (Vet.)	394	—
Epinicus, Comicus (Nov.)	270?	—
Erinna, Lyrica	610?	—
Eriphus, Comicus (Med.)	350?	—
Euangelus, Comicus (Incert.)	..?	—
Eubulides, Comicus (Med.)	350?	—
Eubulus, Comicus (Med.)	375	—
Eudoxus, Comicus (Nov.)	..?	—
Euenus, Elegiacus	450	—
Eunicus, Comicus (Vet.)	394	—
Euphorion	235	—
Euphro, Comicus (Nov.)	280	—
Eupolis, Comicus (Vet.)	429	—
Euripides, Tragicus (Date of first prize)	441	—
Euthycles, Comicus (Vet.)	400?	—
Hegemon, Comicus (Vet.)	413	—
Hegesippus, Comicus (Nov.)	300	—
Heliodorus, Scriptor Eroticus	—	390
Heniochus, Comicus (Med.)	350?	—
Heraclides, Comicus (Med.)	348	—
Hermesianax, Elegiacus	290?	—

	Floruit circa A.C.	P.C.
Hermippus, Comicus (Vet.)	432	—
Hesiodus, Epicus	..?	—
Hipparchus, Comicus (Nov.)	320	—
Hipponax, Iambographus	546	—
Homerus, Epicus	..	—
Ibycus, Lyricus	560	—
Ion, Tragicus	451	—
Laon, Comicus (Incert.)	..?	—
Lasus, Dithyrambicus	503	—
Leonidas Alexandrinus	—	60
——— Tarentinus	280	...
Leuco, Comicus (Vet.)	423	—
Lucianus	—	160
Lycophron, Iambographus (Alexandrinus)	259?	—
Lynceus, Comicus (Nov.)	300	—
Lysippus, Comicus (Vet.)	434	—
Macho, Comicus (Nov.)	230	—
Magnes, Comicus (Vet.)	460	—
Melanippides, Dithyrambicus	520	—
Meleager, Elegiacus	95	—
Menander, Comicus (Nov.)	321	—
Metagenes, Comicus (Vet.)	410	—
Mimnermus, Elegiacus	630	—
Mnesimachus, Comicus (Med.)	..?	—
Moschus, Bucolicus	154	—
Musæus	—	..?
Myrtilus, Comicus (Vet.)	430	—
Nausicrates, Comicus (Med.?)	350?	—
Nicander, Poëta physicus	182	—
Nicochares, Comicus (Vet.)	388	—
Nicoläus, Comicus (Incert.)	..?	—
Nicomachus, Comicus (Nov.?)	..?	—
Nicophon, Comicus (Vet.)	388	—
Nicostratus, Comicus (Med.)	240?	—
Nonnus, Epicus	—	500?
Ophelio, Comicus (Med.)	370	—
Oppianus, Poëta physicus	—	204
Orphica...	—	..?
Panyasis, Epicus	489	—

	Floruit circa A.C.	P.C.
Parmenides, Poëta philosophicus	503	—
Parthenius, Scriptor Eroticus	63	—
Paulus Silentiarius	—	530
Phanocles, Elegiacus	280?	—
Pherecrates, Comicus (Vet.)	436	—
Pherecydes, Minor, Historicus	480	—
Philemon, Comicus (Nov.)	330	—
——— Minor, Comicus (Nov.)	300?	—
Philetærus, Comicus (Med.)	250	—
Philetas, Elegiacus	300	—
Philippides, Comicus (Nov.)	335	—
Philiscus, Comicus (Med.)...	380	—
Philonides, Comicus (Vet.)	430	—
Philostephanus, Comicus (Incert.)	..?	—
Philoxenus, Dithyrambicus	398	—
Philyllius, Comicus (Vet.)...	394	—
Phocylides, Elegiacus	544	—
Phrynicus, Comicus (Vet.)...	429	—
——— Tragicus	511	—
Pindarus, Lyricus	490	—
Plato, Comicus (Vet.)	428	—
Poliochus, Comicus (Incert.)	..?	—
Polyidus, Dithyrambicus	398	—
Polyzelus, Comicus (Vet.)	402	—
Posidippus, Comicus (Nov.)	280	—
Pratinas, Tragicus	499	—
Praxilla, Lyrica	..?	—
Proclus	—	450
Quintus Smyrnæus (or Calaber), Epicus	—	..?
Rhianus, Elegiacus	222	—
Sannyrio, Comicus (Vet.)	407	—
Sappho, Lyrica	610	—
Scymnus, Poeta Geographicus	90	—
Simonides of Amorgus	404	—
——— of Ceos	525	—
Solon, Elegiacus	604	—
Sophilus, Comicus (Med.)...	350?	—
Sophocles, Tragicus ... ... (Date of first prize)	468	—
Sophron, Mimographus	450	—

	Floruit circa A.C.	P.C.
Sosicrates, Comicus (Nov.)	..?	—
Sosipater, Comicus (Nov.)	290?	—
Sotades, Comicus (Med.)	..?	—
Stephanus, Comicus (Nov.)	332	—
Stesichorus, Lyricus	610	—
Stobæus	—	500?
Strattis, Comicus (Vet.)	407	—
Susario, Comicus (Vet)	560	—
Synesius	—	410
Teleclides, Comicus (Vet.)	440	—
Telesilla, Lyrica	510	—
Telestes, Dithyrambicus	401	—
Theocritus, Bucolicus	272	—
Theognetus, Comicus (Nov.)	..?	—
Theognis, Elegiacus	540	—
Theophilus, Comicus (Med.)	330	—
Theopompus, Comicus (Vet.)	390	—
Thugenides, Comicus (Incert.)	..?	—
Timocles, Comicus (Med.)	350	—
Timocreon, Lyricus	471	—
Timon, Sillographus	279	—
Timostratus, Comicus (Incert.)	..?	—
Timotheus, Comicus (Med.)	350?	—
——— Dithyrambicus	398	—
Tryphiodorus, Epicus	—	..?
Tyrtæus, Elegiacus	680	—
Xenarchus, Comicus (Med.)	350	—
Xeno, Comicus (Incert.)	..?	—
Xenophanes, Poeta Philosophicus	538	—